APPLIED POSITIVE PSYCHOLOGY

PRAISE FOR THE BOOK

'This textbook captures the best of the positive psychology initiative, and most importantly, translates it to practice. The authors bring remarkable depth and breadth to the subject matter and do so in a way that is fresh, engaging, relevant, and unusually thoughtful. Everyone who reads this book will derive useful insights about how to live. The closing chapter on ethical and reflective practice is a masterpiece.'
Carol Ryff, University of Wisconsin-Madison

'If you are interested in having a positive impact on people's lives then this book is for you. By firmly placing Positive Psychology in an applied and social context the authors identify its true purpose – to make life better. It does a brilliant job of showing readers how to apply the insights that research has uncovered. It will surely become one of the go-to text books for all students of Positive Psychology.'
Nic Marks, creator of the Happy Planet Index, Five Ways to Wellbeing and Founder of Happiness Works

'If you think you know what positive psychology is, think again! This book offers a new integrative vision for making life better that takes in the body and the brain, culture and society, and childhood and development. Written by the team who lead the Applied Positive Psychology programme at the University of East London you can be sure that the scholarship is cutting edge. A must read for students of positive psychology.'
Professor Stephen Joseph, University of Nottingham, editor of *Positive Psychology in Practice*

'It's hard to think of any discipline that could be more important in modern society than Positive Psychology – the science and practice of improving wellbeing. This book marks a significant coming-of-age for this exciting and rapidly developing field. It provides a grounded, compelling and comprehensive view of the many ways that Positive Psychology can help make life better – from individuals and families to schools, workplaces and communities; from birth and childhood to adult life and old age. If you want to understand what Positive Psychology really is, learn how it works in practice and discover its huge potential to transform our lives and our world then look no further than this superb book. I really can't recommend it highly enough.'
Dr Mark Williamson, Director of Action for Happiness

APPLIED POSITIVE PSYCHOLOGY

TIM LOMAS

KATE HEFFERON

ITAI IVTZAN

integrated positive practice

Los Angeles | London | New Delhi
Singapore | Washington DC

Los Angeles | London | New Delhi
Singapore | Washington DC

SAGE Publications Ltd
1 Oliver's Yard
55 City Road
London EC1Y 1SP

SAGE Publications Inc.
2455 Teller Road
Thousand Oaks, California 91320

SAGE Publications India Pvt Ltd
B 1/I 1 Mohan Cooperative Industrial Area
Mathura Road
New Delhi 110 044

SAGE Publications Asia-Pacific Pte Ltd
3 Church Street
#10-04 Samsung Hub
Singapore 049483

Editor: Michael Carmichael
Assistant editor: Keri Dickens
Production editor: Imogen Roome
Proofreader: Leigh C. Timmins
Marketing manager: Michael Ainsley
Cover design: Wendy Scott
Typeset by: C&M Digitals (P) Ltd, Chennai, India
Printed in Great Britain by CPI Group (UK) Ltd,
Croydon, CR0 4YY

Library of Congress Control Number: 2014936368

British Library Cataloguing in Publication data

A catalogue record for this book is available from
the British Library.

MIX
Paper from
responsible sources
FSC® C013604
www.fsc.org

ISBN 978-1-4462-9862-6
ISBN 978-1-4462-9863-3 (pbk)

At SAGE we take sustainability seriously. Most of our products are printed in the UK using FSC papers and boards.
When we print overseas we ensure sustainable papers are used as measured by the Egmont grading system.
We undertake an annual audit to monitor our sustainability.

CONTENTS

ABOUT THE AUTHORS

Dr Tim Lomas is a Lecturer and Deputy Programme Leader on the MSc in Applied Positive Psychology at the University of East London. Tim undertook an MA (Hons) and an MSc in Psychology at the University of Edinburgh, and completed his PhD at the University of Westminster in 2012. He has published numerous papers on meditation, Buddhism and masculinity. His first academic book, entitled *Masculinity, Meditation and Mental Health*, was published by Palgrave Macmillan in spring 2014.

Dr Kate Hefferon is a Chartered Research Psychologist, Senior Lecturer and Programme Leader of the MSc in Applied Positive Psychology at the University of East London. Kate is the author of numerous peer-reviewed papers, books and book chapters, and has presented at conferences nationally and internationally on positive psychology. Her research interests include posttraumatic growth, resilience, physical activity and embodiment.

Dr Itai Ivtzan is a Chartered Psychologist, Senior Lecturer and Programme Leader of the MSc in Applied Positive Psychology at the University of East London. Itai is also an Honorary Senior Research Associate at University College London. He has published many peer-reviewed journal papers and book chapters, and his main areas of research are spirituality, mindfulness, meaning and self-actualisation.

INTRODUCTION

The philosophers have only interpreted the world, in various ways.
The point, however, is to change it.
Karl Marx

Welcome to *Applied Positive Psychology: Integrated Positive Practice*! It certainly is an exciting time to be studying positive psychology (PP), a rapidly evolving field that is attracting an ever-increasing number of adherents within academia and beyond. It is currently a little over 16 years since Martin Seligman used his 1998 American Psychological Association (APA) presidential address to usher in the innovative new field of PP (Fowler et al., 1999). Of course, many of the concerns of PP – such as the nature of the good life and the pursuit of happiness – have been debated for centuries, millennia even. As such, PP has drawn heavily on antecedent schools of thought, from the perennial legacy of philosophers in classical Greece to twentieth-century humanistic psychology. And yet . . . PP does appear to have captured a spirit of excitement and innovation, a sense that age-old questions are being answered in new ways. Even if we are simply standing on the shoulders of giants, nonetheless PP seems to have brought a fresh perspective to bear on some of humanity's most enduring and important issues. Consequently, we have seen PP flourish within academia, drawing in both new students and established scholars, generating a proliferation of journal articles and international conferences, and attracting funding and interest from diverse sources, not to mention arousing considerable attention in the media and society at large (Biswas-Diener et al., 2011b). In that respect, PP can be regarded as a stunningly successful programme of inquiry, a veritable 'movement' that has addressed some unmet need of our current age (Rusk & Waters, 2013).

In spite of its success, however, or perhaps because of it, however, scholars are beginning to ask some soul-searching questions around what PP actually *is*. In one sense, such questions are simply a sign that PP is reaching a particular stage of maturity in its evolution as a discipline. In another sense, though, the nature of PP has always been a slightly grey area. Is it a separate discipline, a collection of practices, or just an ethos? Initially, some of the pioneering scholars who helped to establish PP, such as Linley and Joseph (2004, p. 4), suggested that PP is *not* a new speciality within psychology, but rather a 'collective identity' unifying researchers interested in 'the brighter sides of human nature'. According to this view, the broad intention underlying the PP movement was to redress what was seen as a 'negative bias' within conventional psychology (Seligman & Csikszentmihalyi, 2000). However, critics have pointed out that once this imbalance *had* been redressed – i.e., topics like happiness had been recognised as legitimate and worthy concerns in psychology – then PP would have 'succeeded' and would logically cease to exist. As Smith (2003, p. 162) argued: 'Psychology in good balance would not need advocates for positive psychology.' One might suggest that with the success of the PP movement, this 'good balance' had indeed been achieved. Thus, given the ever-growing influence and standing of PP, it is an apposite time for a reflective appraisal of what PP actually *is*, and where it might be going.

In this spirit, our book offers one vision of the way forward for PP. We contend that the future lies in recognising PP as a form of applied psychology. There is already an applied aspect to PP (Donaldson et al., 2011), defined as 'the application of positive psychology research to the facilitation of optimal human functioning' (Linley & Joseph, 2004, p. 4). In this respect, there is a growing corpus of positive psychology interventions (PPIs), discussed throughout the book. However, our emphasis on application serves as a more fundamental statement of intent regarding the core ethos of PP, and where it sits in the wider terrain of human action and inquiry. In the *Nichomachean Ethics*, Aristotle (2000 (350 BCE)) constructed a threefold classification of human activities: poiēsis, theōria and praxis. As elucidated in Carr and Kemmis (1986), poiēsis refers to productive and creative disciplines, which strive to generate artefacts. Theōria encompasses contemplative endeavours, which seek to attain knowledge for its own sake. Finally, praxis designates practical occupations which aim to act upon the world through the skilful application of ideas. We contend that PP is best viewed as a form of praxis. The importance of praxis has been emphasised by influential thinkers such as Heidegger (1927) and Arendt (1958). However, perhaps its most eloquent articulation was formulated by Marx (1977 (1845), p. 158), who said that 'The philosophers have only interpreted the world, in various ways. The point, however, is to change it'. For us, this quote captures the spirit of PP.

More specifically, applied positive psychology (APP) seeks to help change people's wellbeing for the better. What is particularly powerful about APP is how it marries Marx's revolutionary spirit of praxis to the empirical rigour of contemporary scientific enquiry. To this extent, we endorse the definition of praxis found in the social sciences, namely, 'practical action informed by theory' (Foster, 1986, p. 96). Thus, our definition of APP – and indeed of PP generally, as we are presenting PP as an intrinsically applied discipline – is '*the science and practice of improving wellbeing*'. The central aim of APP is to generate PPIs, which we define as '*theoretically-grounded and empirically-validated interventions, activities, and recommendations to enhance wellbeing*'. These PPIs are available to all. They can be adopted by practitioners working in other areas of psychology, like clinical psychology. They can be taken up by professionals in other fields, from education to social work. More universally, they can be used by the public generally as a form of scientifically-based self-help. More adventurously, looking to the future, we can even think of developing APP as a separate speciality within psychology: it is feasible that a process of professional accreditation could be developed for PP, leading to chartered status for PP practitioners in a manner comparable to clinical psychology. For now, though, the main concern in this book is to present a comprehensive system of tools and practices that can be used to promote wellbeing. Moreover, we shall do this by using an innovative multidimensional model that offers a genuinely integrated approach to the person and their wellbeing – hence the subtitle of the book, *Integrated Positive Practice* (IPP). We shall do this over eight chapters.

Chapter 1 sets out the theoretical framework that underpins the book, a multidimensional conceptual model of wellbeing – and indeed of the person – which we call the 'Layered Integrated Framework Example' (LIFE) model. This model is adapted from the Integral Framework, formulated by the philosopher Ken Wilber (1995, 2000). Wilber's original framework conceptualises the person as comprising four distinct, yet interrelated, ontological dimensions. These dimensions are produced by juxtaposing two binaries: subjective versus objective and individual versus collective. This juxtaposition creates four 'quadrants': individual-subjective (the mind), individual-objective (the body/brain), collective-subjective (culture) and collective-objective (society). We then adapt Wilber's framework by arguing that each quadrant can be 'layered' or 'stratified' into various levels. For example, we use Bronfenbrenner's (1977) experimental ecology to deconstruct the two collective quadrants according to levels of scale, from micro to macro. As such, by referring to our adapted model using the acronym LIFE, we acknowledge our debt to Wilber, while emphasising our departure from his original model. Finally, we introduce a guiding teleological (i.e., goal-oriented) statement which serves as the motto of the book, namely that the aim of PP is '*to make life better*'. The four quadrants are used to structure subsequent chapters, thus providing the overall framework for the book.

In the second chapter, we begin by focusing on the individual-subjective quadrant, i.e., the mind. Allied to the guiding motif of the book, the theme for this chapter is '*working with the mind to make life better*'. In keeping with the applied perspective of the book, the focus is on interventions that 'work on the mind' – i.e., at an individual psychological level – to enhance wellbeing. Using the stratification of the LIFE model introduced in Chapter 1, we examine the five 'layers' of this domain (although, in separating the levels, we remain conscious that this separation is just a heuristic device, i.e., a way of helping us think about the mind, and does not reflect the complexity of the domain). We begin with consciousness, exploring PPIs related to the development of awareness and attention. To this end we focus on meditation, a pre-eminent topic of interest in PP, looking at practices that have been adopted and adapted in psychology, like mindfulness.

As with the book generally, the emphasis is on how meditation is used in real-life practical contexts, from education to healthcare, and how readers can use it themselves. We then consider the other 'levels' of the LIFE model in turn, exploring PPIs related to embodiment (e.g., body awareness therapies), emotions (e.g., emotional intelligence interventions) and cognition (e.g., narrative restructuring exercises), before briefly touching on the idea of cultivating 'higher' levels of consciousness (which we tentatively refer to as 'awareness+').

In the third chapter, we switch our attention to the 'individual-objective' domain, i.e., the body/brain. Thus the guiding question becomes '*What can we do with the body and the brain to make life better?*' While Chapter 2 covered the subjective pole of the mind–body dichotomy, here we investigate the role of physiological functioning and behaviour in wellbeing. Again, we structure our enquiry using the stratified layers of the LIFE model. We begin with sub-cellular biochemistry, focusing on the impact of molecular genetics on psychological outcomes, and considering applied interventions like gene therapy. Moving 'up' levels, we explore the neural correlates of wellbeing (Urry et al., 2004) – including neurotransmitters, neural networks, and paradigms such as electroencephalography – and practices designed to engage directly with the brain, from neuropharmacology (e.g., psychoactive drugs) to neurofeedback. We then turn to the broader nervous system, where we highlight the value of exercise in promoting wellbeing. Finally, we consider the body 'as a whole', reflecting on what it means for us to *have/be* a body, and exploring the ways we can *use* our bodies to find wellbeing. Here we focus on modes of artistic self-expression – concentrating in particular on dance, art and music – examining how these have been harnessed to improve mental health and to help people flourish.

In Chapter 4 we broaden our horizons by considering how socio-cultural factors influence individual wellbeing. We draw on the useful distinction in the LIFE model between the intersubjective domain (culture, i.e., shared meanings) and the interobjective domain (society, i.e., material processes such as income). Moreover, we see that both of these domains can be stratified according to Bronfenbrenner's (1977) experimental ecology, which identifies different socio-cultural levels, from micro to macro. From an APP perspective, we then consider interventions to improve wellbeing that are specific to each of these levels. We start with the microsystem (i.e., one's immediate social situation, such as one's family), examining PPIs to enhance this, both from an intersubjective perspective (e.g., using PP in couples therapy) and from an interobjective perspective (e.g., enhancing the aesthetics of the environment). We then move up to the mesosystem (i.e., the interaction between microsystems), exploring interventions for children that encompass home *and* school. Next we address the exosystem (i.e., the wider community), outlining some community-level interventions. Above this is the macrosystem (i.e., more encompassing social structures); here we touch upon top–down initiatives, such as governmental policies, to enhance wellbeing.

Finally, we augment Bronfenbrenner's model by considering the eco-system, and the importance of the environment to wellbeing.

Having outlined the four domains of the LIFE model, Chapter 5 takes a more dynamic diachronic perspective (i.e., analysing changes over time), focusing on development throughout the lifespan. The chapter examines the various developmental stages in turn, from birth to old age, thus offering a sense of the existential unfolding of the entire life course. Moreover, in considering development, we of course do so from a *positive* perspective, exploring factors that enable people to flourish at each life stage, and moreover suggesting PPIs/recommendations to *promote* such flourishing. We begin *before* life starts, exploring pregnancy and childbirth. A key thread through these early sections is the idea of positive parenting, i.e., the role that parents/caregivers play in engendering wellbeing in children. As we move into infancy, we focus on the *relations* between children and parents/caregivers, looking in particular at attachment theory and parenting styles. Progressing further, we then follow the child into school, exploring the flourishing field of positive education (Seligman et al., 2009), and then on to the broader notion of positive youth development (Larson, 2000). From there, we examine development across the lifespan (Beck & Cowan, 1996). Finally, as we reach the culmination of the life journey, we reflect upon the possibility of positive aging (Tornstam, 2005).

So, we have covered the domains of the LIFE model, and moreover considered the development of the person over time. In Chapter 6 we then apply the LIFE model, and the idea of APP, to the sphere of activity that dominates much of human existence: work. However, our concern is not only with paid employment. As indicated by its title (Occupations and Organisations), this chapter encompasses any of the ways people substantively and productively occupy their time (from studying or working to volunteering or raising a family), and pertains to any functional group of people (from families and social groups to companies and large organisations). As such, whether 'in work' or not, this chapter is intended to be relevant to all people, outlining ways to enhance wellbeing 'at work' using the four domains of the LIFE model. Focusing on the mind, we look at how to promote the psychological drivers of work engagement, including using one's strengths, developing Psychological Capital (self-efficacy, hope, optimism and resilience), and cultivating meaning at work. Addressing the body, we look at ameliorating work stressors, including ensuring health and safety, reducing workload and enhancing job control. From an intersubjective perspective, we address the importance of organisational culture, with interventions including promoting positive relationships, effective leadership and value-driven inquiry. Finally, in interobjective terms, we reflect on the importance of taking the structural context of work, including its wider political/economic context, into account.

In the penultimate chapter, we turn our attention to a sphere of human activity which is perhaps less concrete and more nebulous than work, but is no less important to many people, namely religion and spirituality. We consider the close connection between religion/spirituality and wellbeing, and look at what PP can learn from the great religious traditions. These traditions have spent centuries developing comprehensive systems of ideas and practices relating to happiness and the nature of the good life; as such, they constitute a deep ocean of wisdom that PP, and psychology generally, has barely begun to appreciate and draw on. As ever, from our applied focus, the emphasis here is on practical lessons that religion/spirituality may have to offer, and activities and interventions we might derive from these. We focus in particular on two spiritual practices: meditation and yoga. Furthermore, we look at the broader religious/spiritual traditions in which these practices were originally developed, namely Buddhism and Hinduism. From Buddhism, we examine teachings around wisdom (e.g., cultivating acceptance of impermanence), universal values (e.g., compassion) and ethics. In terms of Hinduism, we present yoga as a comprehensive system of psycho-spiritual development, paying close attention to Patañjali's eight 'limbs' of yoga. However, although the chapter focuses on meditation and yoga, and on their Buddhist and Hindu roots, we also emphasise that all religious/spiritual traditions may have something to offer PP, and that PP can usefully engage with these in future.

In the final chapter, we turn our attention more directly towards *you*, the reader, as we consider what it might mean to be a PP practitioner. Throughout the book we will have introduced PPIs and activities that we can use to *make life better* and enhance wellbeing. Here, we explore what precautions might be necessary for people to actually use these interventions in practice, in order to safeguard the wellbeing of both clients/participants and practitioners themselves. The chapter focuses on two main concepts that we feel are important for practitioners to take on board: ethical practice and reflective practice. First, we ask what it means to practise ethically. We learn from other applied psychological fields that have already put considerable thought into this issue, especially counselling and psychotherapy. Using the ethical framework developed by the British Association of Counselling and Psychotherapy, we make recommendations for how PP practitioners can develop an ethical practice. Secondly, we explore the importance of reflective practice, introducing Schön (1983), who argued that professionals should develop reflexive self-awareness about their practice, and about their professional development more generally. At a deeper level, the chapter also encourages you to reflect on your own personal journey. We hope that this final chapter will enhance the sense that learning and practising PP can really touch the core of our being, and is an invitation to a personal adventure of development and transformation.

Before we start, though, we want to say a little about the format of the book. Its chapter structure has been taken from the MSc in Applied Positive Psychology programme at the University of East London, which is run by the authors. The book reflects the content of the second year double module of this course, entitled 'Advanced Positive Psychology: Theory and Practice'. This double module is run over the course of eight weekends. Each weekend is centred around a particular theme, and involves between five and seven separate lectures on that particular theme. As you will perhaps have guessed, each of these weekends is represented by a chapter in the book. So, in terms of using the book as a teaching resource, one could think of each chapter as constituting a whole weekend, or, alternatively, as representing five separate lectures (and so the book as a whole could be presented as around 40 lectures over the course of an entire semester or year). In addition, each chapter comprises various pedagogical features; these are designed to enhance the learning experience of students, and indeed are recommended to all readers generally as a way of getting the most out of the book. These features are captured in boxes that stand apart from the main text, sprinkled throughout each chapter, in the following order:

LEARNING OBJECTIVES – AT THE END OF THE CHAPTER YOU WILL BE ABLE TO…

Each chapter begins with a statement of the learning objectives for that chapter. These help orient you to the material contained in the chapter, and describe what you should know after reading it.

LIST OF TOPICS…

At the outset of each chapter we also provide a list of the main topics that will be covered within it.

PRACTICE ESSAY QUESTIONS …

After introducing the chapter, we set two practice essay questions. Often, one of these will ask you to discuss a controversial idea, in order to stimulate debate around a topic. As you read the chapter, you can be thinking of how you might answer these questions in light of the material presented.

RESEARCH AND PRACTICE CASE STUDIES …

As you read through the chapter, we will use these boxes to draw your attention to real-life research, case studies, people and examples that help illustrate the material being discussed.

REFLECTION . . .

As you read, we will also invite you to step back and consider the points being discussed from your own perspective, drawing on experiences and insights from your own life.

TRY ME! . . .

The book generally is full of PPIs and recommendations designed to enhance wellbeing. However, we will sometimes also include brief wellbeing activities for you to try out yourself as you are reading!

PSYCHOMETRIC SCALES . . .

At relevant points, we provide measurement tools relating to the constructs that are being discussed. These will be helpful in conducting research on areas you find interesting.

ART LINKS . . .

As a fun way of illuminating ideas in the text, we will occasionally recommend cultural artefacts (e.g., films, songs, books) that capture the spirit of these ideas, and which you might like to enjoy!

SUMMARY – THIS CHAPTER HAS...

At the end of each chapter, we summarise the material that we have covered within it. Bookended with the learning outcomes, these boxes provide a concise overview of the chapter.

QUIZ...

We also round off each chapter with a quick quiz, featuring 10 questions relating to the material in the chapter, just to check that you've been paying attention! The answers are at the back of the book.

RESOURCES AND SUGGESTIONS…

Finally, each chapter ends with a list of resources – such as websites – that will help you explore the material in more depth, and enable you to pursue your learning further.

1

PREPARING FOR THE JOURNEY

Do not go where the path may lead,
go instead where there is no path
and leave a trail.
Ralph Waldo Emerson

LEARNING OBJECTIVES – AT THE END OF THE CHAPTER YOU WILL BE ABLE TO…

- Take a multidimensional approach to wellbeing
- Use our LIFE model to guide your efforts to promote wellbeing
- Understand and respond to pertinent criticisms of PP
- Conceptualise PP as a form of praxis, and as an applied psychological discipline
- Articulate a motto encapsulating the 'point' of PP
- Engage in integrated positive practice!

LIST OF TOPICS…

- Multidimensionality
- Wilber's Integral Framework
- The LIFE model
- Layering/stratification
- Bronfenbrenner's experimental ecology

- Critiques of PP
- Praxis and applied disciplines
- The mental health–illness circumplex
- PP 2.0/second-wave PP
- Facilitation not prescription

In this first chapter, we are going to lay the groundwork for the book. The metaphor that springs most readily to mind is that of preparing for a journey. We can think of this journey in two respects. First, we are referring to the journey that you as readers will be taking through the book. Together, over these eight chapters, we will be charting a course through the latest empirical and theoretical terrain in PP. Collectively, of course, we shall travel together. However, there will be ample time and opportunities for you to take individual detours, to explore some of the many tangential paths we shall spy along the way, or to rest awhile in a particularly interesting location and explore it in more depth. The second meaning of this hopefully not-too-strained journey metaphor concerns the ongoing adventure of PP itself. Of course, since boldly striking forth into new – or at least underexplored and underappreciated – territory, PP has successfully covered a good deal of ground, attracting an ever-increasing number of interested people along the way. However, given the speed with which PP has raced forward, the time is right to pause and gather our bearings. There is much to be gained from catching a breath and looking around, taking stock of where we have come from and where we are now. Most importantly, we need to consider where we should go from here.

Persisting with this metaphor, our preparation for this journey – your own through the book, and that of PP itself – will focus on two key items that will be helpful on our travels: a map and a motto. In the first part of the chapter, we will articulate a conceptual map of the territory that might be relevant to PP, the terrain that we can explore on our journey. Broadly speaking, this map – i.e., our LIFE model – covers the various 'dimensions' of the person. By elucidating these dimensions, this model will enable us to take a comprehensive approach to wellbeing. This is not the only possible map one could use; nonetheless, you will hopefully be persuaded of its merits and will find it useful. Nor can our map be regarded as complete; it can and *should be* subject to critique and improvement, including by you, our reader. Nevertheless, we hope that it will contain, in Koestler's (1964, p. 22) poetic words, a 'shadowy pattern of truth'. The second part of the chapter will then articulate a motto that will guide us on our journey. This motto is a response to the searching question of what PP is actually *for*. Our answer is that the point of PP is *'to make life better'*. This motto will give purpose to our journey by helping us understand *why* we are travelling and to what end. Equipped with this map and motto, we will then be ready to set off on our adventures!

PRACTICE ESSAY QUESTIONS . . .

- Critically evaluate the LIFE model as a multidimensional approach to wellbeing.
- What relationship does APP have to other applied disciplines such as clinical psychology?

A map to guide us

A map is not the territory it represents, but if correct, it has a similar structure
to the territory, which accounts for its usefulness.
Alfred Korzybski

In this first part, we shall articulate a map of the person; more specifically, a *mul-tidimensional* map. This means we are suggesting that people comprise multiple dimensions, all of which need to be appreciated in order to arrive at a comprehensive understanding of the person. This multidimensional conceptualisation of the person, then, inevitably and automatically facilitates – indeed necessitates – a multi-dimensional appreciation of wellbeing; logically, the two go hand-in-hand. Once we appreciate the various dimensions of the person, we can try to promote wellbeing by targeting *all* these different dimensions. So, what map will we be using? Various multi-dimensional models of the person, and hence of wellbeing, are possible candidates.

One influential model is offered by the World Health Organisation (WHO). Their definition of health – formulated in 1948 and unchanged since – is 'a state of complete physical, mental and social well-being, and not merely the absence of disease and infirmity'. This recognises three main dimensions to the person and their health/wellbeing: physical, mental and social. This same triad is also evident in Engel's (1977) biopsychosocial model of health. In contrast to the prevailing reductive biomedical approach within medicine, Engel sought a more comprehensive understanding of health and illness, one incorporating 'the patient, the social context in which he lives, and the complementary system devised by society to deal with the disruptive effects of illness' (p. 132). More closely related to PP, Jahoda (1958) also formulated a biopsychosocial model, in her case pertaining to 'positive mental health' (the prefix 'positive' reveals her as a key influence on the PP movement). These models have influenced contempo-rary conceptualisations of health and wellbeing.[1] Pollard and Davidson (2001, p. 10) define wellbeing as a 'state of successful performance throughout the life course integrating physical, cognitive and social-emotional function'. This defini-tion also has three dimensions, albeit different ones from those identified by the WHO and Engel, which suggests there is room for debate over what dimensions a multidimensional model should contain. Thus, the LIFE model in this book – detailed below – is by no means the only possible one. However, we feel this may be more comprehensive and useful than the WHO and Engel models, as we explain next.

---

[1] It is worth clarifying here the distinction between health and wellbeing. As de Chavez et al. (2005) elucidate, some definitions position health as a component of the broader notion of wellbeing; conversely, other conceptualisations make health the more encom-passing concept; still other models use the terms synonymously. However, there is growing preference for taking wellbeing as the broader term, and using health to refer specifically to the physical dimensions of wellbeing, which is the way we shall use the terms.

The Layered Integrated Framework Example (LIFE) model

The multidimensional model of the person – and hence of wellbeing – which underpins this book is derived from the Integral Framework, developed by the influential American philosopher Ken Wilber (1995, 2000). We shall briefly elucidate Wilber's framework, before explaining below (in the subsection entitled Layering) how we have adapted it to create our own LIFE model. Wilber's framework is described as an ontological 'map' elucidating 'the basic dimensions of an individual' (Esbjörn-Hargens, 2006, p. 83). What is striking about his framework is the innovative way in which it identifies *four* dimensions, in contrast to the three biopsychosocial dimensions of the WHO, Engel and Jahoda models, described above. These dimensions are produced through the intersection of two binaries that are in themselves common. However, when these binaries are juxtaposed, this creates a framework that is novel and unexpected, and yet also logically appealing and parsimonious.

RESEARCH AND PRACTICE CASE STUDIES . . .

Ken Wilber is one of the most influential philosophers of recent times, and an iconoclastic thinker. In 1968 he dropped out of his graduate studies in biochemistry, and, while working as a dishwasher to pay the bills, immersed himself in spiritual literature, and by 1973 had finished his ground-breaking manuscript, *The Spectrum of Consciousness*. A prolific career followed, including a complete hiatus for four years to care for his terminally ill wife. Wilber is regarded with suspicion in some academic quarters as a 'transpersonal' philosopher. However, this characterisation is misleading – his work attempts to formulate a grand overarching framework incorporating all understanding about existence, including, but most certainly not limited to, transpersonal theories and ideas around spirituality.

The first binary is the **_mind–body dichotomy_**. The interaction between subjective mind and objective body is one of the most intractable issues in the history of thought (Shear, 1998). Indeed, such are the complexities of this issue, it has been labelled the 'hard problem' of philosophy (Chalmers, 2004). A range of perspectives on this have developed over the centuries (Moravia, 1995). Materialistic monism (or reductive/eliminative materialism) grants primacy to the physical body, with subjective mind seen as an illusion or epiphenomenon, as articulated by prominent contemporary philosophers such as Daniel Dennett (1990). Conversely, transcendental monism views mind as the fundamental reality, with material substance essentially a mental construct or creation. Advocates of this view range from idealist philosophers like Schopenhauer (1969 (1819)) to modern quantum physicists (Goswami, 1990). Finally, dualistic perspectives acknowledge the reality of both material body and subjective mind, with various theories taking different positions on the nature of their interaction. This position is perhaps most commonly associated with the influential philosopher René Descartes (2008 (1641)), who thought that the pineal gland in the centre of the brain was the seat of mind–matter interaction. More recently, Chalmers' (1995) dual-aspect theory proposes that the fundamental 'reality' underlying both mind and body is information; this information is then both manifested physically (as the body/brain) and experienced subjectively (as the mind).

REFLECTION . . .

What is your take on the mind–body debate? What do you think is the relationship between the mind and the body/brain? Does the brain 'cause' the mind? Can the mind impact upon the brain? Perhaps matter is an illusion, a figment of mind? Such questions have perplexed philosophers for centuries. Where do you stand?

One such dualistic perspective underlies the dominant paradigm in contemporary consciousness studies, the neural correlates of consciousness (NCC) approach (Fell, 2004). This is based on the premise of 'psychophysical isomorphism', i.e., the view that states of mind are accompanied by analogous neurophysical states. At this early point in our understanding of the brain, this paradigm aims only to chart the neurophysiological correlates of cognitive functions and mental states; our knowledge is not sufficiently advanced to ascertain directional causality (whether the brain 'causes' the mind, or vice versa) or resolve the ontological mind–body problem (i.e., *how* NCCs are connected to conscious states). These unresolved issues are goals for a future research programme, as outlined by Chalmers (2004, p. 1): 'The task of the science of consciousness . . . is to systematically integrate two key classes of data into a scientific framework: third person data, or data about brain experiences, and first person data, or data about subjective experiences.' Nevertheless, the NCC approach certainly does acknowledge the binary reality of subjective mind and objective body/brain. This binary, then, is one of the two dichotomies that form Wilber's Integral Framework.

The second binary is the ***individual–collective dichotomy***. This reflects the notion that there are two fundamental 'modes of existence', which Bakan (1966) identified as 'agency' and 'communion'. On one hand, people exist as discrete individuals. Thus, agency refers to the way people differentiate themselves from others and develop autonomy as free agents. On the other hand, people are also inevitably and inextricably 'nestled in systems of cultural and social networks' (Wilber, 2005, p. 256). (Even in cases of extreme isolation, social relationships were still necessary to bring the individual into existence.) As such, communion concerns the way people are situated within collective networks that sustain their being, whether physically, emotionally or cognitively. The study of these different modes of being has traditionally been fairly segmented within academia, with agency generally more the province of biology and psychology, and communion claimed by various forms of social theory, such as politics or sociology (Giddens & Dallmayr, 1982). However, more recently, theorists have acknowledged the difficulty of studying these two modes in isolation and recognised the need to explore the complex interactions between them. As such, the term 'psychosocial', which actually has a long and distinguished history (Halliday, 1948), is now increasingly prominent across academic fields, from psychology to epidemiology (Martikainen et al., 2002). This psychosocial binary, then, is the second dichotomy that forms Wilber's Integral Framework.

The innovation offered by Wilber's framework is that it juxtaposes these two binaries, creating a 2 × 2 matrix of four quadrants, which we shall refer to as *domains*, as shown in Figure 1. Beginning with the top left of the schematic, we have the subjective-individual quadrant. This is the domain of the mind, an umbrella term encompassing general subjective experience, including conscious thoughts, feelings and sensations (as well as unconscious subjective dynamics). The top right objective-individual quadrant is the domain of the body and the brain, i.e., all aspects of physiological functioning and behaviour. The lower left is the subjective-collective (or 'intersubjective') quadrant. This is the domain of relationships, and the way these produce a common hermeneutic (i.e., interpretative or sense-making) worldspace, including shared meanings and values. We can refer to this domain

	SUBJECTIVE	**OBJECTIVE**
INDIVIDUAL	SUBJECTIVE *Individual conscious experience* **MIND**	OBJECTIVE *Correlated physical substrates* **BODY**
COLLECTIVE	**CULTURE** *Relationships and shared meanings* INTERSUBJECTIVE	**SOCIETY** *Material systems and structures* INTEROBJECTIVE

Figure 1 Schematic diagram of the four quadrants, adapted from Wilber (1995)

as that of culture, as in 'the culture' of a group of people. Finally, the lower right objective-collective (or 'interobjective') quadrant is the domain of society. This encompasses the material and structural aspects of social networks, such as the physical instantiations of communities (e.g., housing infrastructure), or socio-economic processes.

Wilber's framework has begun to be utilised in academia as a way of conceptualising how to promote wellbeing in an integrated, multidimensional way. Hanlon et al. (2010, p. 307) have used it in public health to understand the 'maze of interconnected problems' which impact upon wellbeing. They offer a hypothetical case study, the gist of which is as follows. A person is depressed due to unemployment. From the perspective of the individual-subjective quadrant, their depression can be viewed in terms of distress, understood with cognitive theories of mental illness, and addressed through therapy. From the perspective of the individual-objective quadrant, their depression can be seen in terms of brain dysfunction, understood through neurochemical theories, and addressed through medication. From the perspective of the subjective-collective quadrant, their depression can be considered in terms of cultural meanings around unemployment, understood through theories of social constructionism, and addressed by challenging societal norms. From the perspective of the objective-collective quadrant, their depression can be approached in terms of socio-economic factors that underlie unemployment, understood through economic theories, and addressed with political efforts towards a fairer society. Hanlon et al. argue that all these 'key dimensions of human experience need to be considered, harmonized and acted on as a whole' to fully address mental health issues (2010, p. 311).

REFLECTION . . .

What do you consider to be more important or instrumental in shaping your own wellbeing – your psychological qualities, your physiology, your relationships or your place in society?

Wilber's framework is a powerful tool for conceptualising and approaching wellbeing. However, within PP, while Ken Wilber is spoken of respectfully by many scholars (Walsh, 2001), so far his framework has not yet been harnessed as an overarching model to guide our understanding and our endeavours to promote wellbeing. Currently though, this book makes the case that this framework can indeed help us develop a comprehensive approach to wellbeing. One of the strengths of his framework is that it is 'content free': rather than proposing theories in a given area, it allows scholars to situate extant theories and research from the area under study according to the four-quadrant framework (Esbjörn-Hargens, 2006).

Moreover, we can appreciate the importance of considering theories/concepts from *all* the domains, and examining how they might interrelate. Such considerations form the substance of the book as a whole, and will be explored in depth throughout the chapters. However, we can briefly consider the domains in turn to get a flavour of the concepts relating to wellbeing that can be situated within each, and hence within our own adaptation of this framework, the LIFE model.

The subjective domain is the location for the wealth of constructs directly pertaining to mental health and illness. Here, wellbeing can be conceptualised either positively as the presence of desiderata, such as pleasure, or negatively as the absence of mental illness. The desiderata include the triad of elements that Seligman (2002) suggests comprises the well-lived life. First, the pleasurable life, as reflected in constructs like subjective wellbeing (SWB). Second, the engaged life, which encompasses notions like flow (Csikszentmihalyi, 1990). Third, the meaningful life, as reflected in Ryff's (1989) model of psychological wellbeing (PWB). (Of course, situating these constructs in this domain does not mean they are unconnected to the other domains. Ryff's PWB model includes relationships, which pertain to the intersubjective domain. Indeed, the *point* about the domains is that they are interlinked.) This domain also includes the panoply of desirable psychological qualities embraced by PP, from emotional intelligence (Salovey & Mayer, 1989) to hope (Snyder, 2000). In addition, recent theorising suggests that the remit of PP does not only cover these positive constructs, but extends to 'negative' constructs, such as sadness (Wong, 2011) and depression (Sin & Lyubomirsky, 2009), which we can also situate here. In a way, as the most 'psychological' of the domains, this is the root domain. PP is first and foremost a psychological discipline, pertaining to the mind. The other domains are only relevant to PP to the extent that they impinge upon the mind, e.g., affect a person's subjective sense of wellbeing. Nevertheless, it is helpful to explore the other domains to gain a comprehensive understanding of the range of factors that influence wellbeing.

The objective domain concerns the physiological functioning and behaviour of the body and the brain. First, this quadrant encompasses everything relating to physical health. Larson (1999) has identified numerous models of health, including the WHO model (noted above); the medical model, which defines health as the 'absence of disease and disability' (p. 124); the wellness model, concerned with 'progress towards higher levels of functioning' (p. 129); and the environmental model, pertaining to successful adaptation to one's milieu. These models can all be situated in this domain. Located here too are the diverse health behaviours which impact upon physical wellbeing, like exercise (Hefferon & Mutrie, 2012), and risk behaviours that detract from health, like alcohol use (Farrell et al., 2001). Second this domain includes efforts towards understanding the physiological aspects of states of wellbeing, as per the mind–body connection introduced above. This includes analysis of biological substrates of pleasure, e.g., neuroendocrine biomarkers (Ryff et al., 2006). Similarly, embracing the NCC paradigm, a positive neuroscience research programme has begun exploring the 'neural correlates of wellbeing' (Urry et al., 2004). For instance, trait asymmetric activation of the prefrontal cortex is linked to greater levels of positive affect (Davidson, 2000). More generally, this whole domain can be situated within the broader arena of positive health (Seligman, 2008).

The intersubjective domain covers relationships and the shared culture (e.g., values and meanings) that these generate. One useful overarching construct pertaining to this domain is social capital. This refers to the 'sum total of the resources, actual or virtual, that accrue to an individual (or a group) by virtue of being enmeshed in a durable network of more or less institutionalized relationships of mutual acquaintance and recognition' (Bourdieu, 1986, p. 248). Social capital is an elastic construct which encompasses all types of relationships of relevance to PP. These range from bonds within the home, addressed by specialities like positive relationship science (Fincham & Beach, 2010) and family-centred positive psychology (Sheridan et al., 2004), to relations in the workplace or the classroom, as covered by PP sub-disciplines such as positive organisational scholarship (Cameron et al., 2003) and positive education (Seligman et al., 2009). This domain captures the manifold ways in which relationships are vital to wellbeing, from offering social support (Kawachi & Berkman, 2001) to being sources of self-esteem (Symister & Friend, 2003). The domain also covers the emergent forms of culture generated by relationships. This includes the way cultural systems can generate values and worldviews that can be conducive to wellbeing, like religion (Koenig, 2009), or detrimental, like materialism (van Boven, 2005). Intersubjective concerns also include cultural norms – in relation to phenomena like gender (Lomas, 2013) – that influence behaviour and consequently affect wellbeing.

Finally, the interobjective domain refers to the structural aspects of society: the impersonal processes, institutions and environments which provide the scaffolding for people's lives. These structures range from the material conditions of the built environment to macro-economic forces that influence employment rates. This domain thus encompasses the work of diverse theorists, across different fields, exploring the way these structures impact upon wellbeing. Economists have embraced SWB as an alternative to Gross Domestic Product as a barometer of societal progress (Layard, 2005), and have analysed the impact of various structural factors on SWB, including employment (Lucas et al., 2004) and income (Easterlin, 1995). Other relevant factors include indices used by the United Nations (UN) (2013) to calculate the 'human development index', namely living standards, health outcomes and education provision. Alternatively, the

World Bank has explored the impact of the quality of governance on wellbeing (Kaufmann et al., 2009). Interobjective structural considerations also include the quality of the built and natural environment (e.g., freedom from air pollution), whether at a local community level (Burke et al., 2009) or a wider national or even global level (Thompson et al., 2013).

So, we have outlined the four domains of our map, which will be used to help structure the book, as set out in the Introduction. We will focus in turn on the mind (Chapter 2), the body/brain (Chapter 3), and culture and society (Chapter 4), before using these domains collectively to explore lifespan development (Chapter 5), occupations and organisations (Chapter 6), religion and spirituality (Chapter 7) and becoming PP practitioners (Chapter 8). Thus, we can see how a multidimensional approach provides the architecture for a comprehensive approach to wellbeing, involving the application of PPIs across all four domains. However, before we move on to presenting the other element in our preparation for the journey – namely our motto – our map is not quite complete. It is not simply that map has four different domains; each domain can itself be stratified into a number of levels, as the next section outlines. By taking into account these different levels, our APP approach becomes even more comprehensive. That is, we can devise and apply interventions and activities that are targeted not only towards the various specific domains, but towards different levels within each domain.

Layering

So far we have introduced Wilber's Integral Framework. Now we shall explain how we have adapted his original framework to produce our own Layered Integrated Framework Example (LIFE) model (see also Lomas et al., forthcoming). Essentially, we can introduce further nuance and subtlety to our understanding of wellbeing by viewing each domain as being layered or stratified, thus producing our LIFE adaptation. That is, rather than just conceptualising each domain as an undifferentiated whole, we can develop a more sophisticated understanding by delineating different strands within them. There are potentially many possible ways of 'carving up' the domains, and our approach is by no means the only viable option. (Indeed, Wilber himself identifies different strata within his own model, although his stratification is more a historical-developmental perspective concerning the emergence of particular qualities in human development.) This is why we have named our own adaptation as the Layered Integrated Framework *Example* – our model is just one example of how such layering might be done, and indeed of a multidimensional model more generally. Nevertheless, we hope the particular layering strategy pursued here will prove convincing and helpful. Essentially, our approach is to view each domain as comprising various levels. These can be arranged in order of scale, such that each level encompasses or supersedes the level 'below' it, as shown in

Figure 2.[2] This concept of layering can be explained in more detail by considering the domains in turn.

We will first consider the subjective domain, since, as suggested above, from a PP perspective this is the *root* domain. We can readily identify at least four different phenomenological strata: embodied sensations, emotions, cognitions

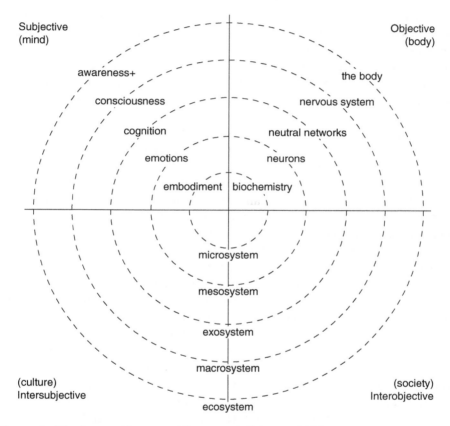

Figure 2 The Layered Integrated Framework Example (LIFE) model

---

[2] In considering the figure, it is worth emphasising that levels that are located on the same concentric circle are not 'equivalent' in any way. For example, the second inner ring features emotions, neurons and mesosystems. These are not functional counterparts; each domain was stratified on its own terms, and these three were placed on the second tier simply because they happened to be the second term in the sequence for that domain. Moreover, there is nothing magical about there being five layers in each domain; as emphasised above, our approach to stratification is just one possible way of layering these domains. It would be perfectly possible and legitimate to stratify each domain with fewer levels, or indeed a greater number of more fine-grained levels.

and conscious awareness. Furthermore, these strata can arguably be viewed as proceeding from 'lower' to 'higher', for two reasons. First, in phylogenetic terms (i.e., the development of the species), we can perhaps see these strata emerging in this sequence: embodied sensations are thought to have emerged much earlier in our evolutionary progression than discursive (i.e., linguistic) cognitions (MacLean, 1990). Secondly, and similarly, this emergent sequence would also apply to ontogenetic development (i.e., the growth of the person), since infants experience sensations before they acquire emotions, followed still later by more complex cognitions (Piaget, 1971). We have also added a more contentious fifth stratum, labelled tentatively as 'awareness+'. This level reflects the work of theorists who propose that conscious awareness can be superseded by yet more advanced phenomenological capacities and higher states of consciousness (Josipovic, 2010), as explained at the end of Chapter 2 and in more detail in Chapter 7.

In PP, our understanding of the role these subjective levels play in enhancing or hindering wellbeing is growing rapidly. Moreover, the field is replete with a cornucopia of PPIs to promote wellbeing at the various levels. First, PP is increasingly attuned to the complex intersections between embodiment and wellbeing (Hefferon, 2013), and various body awareness therapies have arisen that focus on these connections (Gard, 2005). Moving 'up' levels, the importance of positive emotions to PP can hardly be overstated, with a focus on constructs like happiness being almost the core defining feature of the field. In terms of APP, we see an ever-expanding list of PPIs to promote desirable emotions, from compassion (Neff & Germer, 2013) to gratitude (Emmons & McCullough, 2003). At the cognitive level, the relevance of discursive thoughts to wellbeing has long been understood (Beck et al., 1979). Such understanding has generated cognitively-focused PPIs, such as narrative restructuring exercises (Pennebaker & Seagal, 1999). Of course, the various levels are not hermetically sealed, but commingle and interact, as evidenced by constructs bridging emotion and cognition, like emotional intelligence (Mayer & Salovey, 1997) and its associated interventions (Nelis et al., 2009). Finally, the levels of consciousness and even awareness+ are very well catered-for by the phenomenal proliferation of constructs and interventions related to the Buddhist-derived notion of mindfulness (Kabat-Zinn, 2003).

Turning now to the objective domain, here we can arrange the levels into a *holarchy*, i.e., a hierarchy in which each level encompasses the level beneath it (see the box below for the origin of this word). Biochemical molecules and atoms (e.g., sodium ions) are components of neurons; neurons combine to create neural networks; such networks are part of the larger nervous system; and the nervous system is but one element of the whole body. (We can of course identify other viable holarchies, perhaps involving more gradations or highlighting other elements.) In terms of PP, we can examine how each of these levels influences wellbeing, and moreover, design interventions to act on each level. At a biochemical level, mental illness can be understood in terms of the activity of neurotransmitters like serotonin, as in the monoamine deficiency model of depression (Schildkraut, 1965). Interventions at this level aim to alter biochemical 'imbalances', as with selective serotonin reuptake inhibitor (SSRI) treatments (Ferguson, 2001). Such biochemical interventions are at present the sole province of medical disciplines like psychiatry, used in treating mental illness. However, research has demonstrated the positive impact on wellbeing of psychoactive drugs such as psilocybin (Griffiths et al., 2006) and MDMA (Adamson & Metzner, 1988). It is conceivable that medical practitioners will in future harness such substances to proactively promote wellbeing (Sessa, 2007), as discussed in Chapter 3.

REFLECTION . . .

The term *holarchy* originated with the Hungarian intellectual Arthur Koestler (1978). To explain this, we need to introduce another neologism coined by Koestler: the *holon*. Koestler proposed the word *holon*, derived etymologically from the words 'whole' and 'part', to reflect the idea that everything in existence is simultaneously a whole and a part. For example, a person is a whole being, yet is part of a family; a family is a whole unit, yet is nevertheless part of a community, and so on. So, each element in the system, such as the family, is a holon – both a whole unit (relative to the level beneath it, i.e., the individual), and a constituent part (relative to the level above it, i.e., the community). As such, a holarchy refers to this arrangement in which holons are embedded within larger holons, which are in turn themselves nested within still larger holons. In terms of our stratification of the objective domain, and indeed of the intersubjective and interobjective domains (see below), the concept of a holarchy is more appropriate than that of a hierarchy. The latter embeds notions of top–down rule, where higher levels dominate and control their subservient inferior levels. In contrast, in a holarchical arrangement, the relationship between the levels is more complex: each level is somewhat autonomous, and causal influences can proceed up the chain as well as down. What do you think of the holarchy concept?

Moving up the holarchy, we can explore the impact of neural networks on wellbeing. These networks refer to the way mental activities are produced by the interaction of areas distributed throughout the brain (Fell et al., 2010). Relevant methods of analysis include electroencephalography (EEG), which gauges the synchronisation of neural populations (Basar et al., 2001). EEG analysis connects wellbeing to particular patterns of neural activity, such as greater left-sided activation of the brain (Rickard & Vella-Brodrick, 2013). Moreover, from an APP perspective, these beneficial activation patterns can be promoted by interventions such as neurofeedback (Hammond, 2005). Neurofeedback activities can be situated within a larger framework of biofeedback, which can affect the nervous system generally, thus reaching a more encompassing holarchical level. Here, Kleen and Reitsma (2011) combined Heart Rate Variability (HRV) biofeedback training (lower HRV is associated with outcomes like anxiety) with mindfulness to good effect. Stepping up to the whole body, PP has tended to overlook its relevance to wellbeing, as reflected in Seligman's (2008) remark that PP needed to evolve beyond being a 'neck-up' focused discipline. However, work has begun to incorporate the body more into PP, exploring the complex intersections between physical health/illness and constructs like SWB and PWB (Hefferon, 2013). From an APP perspective, there is a panoply of PPIs that work with the body to promote wellbeing, from exercise (Hefferon & Mutrie, 2012) to creating meaning with the body through dance therapy (Puig et al., 2006).

Having outlined our stratification of the subjective and objective domains, we now turn to the two collective domains. As with the objective domain, we can again conceptualise these as being stratified holarchically. For this stratification, we will use Bronfenbrenner's (1977) influential experimental ecology model, which identified six socio-cultural levels, ordered according to scale from the micro to the macro. This model can be used for both domains, as it straddles the two quadrants. That is, one can analyse all levels of his model from either an intersubjective perspective (e.g., shared values) or an interobjective perspective (e.g., structural aspects of that level). We shall consider these levels in turn, from smallest to largest. However, we shall omit the 'smallest' level of his model, since this is not relevant to the intersubjective or interobjective domains; in Bronfenbrenner's original model, the first level is the person themselves (e.g., their cognitive processes). However, in our adapted version, this first level has been massively expanded, becoming in effect the entire subjective and objective domains. (The LIFE model also omits the sixth of Bronfenbrenner's levels, namely the chronosystem, which pertains to change over time. However, consideration of the chronosystem in effect constitutes the entire fifth chapter of this book, which focuses on lifespan development.) As such, in terms of the intersubjective and interobjective domains, we begin the stratification at the second tier of Bronfenbrenner's model, namely the microsystem. As with the other domains, we shall again highlight examples of PP constructs and practices that pertain to each level.

The microsystem refers to the immediate social setting of the person, e.g., their family or workplace. To reinforce the point about Bronfenbrenner's model straddling both domains, we can approach these settings from either an intersubjective (e.g., a family's shared values) or an interobjective (e.g., their material circumstances) perspective. In PP, the importance of the microsystem is recognised in studies highlighting the powerful association between relationships and wellbeing (Phillips et al., 2008). In APP terms, PPIs delivered at a microsystem level include the use of PP activities in couples therapy (Kauffman & Silberman, 2009). The next level is the broader network of the mesosystem, which refers to inter-relationships among different microsystems. Meso-level PPIs may involve working with clients across diverse settings, such as helping students in school *and* supporting them outside school (Sheridan et al., 2004). Indeed, Prilleltensky et al. (2001, p. 151) argue that 'clinical and community interventions are inseparable' (as reflected in the provision of an MSc in Clinical and Community Psychology at our own institution). A larger scale still is the exosystem, which refers to structures that 'encompass the immediate settings', such as the wider community in which the various microsystems are situated (Bronfenbrenner, 1977, p. 515). Community factors, both intersubjective (e.g., social capital) and interobjective (e.g., provision of social services), have a large impact upon well-being (Burke et al., 2009). We can promote wellbeing at the exosystem level through community interventions, like the Well London Project, which works with local communities in terms of health promotion and community develop-ment (Phillips et al., 2012).

REFLECTION . . .

What do you think of Bronfenbrenner's (1977) experimental ecology, and the way we have deployed it in our LIFE model? Do you think this is a helpful way of conceptual-ising our socio-cultural world? Can you think of other possible ways of stratifying the intersubjective and interobjective domains?

The most expansive of Bronfenbrenner's (1977, p. 515) levels is the macrosystem, i.e., 'overarching institutional patterns . . . such as the economic, social, educational, legal, and political systems', of which the other levels are 'concrete manifestations'. Analysis of the impact of the macrosystem on wellbeing focuses on economic and political factors, like quality of governance (Kaufmann et al., 1999), with rec-ognition that wellbeing depends upon 'effective social and political institutions' (Duncan, 2010, p. 165). In terms of APP, we can consider interventions at a policy level, promoting wellbeing by making regulatory frameworks more conducive to this end. Indeed, UN-commissioned analyses of global levels of SWB have led to structural macro-policy recommendations (Helliwell et al., 2013). Finally, we shall take the liberty of adding another level to Bronfenbrenner's original model, namely the global eco-system. The biosphere encompasses all the other systems, since it is the physical matrix that supports their very existence. From a PP per-spective, this means extending our concern with wellbeing to *environmental* well-being, since existentially, our wellbeing is ultimately dependent upon the health of the planet (Smith et al., 2013). This dependence is recognised in recent efforts to take ecological variables into account, such as societal sustainability, when calculating macro-level wellbeing, as in the New Economics Foundation's (NEF) (2013) Happy Planet Index. In terms of APP, as ecological wellbeing depends to some extent on human behaviour, we can devise PPIs that might impact positively on the environment, intervening at any of the levels of Bronfenbrenner's model to influence people in the direction of more sustainable behaviours (Hopper & Nielsen, 1991).

Our motto

So, we have constructed a detailed map of the terrain that APP can be concerned with, and highlighted some of the ways in which we can promote wellbeing across the various domains and levels – these will, of course, be examined in detail throughout the book. As such, we are almost ready to begin our journey! However, before we set off, it will help to avail ourselves of a motto that can help us understand *why* we are travelling, and lend purpose to our mission. To this end, we have constructed a purposeful teleological statement to guide us. This motto was devised in response to us interrogating at length the issue of what PP is actually *for*. Our answer is that the point of PP is *to make life better*. Although this motto initially comes across as plain, even banal, we believe that a number of important concepts are embedded within it that collectively make it a powerful statement of intent. Moreover, the motto also serves as an answer to some trenchant criticisms that have been levelled against PP in recent years (e.g., Lazarus, 2003). In some ways, such critics are the best friends of the PP movement, as they shine a clinical light on its weak points and unacknowledged biases. Responding thoughtfully to such critiques, as this motto seeks to, can only help to strengthen PP.

REFLECTION . . .

What do you see as the 'point' of PP, and what might your own motto be? Whatever phrase you choose as your motto, what are the meanings and nuances embedded within it?

The first component of our guiding statement is the verb 'to make'. This serves to reinforce the idea of PP as a form of praxis, and to designate PP primarily as an applied discipline. As outlined in the introduction, this designation helps address the issue of the *identity* of PP, and whether it even needs to exist *per se* as a going concern (since the movement has arguably gone some way towards fulfilling its original mission, i.e., redressing the negative bias within psychology). Moreover, the word 'praxis' incorporates various other meanings which further help to conceptualise the nature of PP. First, praxis can be defined as 'practical action informed by theory' (Foster, 1986, p. 96). This definition reinforces the notion that PP seeks to promote wellbeing in empirically-validated and theoretically-justified ways, which differentiates it from generic self-help movements. A second key meaning embedded in the term concerns the relationship between the PP practitioner and their participant/client. In the social sciences, praxis has its most committed advocates among politically-minded scholars committed to 'action research' (Kemmis & McTaggart, 1982). In this paradigm, also called participatory research, collaborative inquiry and emancipatory research, researchers and researched *collaborate* in effecting real-world changes. Thus, praxis suggests a non-coercive, non-hierarchical partnership between practitioner and client. So, PP is ideally facilitative rather than prescriptive – encouraging people to determine their own goals and helping them achieve these, rather than paternalistically telling people how to be.

If PP is indeed an applied discipline, we must ask, who is it for and in what circumstances? What differentiates PP from other applied disciplines, like clinical psychology, which are also undoubtedly concerned with improving wellbeing? Until recently, one answer would be that clinical psychology alleviates negative mental states, while PP aims to promote positive states. However, that distinction might not hold any longer. On one hand, some clinical psychologists have argued that their discipline should also focus on positive mental health (Wood & Tarrier, 2010). On the other hand, PP is also beginning to engage with what could be considered to be difficult and challenging states (e.g., finding meaning in suffering). More fundamentally, some theorists have even questioned the validity of labelling particular emotions or outcomes as either 'positive' or 'negative' (Lazarus, 2003), as discussed further below. Another possible answer could be that PP is defined by the use of specific practices, such as gratitude tasks. However, that definition is not especially useful either. To illustrate this, consider mindfulness, a form of meditation that has been embraced by psychology and medicine (as discussed in Chapter 2). Does this count as a PPI? The answer would have to be no, at least not exclusively. In so far as mindfulness has been used in treating physical illness, it can be seen as a medical intervention (Kabat-Zinn et al., 1987). In so far as it has been adapted for mental health disorders, it constitutes a clinical psychology intervention (Teasdale et al., 2000). In so far as it has been harnessed in psychotherapy, it qualifies as a psychotherapeutic tool (Germer et al., 2005). Given the range of uses of mindfulness, not to mention its Buddhist roots, it would be hubristic to 'claim it' as a PPI.

The range of contexts in which mindfulness has been used, however, might offer one possible way of delineating a specific territory for APP, namely that, generally speaking, APP can be defined as the use of wellbeing practices with a *non-clinical* population.[3] For instance, mindfulness has been used in non-clinical settings to promote wellbeing (Smith et al., 1995); in this case, it would qualify as a PPI. In presenting this tentative definition, it is worth saying that the authors engaged in ongoing debate about its merits. We wondered, what about the use of PP in treating mental health problems? We felt this definition would not preclude PPIs being used for this (Sin & Lyubomirsky, 2009); the question is how one conceptualises such problems and categorises people suffering from them. The issue of when 'negative' mental states become classified as clinical disorders is much debated (Flett et al., 1997). We can certainly recognise that there are times when a person is deemed to be experiencing dysphoria, but this is not treated as a clinical issue, either by health professionals or by the person themselves. For instance, a sufferer may ascribe their depression to a legitimate sense of existential anomie, rather than view it as a psychiatric disorder (Szasz, 1960). In such cases, people may have historically tried psychotherapy; now, others may engage with a PP practitioner. APP would thus include interactions that were like 'therapy for people who don't want therapy'. There remains the grey area of interventions that originated in PP – e.g., gratitude exercises – being used in clinical settings. By our rationale, in such circumstances, these would simply be clinical psychology interventions (clinical psychology would thereby expand its own boundaries, taking in exercises that actively promote 'positive' thoughts/emotions).

REFLECTION . . .

Who do you think PP is for, and under what circumstances? What do you think of our designation of PP as the use of wellbeing practices with a *non-clinical* population? Do you agree that, even with such a designation, PP might still be used in treating mental health problems? The ideas in this chapter are just suggestions – you may construe the nature and role of PP differently. How would you demarcate the 'territory' for PP? Do we even *need* to specify a territory in this way? Reflect on your opinions.

---

[3] This delineation overlaps to some extent with the field of coaching psychology as defined by Grant (2006, p. 12): 'The systematic application of behavioural science to the enhancement of life experience, work performance and well-being for individuals, groups and organisations who do not have clinically significant mental health issues.' However, following Biswas-Diener (2009), we reserve the term 'coaching' for interactions involving a one-to-one 'professional relationship' between a coach and client – akin to psychotherapy, except helping 'functioning people perform even better' (p. 546). Our vision for PP is much broader than this, including, but certainly not limited to, such interactions – as elucidated in this book. As such, we could view coaching as a subset of PP (though those in coaching psychology may not agree!), as discussed in Chapter 6.

At this point, given that we are suggesting that PP might be used in ameliorating mental health issues, it is worth updating a common PP metaphor: the mental illness–health continuum. A founding image used in articulating a role for PP was that whereas fields like clinical psychology just aimed to bring people from '–5' (i.e., mental illness) to '0' (i.e., absence of mental illness), PP could take people up to '+5' (i.e., positive mental health). This image of a single continuum from illness to health implies that PP is only relevant once people reach this metaphorical '0', i.e., are free from mental health problems. However, we reject this implication, as PP may be useful in helping treat mental illness, e.g., as an adjunctive intervention (Sin & Lyubomirsky, 2009), as argued above. More fundamentally, we also disagree that mental illness and health are mutually exclusive, that one can only flourish if free from mental illness. A fascinating study suggested that a small minority of people score highly on measures of depression and flourishing *simultaneously* (Keyes, 2002). Indeed, there has long been a cultural association between mental illness and certain aspects of flourishing, especially creativity (Kaufman, 2001). We contend, then, that the continuum metaphor might be better configured as a circumplex, as shown in Figure 3. Here, mental illness ('–5' to '0') and mental health ('0' to '+5') are represented as separate orthogonal dimensions. An individual might be judged to be at a particular point on *both* dimensions – suffering with mental health issues to some extent *and* also flourishing to some extent – thus locating them somewhere in the two-dimensional space of the model. And, wherever they are 'located', we argue that PP can play a role in making their life better.

The second component of our guiding teleological statement is the noun 'life', which nicely reflects the LIFE acronym we have chosen for our multidimensional model of the person. The choice of this word as the target of PP serves to drastically widen the scope of the discipline. In many ways, this expansion is *already*

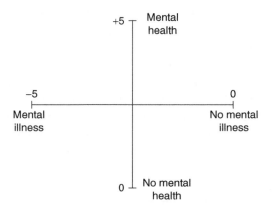

Figure 3   The mental illness–health circumplex

taking place within PP – this motto simply recognises and conceptualises this. We might consider this 'widening' in three respects: going beyond the mind, beyond the individual and beyond the species. Here the LIFE model really helps to clarify matters, since our vision for the enlarged scope of PP encompasses all domains and levels of the model. First, PP is beginning to go beyond the mind by incorporating the whole body, both in terms of embodiment (the first level of the subjective domain) and physiology (the whole objective domain) (Hefferon, 2013). Second, PP is starting to go beyond the individual by considering their socio-cultural context, as reflected in the entire intersubjective and interobjective domains of the model. Finally, PP is even starting to go beyond humankind by taking into account the wellbeing of the environment, as represented by the addition of the eco-system level. Thus, by seeking to make 'life' better, we are not aiming to simply improve the mind, or even just make the individual better, but to improve all aspects of life: individual functioning (both subjective and objective), social contexts at all levels of Bronfenbrenner's model (in both intersubjective and interobjective terms) and finally the biosphere that actually sustains life.

Expanding our focus in this way helps answer various criticisms of PP. First, going beyond the mind to incorporate the body addresses a historical lack of attention to the corporeal in PP (Hefferon, 2013). Second, going beyond the individual to consider social contexts answers one of the most pernicious critiques levelled against PP – its tendency towards an individualistic conceptualisation of wellbeing. From a critical perspective, PP is accused of promulgating a culturally-specific version of the good life, drawing upon a North American tradition of individualism in which happiness is seen as a private concern, achieved through self-determined choices (Becker & Marecek, 2008). While some attention is paid to social contexts in PP – indeed, institutions are one of the 'three pillars' of personal fulfilment (Peterson, 2006a) – analysis of these is largely restricted to what Bellah et al. (1996, p. xxv) call 'social in the narrow sense', i.e., limited to local settings. For instance, it is recognised that positive family relationships contribute to SWB (Reis & Gable, 2003). However, there has been little critical analysis of the way political, cultural and socio-economic factors impinge upon wellbeing, or of structural factors that might affect a person's ability to flourish, such as educational and economic opportunities (Prilleltensky & Prilleltensky, 2005). These are important issues, which we discuss in depth in Chapter 4 (and will generally seek to be cognizant of throughout the book). As such, by articulating a stratified multidimensional model of wellbeing, we can begin to redress such critiques.

The third component of our guiding teleological statement is the adjective 'better'. This is chosen as being deliberately ambiguous and polysemantic. Dictionary definitions attribute a range of meanings to the term, including more useful, satisfactory, effective and desirable, and greater in excellence or quality. Thus, although the word is value-laden – seeking positive change – it does not ascribe a particular form to these improvements. Most notably, it avoids positioning 'happiness' as the goal of PP. This is important for various reasons. First, eschewing the word 'happy' as a goal helps neutralise the prominent criticism of PP as being 'happyology' (Peterson, 2006a). As Peterson laments, this has led to PP being linked to the 'ubiquitous smiley face' in media coverage of the field. There are various dangers inherent in this depiction of PP. There is a risk of PP being viewed as just another self-help movement based around positive thinking. This lends the impression that PP is simply old wine in new bottles, rehashing the tropes of previous movements centred on the power of positive thoughts (Becker & Marecek, 2008), such as the 'New Thought' trend associated with Phineas Quimby (2007 (1846–1865)). More perniciously, an undue emphasis on happiness has generated accusations that PP promotes a 'tyranny of positive thinking' (Held, 2004, p. 12), making happiness normative to the extent that failure to experience positivity is viewed almost as a moral failing (Ehrenreich, 2009).

Avoiding the term 'happy', however, is not just about distancing PP from antecedent ideologies, thus hoping for a better critical reception. Rather, it reflects a growing appreciation in PP of the nuances of emotions. PP has sometimes been guilty of promulgating a simplistic Manichean dichotomy, where positive emotions are associated with happiness and are therefore unreservedly good, while negative emotions are coterminous with unhappiness and thereby unreservedly bad (Lazarus, 2003). However, a more nuanced treatment of emotions is emerging, a trend labelled the 'second-wave' of PP (Held, 2004), or 'positive psychology 2.0' (Wong, 2011). Positive emotions/qualities can have maladaptive outcomes, e.g., optimism is linked to under-appreciation of risk (Peterson & Vaidya, 2003). Conversely, dysphorias may actually serve to promote wellbeing, e.g., anxiety can alert us to threats. Indeed, Lazarus (2003) questions the very possibility of classifying emotions as positive or negative, as many emotions are co-valenced, with their impact contextually determined. For example, love can be either agony or ecstasy, depending on whether it is reciprocated. At a deeper philosophical level, there is an inherently dialectical relationship between positive and negative emotions, which are by definition conceptually co-dependent (Ryff & Singer, 2003). Just as 'up' only exists if 'down' is recognised, 'positive' only has meaning if 'negative' also exists. Trying to eradicate the 'negative' is thus as nonsensical as trying to abolish 'down'. Thus, Resnick et al. (2001) urge us to avoid polarising psychology into good and bad, but to appreciate the complexities of the good life.

REFLECTION . . .

Think about the complexities of your own emotions. In what circumstances might emotions normally deemed 'positive' inhibit flourishing, or 'negative' emotions actually be conducive to wellbeing?

Thus, the vagueness of the word 'better' means these complexities are recognised. Moreover, it is an admission that our understanding of how to inculcate and promote the good life is always incomplete and provisional. Finally, reflecting the point about expanding the scope of PP, using 'better' prevents an undue individualistic focus on private emotional states, and extends our focus to improving social conditions – for we cannot speak of making social contexts 'happier', only making them 'better' so that they may be more conducive to happiness. That said, we do need some way of assessing what 'better' means in the context of PP. This judgement lies primarily with the people who are the subject of PPIs, i.e., their assessment of whether their life has been made better. Crucially, the person themself will determine the basis on which they make this assessment. This autonomy mirrors current measures of life satisfaction (e.g. 'Are you happy with your life?') which represent a 'global assessment of a person's quality of life *according to a person's chosen criteria*' (Shin & Johnson, 1978, p. 477, our italics). Moreover, this autonomy reflects the idea, raised above in relation to praxis, that PP should be facilitative, not prescriptive. The person themself determines what 'better' consists of, and whether this has indeed been achieved.

So, we have constructed our map, and articulated our motto. One final issue remains: the name we give to our endeavours! In recent years, a profusion of positive disciplines has emerged, including positive education (Seligman et al., 2009), positive psychotherapy (Seligman et al., 2006), positive health (Seligman, 2008) and positive sociology (Stebbins, 2009). While these disciplines are often treated as subsets of PP, the broader terms positive social science (Seligman, 1999) and even positive science (Sheldon, 2011) have been used to encompass these approaches. However, a better overarching label might be Integrated Positive Practice. The word 'integrated' encapsulates the multidimensional nature of wellbeing, and is a key term in our LIFE acronym. The phrase 'positive practice' is useful, since by eschewing the word 'psychology' it is able to embrace all the various positive disciplines as an overarching conceptual term. The word 'practice' also overlaps conceptually with the term 'praxis' and thus serves to emphasise the applied nature of the discipline. At the same time, we can still recognise PP (i.e., psychology) as being the root of the varied positive disciplines: whether we are engaging in positive neuroscience or positive sociology, ultimately, the fundamental test of our interventions – at whatever level of scale – is whether people subjectively *feel better* about their lives as a result. Thus, the critical outcome will always be a subjective assessment of improvement (hence our assertion above about the subjective domain being the root quadrant). That being said, we hope the phrase Integrated Positive Practice will help lift our visions to new horizons and empower us to approach and engage with wellbeing in a comprehensive and multidimensional way. And so. . . the journey begins!

SUMMARY – THIS CHAPTER HAS...

- Articulated the desirability of taking a multidimensional approach to wellbeing
- Introduced Ken Wilber's Integral Framework and Bronfenbrenner's experimental ecology
- Presented our own multidimensional LIFE model as the conceptual map for this book
- Articulated a motto for PP, namely *to make life better*
- Used this motto to identify PP as a form of praxis, and as an applied psychology discipline
- Used this motto to expand the focus of PP beyond the mind and beyond the individual
- Used this motto to take a more nuanced approach to conceptualising emotions

QUIZ...

1 In what year did the WHO formulate its definition of health?
2 What is the dominant mind–body paradigm within consciousness studies?
3 Who identified agency and communion as being the two fundamental modes of being?
4 Which domain pertains to relationships, the intersubjective or interobjective?
5 Who coined the terms 'holon' and 'holarchy'?
6 What level did our LIFE model add to Bronfenbrenner's original experimental ecology?
7 Who said 'The philosophers have only interpreted the world, in various ways. The point, however, is to change it'?
8 In the social sciences, what is another name for 'action research'? (3 possible answers)
9 In order of increasing scale, which level comes after 'micro' in Bronfenbrenner's ecology?
10 Who was the originator of the 'New Thought' movement?

RESOURCES AND SUGGESTIONS...

- You can find more information about Ken Wilber at www.kenwilber.com, and more on the Integral Framework generally at www.integralinstitute.org.
- In terms of the frameworks outlined in this chapter, you may not be persuaded by Wilber and Bronfenbrenner's models, or by our adaptation of these in the form of our LIFE model. That's OK! Other multidimensional frameworks exist, like Layder's (1993) research map, which you could use instead. In terms of the use of conceptual maps in academia generally, *Visualizing Social Science Research: Maps, Methods, & Meaning*, by Wheeldon and Ahlberg (2011), is well worth a read.

THE MIND

God grant me the serenity to accept the things I cannot change,
the courage to change the things I can,
and the wisdom to know the difference.
Reinhold Niebuhr

LIST OF TOPICS…

- Consciousness, awareness and attention
- Types of meditation
- Mindfulness-based interventions
- Embodiment
- Body awareness therapies
- Emotional intelligence
- Meaning, coherence and purpose
- Logotherapy
- Narratives
- Personal projects
- Possible selves
- Awareness+

In Chapter 1 we introduced our LIFE model, identifying four fundamental domains of the person: subjective (mind), objective (body), intersubjective (culture) and interobjective (society). We also presented PP as a form of praxis, and articulated a motto to reflect this, namely that the point of PP was *to make life better*. In this second chapter, we focus on the subjective domain, i.e., the mind. Aligning this focus with the central motto, this chapter is about *working with the mind to make life better*. What this means is that we are concerned here with strategies to enhance wellbeing that are primarily internal and introspective. This is in contrast to strategies that involve actions and behaviour (these feature in Chapter 3, which focuses on the body), or strategies that concern relationships (these are discussed in Chapter 4, which pertains to culture and society). In essence, then, we are looking at psychological techniques for enhancing wellbeing, the kind a person might be able to do sitting alone at home (i.e., they don't necessarily require movement, or other people).

Our approach to this subjective domain can be further clarified by the idea of stratification introduced in Chapter 1. We stratified the subjective domain into five levels: embodiment, emotions, cognitions, consciousness and awareness+. Here we will consider each of these levels in turn. However, it is important to emphasise that these levels are not rigidly compartmentalised, and our discussion of each level will incorporate aspects from the other levels. For example, for the emotional level, we focus on the construct of emotional intelligence; while evidently about emotions, this involves both emotional awareness (i.e., consciousness) and ratiocination (i.e., cognitions). So, although the chapter is structured into parts according to the levels, we will strive to remain cognizant of the complex interrelationships between the various levels. In structuring the chapter, in one sense, it would be logical to proceed 'up' the levels of the domain, from embodiment to awareness+. Indeed, for the objective domain (Chapter 3) and the intersubjective and interobjective domains (Chapter 4), we do structure our presentation in this way, starting at the smallest/lowest level and going outwards/upwards. However, for this chapter our approach is different: we begin with consciousness, since this level is the *key* to this domain. As we shall see, from an APP perspective, by consciousness we mean developing skills of attention and awareness. All the other levels then involve bringing attention/awareness to bear on the contents of that particular level (e.g., reflecting on our emotions). So, we start with consciousness, then consider embodiment, emotions and cognitions in turn, before finishing by touching on awareness+.

PRACTICE ESSAY QUESTIONS . . .

- Critically evaluate the differences and similarities between the overlapping constructs of consciousness, awareness, attention and mindfulness.
- How can APP help people cultivate a sense of meaning in life?

Consciousness

We begin by considering consciousness. As we have suggested, this 'level' is the key to this domain – from an APP perspective, the development of attention and awareness generally underpins all of the activities pertaining to the other levels; e.g., when we explore the emotional level in the third part of the chapter, PPIs in this area involve enhancing people's awareness of their emotions. As such, the cultivation of attention/awareness is the foundation for our approach to this domain, and the skills we outline in this first section run as threads throughout all the other sections, suffusing the chapter as a whole. So, what do we mean by consciousness? It is a nebulous, complex word, with a range of different meanings (Keenan et al., 2005). In a medical context, consciousness often refers simply to alertness (i.e., responsiveness to stimuli). In contrast, other uses of the term imply higher-order forms of self-awareness. The fact that words are polysemantic is, of course, fine – one just needs to be clear about the way one is using them. In this spirit, then, we are using consciousness here to refer collectively to two related concepts: awareness and attention. This section will discuss the relevance of these concepts to wellbeing and, moreover, highlight practices – mainly involving meditation – for developing these. Before this, however, we must clarify what we mean by awareness and attention, as although often used synonymously, they are distinct constructs (Koch & Tsuchiya, 2007).

Awareness refers generally to subjectivity, i.e., the 'conscious registration of stimuli, including the five senses, the kinaesthetic senses, and the activities of the mind' (Brown et al., 2007, p. 212). In contrast, attention encompasses the cognitive mechanisms that control what enters awareness (Fell, 2004). As Austin (1998, p. 69) articulates the distinction, awareness implies sensate 'reactivity', while attention is a 'searchlight': 'Attention reaches. It is awareness stretched *toward* something. It has executive, motoric implications. We attend *to* things.' Moreover, both awareness and attention can be further deconstructed. Awareness can be subdivided into phenomenal awareness (a catch-all term for the subjective experience of qualia) and access awareness (phenomenal experience being used for 'reasoning and rationally guiding speech and action'; Block, 1995, p. 227). Phenomenal awareness can itself be subdivided according to the various sensory modalities (e.g., visual awareness), as well as proprioceptive (body position) and interoceptive (internal sensations) awareness. There are also higher-level forms of meta-awareness, such as of oneself and one's mental processes. Attention is likewise theorised as being modular, with functionally distinct but overlapping networks (Posner & Petersen, 1990). Sustained attention concerns the intensity of one's focus, involving extended ongoing readiness for processing stimuli over time. Two other networks pertain to selectivity: executive attention describes top–down monitoring of competing stimuli, while selective attention is when resources are allocated to specific stimuli. Additionally, attention switching is 'the ability to change attentive focus in an adaptable and flexible manner' (Mirsky et al., 1991, p. 112).

As we shall see, awareness and attention are not just psychological processes, but *skills* that can be trained and developed. Moreover, such development has been associated with enhanced wellbeing. As such, from an APP perspective, the key question is how can these skills be developed? The activity that above all others is most strongly linked to this development is meditation. The word 'meditation' is actually an umbrella term for a diverse range of practices. However, in contemporary psychological terms, the common element among all these practices is the training and development of awareness and attention. As Walsh and Shapiro (2006, pp. 228–229) put it, meditation refers to 'a family of self-regulation practices that focus on training attention and awareness in order to bring mental processes under greater voluntary control and thereby foster general mental well-being'. Taking this definition as a starting point, we can further differentiate various kinds of meditation practices. Mikulas (1990) suggests we can classify such practices according to four parameters, all of which relate to the skilful deployment of awareness/attention: behaviours of mind, object, attitude and form.

First, *behaviours of mind* refers to the *type* of awareness/attention. Meditation practices are classified according to two main types: focused attention (FA) and open monitoring (OM) (Lutz et al., 2008). In Pali, the Indian language of early Buddhist texts (many meditation practices derive from Buddhism, as discussed further in Chapter 7), these are referred to as *samatha* and *vipassana* respectively. FA-type practices primarily involve sustained attention on a particular object, like the breath. However, they also utilise the other attention networks: executive (to stop the mind 'wandering'), switching (disengaging from distractions) and selective (redirecting focus back to the meditative object). In contrast, OM does not involve focusing attention on particular stimuli, but is a broad receptive awareness – an 'open field capacity to detect arising sensory, feeling and thought events within an unrestricted "background" of awareness, without a grasping of these events in an explicitly selected foreground or focus' (Raffone & Srinivasan, 2010, p. 2). OM is more commonly referred to as mindfulness, defined as 'the awareness that arises through paying attention on purpose, in the present moment, and nonjudgmentally to the unfolding of experience moment by moment' (Kabat-Zinn, 2003, p. 145). The term itself derives from the Pali word *sati*, which carries connotations of being watchful and alert (Kiyota, 1978). We shall return to mindfulness below, since this is the practice that has emerged as the pre-eminent focus of clinical and academic attention in the West. First, though, we shall briefly touch upon the other parameters.

The second parameter is the *object* of attention/awareness in meditation. One's focus can be directed inwardly to any of the levels of the subjective domain, e.g., on the embodied sensations of breathing. Mindfulness 'proper' involves letting all qualia (e.g., emotions or thoughts) just 'pass through' one's awareness, like clouds drifting across the sky. One may also concentrate on specific cognitions, including mantras (repeated words/phrases), koans (paradoxical statements/questions, used in Zen Buddhism, that arrest discursive thought, like 'What is the sound of one hand clapping?'), and imaginative images (e.g., of Buddhist 'deities'; Vessantara, 2002). Attention can also be directed outwardly to visual stimuli, like religious icons or mandalas (meaningful geometric patterns, used in Tibetan Buddhism), and auditory or olfactory stimuli (e.g., bells, incense). In fact, one can attend to anything in a meditative way – the Dalai Lama describes meditation as 'a deliberate mental activity that involves cultivating familiarity, be it with a chosen object, a fact, a theme, a habit, an outlook or a way of being' (Gyatso, 2006, p. 98). Intriguingly, from this perspective, many activities that we do not currently conceive of as being forms of meditation – including various PPIs – can be viewed as meditative practices. This would include PPIs like the 'three good things' exercise (Seligman et al., 2005), since this involves the deliberate contemplation of a beneficial mental 'object' (i.e., reasons for gratitude). Defined broadly in this way, meditation can be viewed as the exemplar activity for the subjective domain, the root of all introspective PPIs.

ART LINKS . . .

One of the most emotionally moving forms of meditation can be listening mindfully to music (Diaz, 2010). Play your favourite piece of music – preferably something relatively soothing! – and try to really be aware of its sonic textures and dynamics. Whatever thoughts or feelings emerge while listening, take note of them, then return to the music. As a recommendation, arguably one of the most beautiful and meditative pieces of music in the world is *Spiegel im Spiegel*, by the Estonian composer Arvo Pärt. Find a version (e.g., on YouTube), tune in, close your eyes and let the music wash over you!

The third parameter is *attitude*: meditators are exhorted not to pay attention in 'a cold, critical' way, but to imbue their awareness/attention with positive emotional qualities (Shapiro et al., 2006, p. 376). These range from relatively neutral (e.g., acceptance) to more positive (e.g., kindness). For example, Kabat-Zinn (2003, p. 145) recommends mindfulness be conducted with an 'open-hearted, friendly' and 'affectionate, compassionate quality'. However, qualitative studies show that people can find it difficult to generate such attitudinal stances, especially if one has tendencies towards self-criticism (Lomas, 2014). As such, there are specific meditations designed to promote these positive qualities. The *metta bhavana* (*metta* is a Pali term translated as loving kindness, and *bhavana* means practice) has recently been embraced by PP scholars, operationalised as 'loving kindness-meditation' (LKM) (Fredrickson et al., 2008). In a five-stage process of guided emotional imagery, practitioners are encouraged to generate positive feelings for themselves, then extend these outwards, first to a close friend, then to increasingly wide circles of people. We shall invite you to try out LKM for yourselves in Chapter 7, when we explore the deeper Buddhist context of this practice. Going further, some practices involve devotional stances of reverence (although Buddhism is not usually seen as theistic, some traditions revere the Buddha and other figures as deities; Vessantara, 2002). We will return to the role of meditation in generating positive qualities below in the section on emotions.

Finally, *form* concerns the various physical postures in which one can practise. The iconic pose is the full-lotus (crossed-legs, both feet resting on opposing thighs). However, this can be hard, especially for those with musculoskeletal issues. As such, any form of sitting is fine as long as one has a secure 'base' and keeps the back straight (Ong, 2007). There are also dynamic forms. Foremost among these is yoga, a Hindu system of psychospiritual development that predates and gave rise to Buddhism (Feuerstein, 2002). As discussed in depth in Chapter 7, yoga involves various branches, one of which – Hatha yoga – involves physical postures that 'unify body and mind' by training attention on the body (Sawni & Breuner, 2012). Indeed, one can undertake any movement in a meditative way. For example, one could walk mindfully, an activity that is particularly useful for people who may find it difficult to sit still and concentrate, like people with attention-deficit disorders (Zylowska et al., 2008). The idea of meditative movement also connects to the concept of flow, a state of absorption attained when tasks are neither too easy to be boring nor too challenging to elicit anxiety (Csikszentmihalyi, 1990). (That said, although there are conceptual overlaps between flow and meditative states, they cannot necessarily be equated; the latter is something we may consciously enter, whereas the latter arguably cannot be willed but 'just happens' if circumstances are opportune.) In fact, any physical activity in which a person feels connected to their body and/or appreciates the physical dimension of the activity for its own sake (e.g., if one enjoys the sensation of swimming) can be regarded as a type of meditation. We shall return to the idea of using meditation to connect with one's body below in the section on embodiment. More broadly, any non-sitting form of meditation – e.g., being mindful of one's actions – can be labelled generically as meditation-in-action (Bruce & Davies, 2005).

PSYCHOMETRIC SCALES . . .

How mindful are you? The Mindful Attention and Awareness Scale (Brown & Ryan, 2003) is a set of statements about your everyday experience. Using the 1–6 scale below, indicate how frequently or infrequently you currently have each experience. Please answer according to what *really reflects* your experience, not what you think your experience *should* be. 1 = *almost always*, 2 = *very frequently*, 3 = *somewhat frequently*, 4 = *somewhat infrequently*, 5 = *very infrequently*, 6 = *almost never*.

Answer

1 I could be experiencing some emotion and not be conscious of it until some time later. _____

2 I break or spill things because of carelessness, not paying attention, or thinking of something else. _____

3 I find it difficult to stay focused on what's happening in the present. _____

4 I tend to walk quickly to get where I'm going without paying attention to what I experience along the way. _____

5 I tend not to notice feelings of physical tension or discomfort until they really grab my attention. _____

6 I forget a person's name almost as soon as I've been told it for the first time. _____

7 It seems I am 'running on automatic' without much awareness of what I'm doing. _____

8 I rush through activities without being really attentive to them. _____

9 I get so focused on the goal I want to achieve that I lose touch with what I am doing right now to get there. _____

10 I do jobs or tasks automatically, without being aware of what I'm doing. _____

11 I find myself listening to someone with one ear, doing something else at the same time. _____

12 I drive places on 'automatic pilot' and then wonder why I went there. _____

13 I find myself preoccupied with the future or the past. _____

14 I find myself doing things without paying attention. _____

15 I snack without being aware that I'm eating. _____

Total _____

To ascertain your level of mindfulness, please add together the scores for all the items. The higher your total score, the greater your general level of mindfulness.

Thus, meditation encompasses a diverse range of practices. However, most of the clinical/academic attention has focused on one particular practice: mindfulness. This interest was initially generated by a pioneering Mindfulness-Based Stress

Reduction (MBSR) programme founded by Kabat-Zinn (1982), a ten-week intervention for the treatment of chronic pain. This involved weekly sessions in which people were instructed in mindfulness practices, together with homework exercises to encourage mindfulness in everyday life. By the end, 50% of the patients reported a reduction in subjective pain of at least 50%, together with reductions in psychiatric symptomology. According to Grossman et al. (2004, p. 36), the success of MBSR is predicated on six premises: (1) people are often unaware of their moment-to-moment experience, operating on autopilot; (2) mindfulness is a skill that can be trained; (3) development is gradual and progressive, requiring practice; (4) better moment-to-moment awareness produces a 'richer and more vivid sense of life'; (5) persistent non-judgemental awareness of mental content leads to less distorted perception and cognition; and (6) more accurate perception and cognition can enhance efficacy and control of actions. In terms of alleviation of pain, point (5) is the most salient. That is, in mindfulness, one learns to 'de-centre' – to 'observe one's thoughts and feelings as temporary, objective events in the mind, as opposed to reflections of the self that are necessarily true' (Fresco et al., 2007, p. 237). Thus, while participants may have still felt pain, they were able to cultivate a more detached 'relationship' with it that was less distressing.

RESEARCH AND PRACTICE CASE STUDIES . . .

Jon Kabat-Zinn obtained his PhD in molecular biology from the Massachusetts Institute of Technology in 1971. After hearing a talk on Buddhism by Philip Kapleau Roshi, Kabat-Zinn became a student of the Zen master Seung Sahn. Jon was in his mid-30s, teaching at the Massachusetts Medical Center in the late 1970s, when he formulated an idea for using meditative practices in the treatment of chronic pain. He received permission from the hospital authorities to work with, almost as a measure of last resort, patients considered 'untreatable.' The rest, as they say, is history…!

Since the success of the MBSR course, interest in mindfulness has exploded, with over 500 studies in 2012 alone (Shonin et al., 2013a). MBSR has successfully enhanced wellbeing in patients suffering with diverse health conditions, including cancer and HIV/AIDS (Zeichner et al., 2013), as well as in non-clinical groups, like workers in high stress occupations (Walach et al., 2007). Moreover, various adaptations of the MBSR protocol have been developed, most notably mindfulness-based cognitive therapy (MBCT), designed to prevent depressive relapse (Zindel et al., 2002). The theoretical basis of MBCT is the differential activation hypothesis: previously depressed people are susceptible to relapse because of 'dysphoria-activated depressogenic thinking', i.e., negative thought patterns associated with previous depressive episodes can be reactivated by negative emotions (Teasdale et al., 2000, p. 615). However, in MBCT, attention training increases emotional awareness and understanding, enabling people to decentre from their cognitions, helping prevent a 'downward spiral' of negative thoughts and worsening negative affect (which might otherwise lead to relapse). In randomised controlled trials, MBCT is found to significantly reduce relapse rates for those with three or more previous episodes of depression (Ma & Teasdale, 2004). Consequently, in 2004, the UK National Institute for Health and Care Excellence approved MBCT as a treatment for recurrent depression. Since then, MBCT has also been developed for use with other clinical problems, including anxiety (Evans et al., 2008) and bipolar disorder (Weber et al., 2010).

It is fascinating to trace the evolution and transmission of the idea of mindfulness, from its Buddhist origins to MBSR, and onwards into further adaptions. There are novel mindfulness-based treatments for smoking cessation ('surfing the urge'; Bowen & Marlatt, 2009); the treatment of eating disorders ('mindful eating and living'; Dalen et al., 2010); multiple sclerosis ('mindfulness of movement'; Mills & Allen, 2000); PTSD-related sleep disorder ('mind–body bridging'; Nakamura et al., 2011); people with learning difficulties and/or conduct disorders ('mindfulness on the soles of the feet'; Singh et al., 2003); and for chronic heart failure (a 'mindfulness based psychoeducational approach'; Sullivan et al., 2009). Various labels have been proposed to encompass these diverse meditation-related interventions, including mindfulness meditation practices (MMPs; Kabat-Zinn, 1982), awareness training programmes (ATPs; Nakamura et al., 2011) and Buddhist-derived interventions (BDIs; Shonin et al., 2013b). However, all these acronyms are imperfect: MMPs exclude other meditation practices; ATPs neglect the role of attention; and BDIs overlook the possibility of interventions based on other religious forms of meditation. As such, we will use 'meditation-based practices' (MBPs) as our overarching term. Given that MBPs are *the* exemplar PPI of the subjective domain, we shall hear more about MBPs throughout this chapter, and indeed the book. However, the evolution of MBPs is ongoing. Indeed, one such exciting mindfulness-based intervention is currently being developed at the University of East London (UEL) by the authors, led by Itai Ivtzan, as outlined in the box below. Perhaps future innovations in the use of MBPs will be developed by *you*, the reader!

RESEARCH AND PRACTICE CASE STUDIES . . .

Prominent mindfulness interventions like MBSR were originally developed as clinical therapies for physical and mental health issues. Such interventions have also been deployed in non-clinical settings, and to that extent, according to our formulation in Chapter 1, could be regarded as PP interventions. However, the ethos of such programmes nevertheless remains about alleviating negative states such as stress and anxiety, rather than embracing the PP spirit of actively promoting flourishing. Alleviating such states is of course valuable, and readers looking for remedies for these are encouraged to engage with MBSR, or a similar programme. Other people, though, may be fortunate enough not to be unduly burdened by states like anxiety, and may be looking to develop the kinds of outcomes that PP has come to specialise in, such as meaning. Thus, the University of East London MAPP (MSc in APP) team, comprising faculty members and students, is developing an eight-week Mindfulness Based Well-Being (MBWB) programme, integrating PP and mindfulness. The programme features numerous PPIs suffused with mindfulness practice, including interventions relating to autonomy, gratitude, self-compassion, relationships, environmental mastery, positive emotions, meaning and self-growth. We feel this programme captures the spirit of compassion and liberation that flowed through the original Buddhist teachings on mindfulness, a spirit which was to some extent lost as mindfulness was harnessed by Western psychology (Shapiro et al., 2006), as discussed in Chapter 7. Mindfulness research has largely focused on the self-regulatory processes of meditation, like the attentional mechanisms outlined above. While these processes are important for understanding mindfulness, they are only the starting point of the meditative journey, and overlook the notion that the practice of meditation was originally an invitation for love, compassion, acceptance and meaning. We aim to invite mindfulness back to its original intention of expanding psychological and spiritual wellbeing. We cannot think of a more appropriate home for that than PP.

Embodiment

Having introduced the idea of developing attention/awareness, we can now explore the other levels of the subjective domain. As we shall see, from an APP perspective, attention/awareness skills are a thread running through all the levels, with PPIs designed to engender attention/awareness *of* each level. So, starting with the 'lowest' level – embodied sensations – there are practices to help people attend to and become aware of their body. Before considering these, it is worth just reflecting on the complex semantics of the concept of the body. When people discuss the mind–body problem (introduced in Chapter 1), 'body' generally refers to the objective domain of our LIFE model, i.e., the physiological organism (including the brain), in distinction to subjective phenomenological experience. However, *part* of this phenomenological experience includes the felt experience of our own bodies. This felt experience is captured by the term 'embodiment', defined as 'the subjectivity of the lived body' (Turner, 2001, p. 253). There is increasing appreciation in PP of the complex intersections between embodiment and wellbeing (Hefferon, 2013), and the value of developing body awareness (BA). BA constitutes an 'overall concept for experience and use of the body, representing body consciousness, body management and deepened body experience' (Roxendale, 1985, p. 10). Scholars are beginning to understand the means towards cultivating BA as a route to wellbeing (Mehling et al., 2009).

REFLECTION . . .

How aware are you of your own body? Do you have a tendency to get lost in abstract thoughts, as if you were a disembodied mind? Even if that is the case, most of us engage in particular activities that are rewarding partly because they put us in touch with our bodies, from sex to sport, and really allow us to feel a powerful sense of being an embodied entity. What activities generate this sense for you?

This appreciation of the value of BA is relatively new in academia. Previously, BA was predominantly studied in relation to anxiety or panic disorder, where it was thought that over-attention to symptoms or body reactions had adverse consequences. Cioffi (1991) suggested that high BA was connected to 'soma-tosensory amplification' (i.e., tendencies to experience somatic qualia in an intense and often noxious way), engendering hypochondriasis, anxiety and som-atization. More recently, though, it has been suggested that attending to one's embodied experience can be conducive to physiological and psychological well-being (Mehling et al., 2009). Studies involving patients with chronic back pain found that those who focused on its sensory components experienced reduced subjective pain compared to patients who tried to suppress their pain (Burns, 2006). Indeed, attending to pain in a non-reactive way was the premise of the first mindfulness intervention, MBSR, which was specifically created for people with chronic pain (Kabat-Zinn, 1982), as outlined above. Moreover, BA is not only conducive to wellbeing in the context of physical pain, but is associated generally with wellbeing in non-clinical populations, where self-reported trait levels of BA correlate with SWB (Brani et al., 2014). Moreover, from an APP perspective, BA is not only desirable, it can be *cultivated*.

First, as noted above, certain forms of meditation are specifically designed to help people develop BA and become more connected with their embodied experience. Foremost among these is yoga, which includes a branch involving physical postures designed to engender BA (Sawni & Breuner, 2012). As with mindfulness, yoga has been found to alleviate mental health problems like depression, and as such is beginning to be used as a clinical intervention (Khalsa, 2007). Similarly, Tai Chi was initially developed as a martial art in ancient China, where it is thought to have first been systematised by Taoist monks around the twelfth century CE (Levine, 1984). Contemporary forms of Tai Chi often harness the slow 'training moves' of the original martial art to create a gentle, flowing sequence of dance-like movements that have been described as a 'Mind–Body Movement Therapy' (Yeh et al., 2004, p. 541). As with meditation and yoga, Tai Chi has begun to be developed and used as a wellbeing intervention, such as helping to prevent falls by elderly people (Voukelatos et al., 2007). Likewise, Yeh et al. found that Tai Chi enhanced quality of life and functional capacity in a group of patients suffering from chronic heart failure.

TRY ME! . . .

A lovely meditation designed to help people connect with their embodied experience is the *body scan*, a component of the MBSR programme (Ditto et al., 2006). To try this, after reading these instructions, lie down flat on the floor (on your back), close your eyes, and slow your breathing down. Start by moving your attention to the little toe of your left foot. Try to really become aware of the sensation in your toe – what does the toe feel like? Is it hot or cold, tingly or dull, tensed or relaxed? In this way, proceed slowly all around your body: move up your left leg, then up your right leg, continuing onto your torso, down each arm, then up to your face, culminating in the crown of your head. The body scan is very relaxing (e.g., it reduces blood pressure; Ditto et al., 2006) and can even help people fall asleep by reducing tension in their body. The value of this practice is not only recognised by Buddhism: the mother of one of the authors (Tim Lomas) recalled *her* mother teaching her the very same technique when she was a child – back in working-class London in the 1950s – whenever she couldn't sleep, even though her mother had never heard of Buddhism or meditation! Why not give it a try yourself?

In addition to these meditative practices, there are a range of therapies designed to help enhance BA, referred to collectively as body awareness therapies (BAT; Gard, 2005). Prominent BATs include Basic Body Awareness Therapy (BBAT; Gyllensten, 2001), Feldenkrais therapy (Feldenkrais, 1977), the Mensendieck system (Mensendieck, 1937) and Pilates (Latey, 2001). These therapies deploy a mix of practices to help foster BA. BBAT incorporates massage, breathing regulation and mindfulness of movement. Likewise, Feldenkrais therapy involves highly structured verbally directed movement explorations, and 'functional integration' sessions in which the practitioner touches/moves the client's body to promote new motor patterns (Wildman, 1988). The Mensendieck system involves pedagogical exercises to help people become aware of and alter 'suboptimal patterns of movement' (Bongi & Del Rosso, 2012, p. 174). Finally, Pilates involves individually-tailored sessions in which practitioners assist clients in engaging in slow deliberate movements, using floor mats and equipment

(Latey, 2001). BATs are beginning to be used with clinical populations as treatments for physical disorders such as fibromyalgia (widespread chronic pain, and a heightened response to pressure; Gard, 2005), and mental health issues like personality disorders (which are thought to be linked to BA deficiencies, like distortions of body image; Skatteboe et al., 1989). However, BATs can be of value in non-clinical settings too, as higher levels of BA are generally associated with greater wellbeing (Brani et al., 2014). Indeed, BATs are increasingly popular in society at large. For example, it is estimated that Pilates is practised by at least 10 million people worldwide (Cruz-Ferreira et al., 2011).

Emotions

We now turn our attention to the next level of the subjective domain, considering the development of emotional skills through PPIs. The word *skills* is crucial here. We are not concerned simply with PPIs and activities that promote positive emotions. Indeed, from one perspective, since the desired outcome of APP is to help people feel better, *many* PPIs are ultimately concerned with engendering positive emotional outcomes. That is, we can intervene at any of the levels in any of the domains of the LIFE model, but the dependent variable is still often likely to involve an assessment of whether the intervention has generated positive emotions, e.g., a measurement of SWB. (This is why we referred to the subjective mind in Chapter 1 as the *root* domain in PP.) Rather, what we are concerned with in this section is people's ability to *work with* their own emotions. The emphasis is not on emotional outcomes *per se* (e.g., SWB), but on emotional management *skills*. Specifically, we will be concentrating on emotional intelligence (EI), and on PPIs that can help develop EI.

This emphasis on EI is important in light of the complexities of emotions, discussed in Chapter 1. We suggested that emotions could not be simply categorised a priori as positive or negative, as emotions are generally covalenced (Lazarus, 2003). Moreover, whether a particular emotion is conducive or not to wellbeing depends on context. For example, forgiveness is usually portrayed as adaptive (Lawler-Row & Piferi, 2006); however, in some situations, like an ongoing abusive relationship, it may be harmful to wellbeing as it may inadvertently help to perpetuate the abuse (McNulty, 2011). So, while being able to forgive is useful, more important is deploying forgiveness skilfully and knowing *when* to forgive. This knowledge is a meta-emotional skill, i.e., involving the ability to reflect on and reason about emotions. A similar point can be made regarding coping. There are three main types of coping strategy (Carver et al., 1989): problem-focused strategies, which target the stressor (e.g., solving the problem); emotion-focused strategies, which target one's reaction to the stressor (e.g., trying to stay calm); and avoidance-focused strategies, where the issue is dodged. The question of which strategy is the most effective depends on the nature of the stressor. Problem-focused strategies are good if the issue can be solved. However, if it does not admit a solution (e.g., if the issue is one's mortality), emotion-focused strategies are better (Cohen et al., 2005). The value of adapting one's response according to the nature of a given stressor is captured poetically in the well-known serenity prayer that opens this chapter, attributed to the twentieth-century theologian Reinhold Niebuhr, which is used therapeutically by groups such as Alcoholics Anonymous: God grant me the serenity to accept the things I cannot change, the courage to change the things I can, and the wisdom to know the difference. Thus, more important than knowing various strategies is having the meta-coping ability to know *which* strategy to use in which situation.

TRY ME! . . .

List all the coping strategies you use when you are feeling stressed/distressed. Next to each one, note down the types of situation in which you use that strategy. Then reflect on *why* you are drawn to that strategy in that situation. This can help us think about how we *strategically* manage our emotions.

So, our focus here is on emotional management skills. There are various conceptually-related theories of emotional management, including emotion work (Hochschild, 1979), emotion regulation (Gross, 1999) and emotional intelligence (EI) (Mayer & Salovey, 1997). We will focus on the latter, since we have found this to be a particularly hepful construct. There are three main types of EI model (Mayer et al., 2008). Specific ability approaches highlight individual capacities important to EI, like the ability to discern people's emotions from their facial expressions (Baron-Cohen et al., 2001). Mixed model approaches offer very broad definitions of EI that include personality dispositions which are arguably not strictly EI skills, such as self-regard. Finally, integrative models conceptualise EI as a global ability; foremost among such models is Mayer and Salovey's (1997) schema, which conceptualises EI as comprising four hierarchical branches:

- Emotional awareness and expression
- Emotional facilitation of thought (the ability to generate emotions)
- Understanding emotional patterns
- The strategic management of emotions

The lower two branches are collectively labelled 'experiential EI'. These involve information processing of emotional stimuli. The higher two branches are together referred to as 'strategic EI'. These concern the strategic management of information processed by the lower branches. This model reinforces the point above about the LIFE levels being interrelated: although this discussion is situated in the emotional level, the EI construct is essentially about the synthesis of emotion and cognition, as it refers to 'abilities that join intelligence and emotion to enhance thought' (Mayer et al., 2008, p. 511). The reason their EI model is conceptualised as hierarchical is that the lower two branches are precursors for the higher two branches. For example, one must first be aware of something before one understands it. Indeed, a study with meditators found that these branches were developed – though practising meditation – in a somewhat sequential fashion (Lomas et al., 2013b). This section will be structured according to this model: we will outline each branch in turn, and highlight PPIs that may help to develop that particular facet of EI.

The first branch is emotional awareness and expression. This branch has already been largely covered by the section on consciousness above. Many MBPs, especially mindfulness, involve becoming aware of one's phenomenological world, including one's emotional experience. As such, the exemplar PPI for developing emotional awareness is mindfulness meditation. Indeed, most interventions aimed at developing EI invariably include a mindfulness component. However, we can augment mindfulness with other strategies to enhance emotional awareness. Hsu et al. (2010) developed an 'affective self-awareness' intervention for pain reduction in people with fibromyalgia. This featured mindfulness exercises, which were augmented by three further components: education (using case studies to teach a biopsychosocial model of chronic pain); written emotional disclosure about stress (30 minutes daily, involving free-writing prose, unsent letters and imagined dialogues); and gradual re-engagement in activity (helping to overcome reluctance to engage). From an integrated perspective, consciousness techniques (i.e., mindfulness) worked together with emotional (disclosure), cognitive (writing tasks) and behavioural practices (activity tasks) to enhance emotional awareness.

The second branch is emotional facilitation of thought, i.e., the 'ability to generate emotions' (Day & Carroll, 2004, p. 1444). Here, we are interested in PPIs that help people generate emotions in order to promote wellbeing. PP boasts a wealth of such PPIs, and many more are conceivable. LKM, outlined above, is effective in both clinical (Johnson et al., 2009) and non-clinical contexts (Fredrickson et al., 2008). Another desirable quality is gratitude. A popular PPI in this respect is counting one's blessings, the psychological benefits of which have been recognised by religions for centuries. Keeping a gratitude journal (noting things for which one feels grateful) has a positive impact on SWB (Emmons & McCullough, 2003). Research suggests the optimum 'dosage' for this activity is once per week; doing it more frequently risks the activity becoming stale (Lyubomirsky et al., 2005). One does not even need to keep a journal, but could simply reflect on reasons for gratitude. From the broad perspective of meditation introduced above, this would constitute an FA meditation practice. Indeed, there are already MBPs centred on inculcating gratitude, as found in the Japanese psychotherapeutic technique of Naikan therapy (Yoshimoto, 1972), deployed by Chan (2010) in an eight-week gratitude intervention for teachers in Hong Kong. In terms of developing other PPIs, given that meditation can simply involve sustained reflection on particular intentional objects (e.g., emotions or thoughts), logically, we could ask people to reflect meditatively upon any positive emotion as a means of increasing that emotion.

REFLECTION . . .

LKM encourages practitioners to generate loving-kindness. Gratitude journals involve reflection on things in life for which one is grateful. What kind of other positive qualities and emotions might we encourage people to dwell on, and what kind of PPIs might we develop to help them do so?

The third branch is emotional understanding. This gauges the extent to which people comprehend the subjective psychodynamics of their own emotional experience. For example, in one psychometric test for EI – the Mayer Salovey Caruso Emotional Intelligence Test (MSCEIT; Mayer et al., 2002) – some questions concern the way emotions 'blend', e.g. 'Which two emotions together are closest to contempt: (*a*) sadness and fear or (*b*) anger and disgust?'. In terms of developing emotional understanding, again, mindfulness is an exemplar activity in this regard: interviewing men who meditate, Lomas (2014) found that, through repeated introspection, these meditators developed sophisticated insights into their own psychodynamics. While some insights were idiosyncratic, there were common understandings which are more widely relevant. Two stood out. The first is that emotions are embodied, felt viscerally in the body. This is reflected in Damasio et al.'s (1996) somatic marker hypothesis, which suggests that sensations convey information that helps us process our emotive reactions, as reflected in Schnall et al.'s (2008) notion that disgust is an 'embodied moral judgment'. The second is that emotions are transient, an insight that practitioners felt was captured in the phrase '*this too will pass*'. Moreover, meditators were able to combine these two insights to help them cope with dysphoria. When in distress, practitioners would often focus on its somatic components, rather than its emotional or cognitive aspects. By attending to this visceral dimension, they could observe their distress changing and ideally dissipating. These insights are combined in a guided meditative activity, detailed in the box below, that you might like to try.

TRY ME! . . .

- Sit quietly and comfortably, and take a few moments to feel your breath slowing down.
- As you sit, allow yourself to acknowledge any negativity you may be feeling.
- As you acknowledge this, rather than trying to think about your suffering, or dwelling on its origins and trying to work out solutions, see if you can *feel* it in your body.
- Perhaps you're anxious – maybe this can be felt as a nervous energy in your chest?
- Or maybe you're feeling sad – perhaps this is a dull heaviness in your stomach?
- Whatever your emotion, try to explore the way it is physically expressing itself as a sensation.
- Having found the physical location of your emotion, turn towards this sensation with a kind, curious, forgiving type of awareness.
- You are not trying to change, amplify or get rid of the sensation. You are simply just letting it be, and observing how it feels.
- Now try to describe the sensation. If it were a colour, what colour? If a shape, what shape?
- As you observe the sensation with a kindly curiosity, perhaps you notice it changing, taking on a different form, maybe shrinking in size.
- Maybe the change is small, almost imperceptible, but nevertheless it is there.
- As you notice this change, reflect on the idea that feelings and sensations are not solid objects, existing permanently through space and time, but are ever changing and evolving.
- As you reflect on this idea, say the phrase '*This too will pass*'.
- As you continue to breathe in and out, while staying focused on the sensations in your body, softly repeat this phrase with each out-breath.
- Continue for as long as you are comfortable doing so.

The final branch is strategic emotional management. This means not only having strategies to generate particular emotions, but knowing which strategy is best suited to a specific situation. This higher-level skill is to some extent simply a culmination and synthesis of the previous three branches – being aware of one's emotional state, understanding how best to change it and being able to do so. Thus, PPIs aimed at the other branches will contribute to the development of emotional management. However, there are also PPIs which target all four levels, and so explicitly develop this branch. For instance, Nelis et al. (2009) devised a four-week intervention (one session per week). Session 1 focused on emotional understanding (branch 3), featuring explanations of the key concepts and role-play to illustrate the importance of EI. Session 2 involved identifying emotions (branch 1), especially in other people, through decoding facial expressions and empathic communicaton. Session 3 dealt with expressing and using emotions (branches 1 and 2), such as using emotions to solve problems. Finally, session 4 covered emotional management: this included theoretical group discussions around coping strategies and their effectiveness, role-play activities and meditative 'mind–body' exercises. Alternatively, an intervention used by the South African cricket academy involved ten three-hour sessions (Crombie et al., 2011). Each session emphasised all four branches, combining theoretical discussion, experiential case studies and personal exercises.

Cognitions

Progressing up the levels, we turn our attention to cognition, and in particular, discursive thoughts. The term 'cognition' can be used to refer to all mental processes, including attention mechanisms. However, our interest here concerns *thoughts* specifically, as in '*what are you thinking?*' There is an intimate connection between thought structures and wellbeing, as recognised by cognitive theories of mental disorder (Beck et al., 1979). Depression, for instance, is linked to a dysfunctional attributional style which interprets negative events as internal (self-caused), stable (connected to enduring factors) and global (universally applicable), as encapsulated in the fatalistic response '*I'm always bad at everything*' (Abramson et al., 1978). Cognitive therapy thus aims to challenge and reconfigure these depressogenic thought patterns (Beck et al., 1979). Although PP practitioners may not generally be practising therapists, PP has been influenced by therapeutic techniques, including those of cognitive therapy. So, from an APP perspective, there are various PPIs that help promote or reconfigure thought patterns to enhance wellbeing, which we can collectively refer to as cognitive restructuring exercises.

For the most part, such exercises are not about promoting what might be pejoratively termed 'positive thinking'. The aim is usually to generate a deeper reflective process, and the desired outcome is often to enhance people's sense of *meaning* in life. That is not to say such PPIs *cannot* focus on positive reflections. We have already seen, in the case of the gratitude journal, that PPIs can involve thinking about 'positive' aspects of life (Emmons & McCullough, 2003). Similarly, the 'three good things' journal involves nightly reflections on positive events that day (Seligman et al., 2005). However, such activities are not simply 'positive thinking', as they do not involve inventing positive content, but are attention-focusing exercises which encourage people to notice what is *already* positive about their life. These exercises can have a potent impact on wellbeing: Burton and King (2004) asked students to write about intensely positive experiences for 20 minutes a day on three consecutive days. Relative to a control group, who wrote about a neutral topic, the PPI not only enhanced positive mood, but was associated with increased longitudinal physical wellbeing (gauged by fewer health centre visits for illness over the subsequent three months). You could try this now!

> **TRY ME! . . .**
>
> 'Think of the most wonderful experience or experiences in your life, happiest moments, ecstatic moments, moments of rapture, perhaps from being in love, or from listening to music, or suddenly "being hit" by a book or painting or from some great creative moment. Choose one such experience or moment. Try to imagine yourself at that moment, including all the feelings and emotions associated with the experience. Now write about the experience in as much detail as possible, trying to include the feelings, thoughts, and emotions that were present at the time.' (Burton & King, 2004, p. 155)

Going beyond noticing or reminiscing about positive events, some PPIs involve deeper reflection on one's life and self-identity. As noted above, such PPIs are often about promoting a sense of *meaning*. It is generally agreed that meaning is crucial for a flourishing life, as reflected in seminal PP theories such as Ryff's (1989) PWB theory, and Seligman's (2012) PERMA (positive emotions, engagement, relationships, meaning, and achievement) model. There are many ways of conceptualising meaning. However, Mascaro and Rosen (2006, p. 170) argue that 'theorists converge' in agreeing that meaning has two fundamental components: coherence and purpose. These components respectively address two fundamental existential needs: for comprehensibility (understanding existence) and significance (existence having value) (Janoff-Bulman & Yopyk, 2004). From an APP stance, we are interested in exercises that help to *promote* meaning. The notion that we can intervene to help people find meaning was powerfully articulated by Frankl (1963), who developed logotherapy, which literally means 'healing through meaning' (Southwick et al., 2006). Logotherapy uses various techniques to engender meaning, including 'self-distancing' (learning to observe the self, with parallels to the notion of decentring), Socratic dialogue (a questioning technique that elicits the client's own insights) and deflection (redirecting attention from the self towards others or meaningful goals). Logotherapy has a similar ethos to PP, including a focus on 'a patient's strengths' and a 'radically optimistic view of human potential' (Southwick et al., 2006, p. 163). Inspired by pioneers like Frankl, and therapies such as logotherapy, PP is beginning to develop PPIs aimed at generating coherence and purpose, as discussed in turn below.

RESEARCH AND PRACTICE CASE STUDIES . . .

Viktor Frankl's work on logotherapy was shaped by traumatic experiences during the holocaust. Born in Vienna in 1905, Frankl was a neurologist and psychiatrist. In 1942 he was taken to the Theresienstadt ghetto, and in 1944 was transferred to Auschwitz, then to a series of other camps where he worked as a slave labourer and then a physician. During that time, he lost his wife and almost his entire family. His life's work so far – *The Doctor and the Soul* – was also destroyed (he had sewn it into the lining of his coat, which was taken from him). Amid all the tragedy, Frankl developed his powerful existential insights. In particular, he found that those who were better able to withstand the horrors of the camps were those who felt they had something to live for. He felt that this affirmed Nietzsche's (1976 (1888), p. 468) aphorism that 'If we have our own why of life, we shall get along with almost any how'. Poignantly, among the most powerful sources of salvation was love, even if, as with Frankl, one's beloved had been lost: 'I understood how a man who has nothing left in this world still may know bliss, be it only for a brief moment, in the contemplation of his beloved' (Frankl, 1963, p. 69).

A potent way to generate **coherence** is through constructing a meaningful *narrative* about one's life. Narratives are fundamental to our understanding of our self and our life, even if there are elements of creativity in the way we construct these. As Frank (1997, p. 22) put it, the 'stories we tell about our lives are not necessarily those lives as they were lived, but those stories become our experience of those lives'. Crucially, our narratives can impact on our wellbeing. Ridge and Ziebland (2006) examined how people with depression went about making sense of their illness. Recovery was helped if people were able to narrate a story that gave meaning to their illness, e.g., viewing it as part of a spiritual journey. In light of the importance of narratives to meaning-making, various forms of narrative therapy have been developed in which the therapeutic encounter is used to help the client explore their narratives and construct more fulfilling ones (Morgan, 2000). Whether these constitute PPIs or not is an interesting point. Based on our formulation in Chapter 1, if used with a non-clinical population, they arguably could be. That said, as noted above, PP practitioners may not be qualified therapists, and taking on a therapeutic role would then be ethically problematic. (We discuss issues around ethics and safeguarding further in Chapter 8.) Nonetheless, as practitioners we can still learn from such therapies, and endeavour to develop appropriate PPIs based on these.

Narrative therapies are not just designed to help people cope with challenging life experiences, but to find meaning and even posttraumatic growth (Tedeschi & Calhoun, 2004) in these experiences. Garland et al. (2007) developed a six-week intervention (one session per week) for cancer patients. Through creative arts (e.g., journalling, creative writing and drawing) participants were encouraged to engage in narrative self-exploration. The first two weeks explored the theme 'who am I?' (one's journey in life so far), the middle two weeks asked 'how am I'? (current emotions and issues) and the final two weeks considered 'how can I heal?' (using the illness journey as a catalyst for finding meaning and moving forward). There are a range of similar interventions in the literature, designed for particular challenges. Ando et al. (2010) developed an intervention for bereavement, conducted by a clinical psychologist. In the first of two sessions, the client reflects on their positive memories of the deceased person and of caring for them. The session is recorded and transcribed, and in the interim the psychologist makes an album by identifying key words in the session transcript and finding photos/drawings to match these words. In the second session, the album is viewed and discussed. Other notable interventions include life review therapy (Davis, 2004) and reminiscence activities (Cook, 1998), designed for older people. All these interventions encourage meaning-making narrative reviews of one's life, and are reported as being conducive to wellbeing (e.g., reducing depression and enhancing spirituality).

> **REFLECTION . . .**
>
> We make sense of all that has happened to us in our lives by connecting these events and experiences into an overarching story/narrative. What is 'the story' of your life? Struggling through adversity and overcoming the odds? Meandering peacefully? Fulfilling a destiny? Might it be possible to construct a different kind of narrative around your life experiences, one that makes these more meaningful?

A second key component of meaning is a sense of ***purpose***. There are various ways in which we might help people find purpose in life, including cognitive interventions (hence the inclusion of this topic in this chapter on the mind). A useful construct in relation to purpose is Little's (1983) concept of personal projects – 'extended sets of personally relevant action', from 'the mundane acts of a Monday afternoon to the galvanising commitments of a lifetime' (Little et al., 1992, p. 502). The key to meaning is achieving integrity of identity, values and action, i.e., what one does is reflective of who one is and what one values. From an APP perspective, we can try to promote goal integrity through PPIs, like Sheldon et al.'s (2002) 'goal training program'. In this, participants completed a pre-intervention questionnaire, listing personal goals. They then rated their motivational reasons for pursuing these goals according to the five types of regulation of self-determination theory (Deci & Ryan, 2000): extrinsic (reward/punishment);

introjected (internalised reward/punishment); internalised (conscious valuing); integrated (synthesis with self); and intrinsic (inherent satisfaction). Participants furthermore linked the goals to higher-level long-term objectives, e.g., personal growth, friendship and societal contribution. Then followed a 60-minute group session: participants reflected on their goals, and were given strategies to help them pursue these effectively, including ideas for developing autonomy, such as 'own the goal' (reflecting on the deeper values that the goal expresses) and 'make it fun' (increasing one's intrinsic enjoyment of it). A week later, participants received a 30-minute individual counselling session to build upon insights from the group session. Thus the activity engendered a sense of purpose by encouraging reflection on the integrity of one's personal projects.

Another useful construct relating to purpose is the idea of 'possible selves' (Markus & Nurius, 1986). These are motivational cognitive constructs that give form and meaning to people's hopes and fears about what they might become in life, generating incentives and goals for future behaviour. From an APP perspective, simply reflecting on one's 'best possible' future self is linked to SWB (King, 2001). More comprehensive interventions also exist. Oyserman et al. (2002) devised a nine-week, school-based PPI, centred on helping students 'to imagine themselves as successful adults', and connecting these future selves to current school engagement. Sessions included reflections on adult images (a concrete experience of imagining adulthood); time lines (concretising connections between present and future); possible selves and strategies boards (connecting current behaviour to adult attainment); and solving problems (breaking issues into manageable parts, and making school-related plans for the future). In later sessions, parents were also brought in to help cement the progress that was taking place. The intervention enhanced students' bonding to the school and their concern with doing well, and, moreover, reduced behavioural and attendance issues, particularly in boys. As such, not only do we see the value of having purpose in life, there are innovative PPIs that can actually help engender this in people.

Awareness+

Finally, we can briefly touch upon the notion of awareness+. This is a term which we are using to describe the idea that people can access and cultivate 'higher' states of consciousness. Here we are entering somewhat esoteric territory, involving concepts that are hard to conceptualise and articulate. Essentially, awareness+ refers to the idea that one's ordinary waking state of consciousness is not the only possible state, and that more 'refined' states can be cultivated. 'Normal' consciousness involves a dualistic subject–object construct (Josipovic, 2010). That is, we experience ourselves as a subject (i.e., an individual entity) that perceives and interacts with external objects (i.e., other material entities, such as people). However, it is argued that it is possible to 'transcend' this ordinary state, and develop advanced states of consciousness in which this subject–object dichotomy is no longer experienced. In this state, the person would cease to make a distinction between qualia that supposedly pertained to them (e.g., the interoceptive sensations of their body) and qualia that apparently derived from sources external to them (e.g., outside sounds). Instead, there would just be a general 'field' of consciousness, encompassing all these qualia without distinction, thus avoiding the creation of the subject–object dichotomy (Wilber, 2007). These advanced states of consciousness are associated with spiritual practices and development; thus, we discuss the possibility of awareness+ at greater length in Chapter 7, which focuses on religion and spirituality.

SUMMARY – THIS CHAPTER HAS…

- Explained the differences between consciousness, awareness, attention and mindfulness
- Identified four parameters for differentiating different meditation practices: behaviours of mind (i.e., type of attention – FA versus OM), object (i.e., of attention), attitude and form
- Described the diversity of meditation-based practices and interventions
- Explored the importance of embodiment, and interventions to enhance body awareness
- Articulated a four-branch model of EI, and highlighted PPIs relevant to each branch
- Introduced PPIs/therapies centred on cognitive restructuring, designed to engender meaning
- Touched upon the idea of cultivating higher states of consciousness

QUIZ…

1 What are the four modular components of attention mentioned in the text?
2 What do the acronyms FA and OM stand for?
3 In what subject did Jon Kabat-Zinn complete his doctorate?
4 Where did the first MBSR intervention take place?
5 We have used the acronym MBPs (meditation-based practices) to encompass the various interventions related to meditation. What other three acronyms are mentioned in the chapter?
6 In terms of emotional understanding, what were the two main insights into the nature of emotions reported by meditators in the study by Lomas (2014)?
7 What is the highest branch of Mayer and Salovey's (1997) hierarchical EI model?
8 According to Mascaro and Rosen (2006), what are the two key components of meaning?

9   Where was Viktor Frankl born?

10   What two constructs were highlighted relating to a sense of purpose in life?

RESOURCES AND SUGGESTIONS...

- For meditation resources, two of the most informative websites are the US National Institute of Health (www.nccam.nih.gov/health/meditation/overview.htm) and the UK mental health foundation (www.bemindful.co.uk).
- Regarding emotional intelligence, assessment information can be obtained through Multi-Health Systems Inc. (www.mhs.com).
- In terms of meaning, Viktor Frankl's work is highly recommended, including *Man's Search for Meaning: An Introduction to Logotherapy* (1963) and *Recollections: An autobiography.* Other good books addressing meaning from a psychotherapeutic perspective include *Existential Therapy*, by Yalom (1980) and *Tales of Un-Knowing: Eight Stories of Existential Therapy*, by Spinelli (1997). From a literary perspective, classics of existentialism include *La Nausée* [*Nausea*] by Sartre (1964 (1938)) and *L'Etranger* [*The Stranger*] by Camus (1942).

THE BODY AND
THE BRAIN

There is more wisdom in your body
than in your deepest philosophy.
Friedrich Nietzsche

LEARNING OBJECTIVES – AT THE END OF THE CHAPTER YOU WILL BE ABLE TO…

- Deconstruct the body according to the stratified layers of the LIFE model
- Appreciate the dynamics of the mind–body relationship
- Approach wellbeing from a biochemical perspective
- Reflect on the role of genetics in psychological outcomes
- Consider the relationship between neural functioning and positive mental states
- Understand the contribution to wellbeing played by elements of the nervous system
- Appreciate the importance of expressions of the body, such as dance, art and music

LIST OF TOPICS…

- Psychosomatic and somatopsychic effects
- Biochemical 'building blocks'
- Genetics and gene therapy
- Nutrition
- Neurotransmitters
- Neural networks
- Electroencephalography and neurofeedback
- The nervous system
- The 'fight/flight' response
- Physical activity and exercise
- Phenomenology and 'the gaze'
- Dance and movement
- Art and aesthetics
- Music appreciation and practice

Here we turn our attention to the body and the brain. Thus, the chapter forms a conceptual counterpart with the previous one: whereas Chapter 2 covered the subjective pole of the mind–body dichotomy, now we explore the objective realm, considering physiological functioning and behaviour. As we saw in Chapter 1, the mind–body relationship has perplexed philosophers for centuries, with a range of perspectives emerging over the years (Moravia, 1995). *Materialistic monism* favours the physical body/brain as the fundamental reality. Conversely, *transcendental monism* grants primacy to the mind, with matter a mental creation. Finally, dualist perspectives acknowledge the reality of both mind and body/brain. We argued that the pre-eminent paradigm in contemporary consciousness studies, the neural correlates of consciousness (NCC) approach, was a form of dualism (Fell, 2004). This approach holds that mental states are accompanied by analogous neurophysical states, but remains agnostic on issues of causality (whether the brain 'causes' mind, or vice versa). This is the paradigm that informs this book, and particularly this chapter. Rather than granting primacy to either the mind or the body/brain, we are interested in the *relationship* between them. We can conceptualise this relationship either in 'psychosomatic' terms (where subjective mental states engender physiological outcomes) or 'somatopsychic' terms (where physiological processes facilitate particular mental states) (Hefferon, 2013). Ultimately, we will endeavour to keep both perspectives in mind.

Our concern with physiology is not simply theoretical. From an APP perspective, we are interested in *harnessing* these body–mind associations, actively *working with* the body/brain to promote wellbeing; that is, if we determine that particular physiological processes – e.g., certain brain-wave patterns – are associated with mental wellbeing, then we can endeavour to actively *facilitate* these processes, thus enhancing wellbeing. As with the previous chapter, we will structure our enquiry using the stratified layers of the LIFE model. We begin with sub-cellular biochemistry, identified as the 'lowest' stratum of the objective domain, focusing on the impact of molecular genetics on psychological outcomes. Moving 'up' levels, we consider neurons and neural communication, looking at the functional neuroanatomy of wellbeing (Kringelbach & Berridge, 2010). We then turn to the broader nervous system, concentrating in particular on the value of exercise on wellbeing. Finally, we consider the body 'as a whole', reflecting on what it means for us to *have/be* a body, and exploring the ways we can *use* our bodies to find wellbeing, focusing on modes of self-expression such as dance, art and music. From our applied perspective, the overriding concern is with identifying practices that impact upon each particular level, thus giving a sense of how we can work with the body to make life better.

- Critically evaluate the argument that genes influence psychological outcomes to such an extent that interventions to improve our wellbeing are ultimately futile.
- What role does the brain play in our experience of wellbeing?

Biochemistry

We begin our tour of the objective domain by considering biochemistry. Of course, in one sense, the entire body is essentially a biochemical entity. However, in this first part we are using biochemistry as a catch-all term to encompass all the fundamental sub-cellular 'building blocks' of the human body.

Here, we can really appreciate that our choice to stratify our LIFE model into five layers was just that, a choice, and that one could delineate a far greater number of levels, deconstructing matter into ever smaller parts. The body comprises billions of cells; cells are created from proteins (as well as lipids, carbohydrates and nucleic acids); proteins are formed of amino acids; amino acids are made up of atoms; and atoms are constituted from vanishingly small sub-atomic particles that barely seem real at all (Toates, 2011)! Entire scientific fields are dedicated to exploring the wonders and complexities of all these layers of matter. However, for our purpose here, which is just to highlight the *relevance* of physiology to wellbeing rather than explore these layers in depth, we shall simply refer to all the sub-cellular strata as *biochemistry*. Biochemistry is, of course, staggeringly complex, and we cannot even begin to do justice to the myriad ways that biochemical factors can influence our wellbeing. Rather, our intention is simply to draw your attention to the impact of physiological factors on wellbeing by highlighting a few choice examples. Indeed, every section of this book – each level in a given domain – is really only a brief introduction to a whole complex field of enquiry. Thus, readers are encouraged to follow up areas of interest in greater depth by engaging with the literature in that area.

In order to demonstrate the relevance of biochemistry to wellbeing, we will touch upon one facet of biochemistry: genetics. To deploy a simplistic metaphor, genes constitute the 'recipe' for the creation of the human body. Our genetic information is coded from the molecule deoxyribonucleic acid (DNA), formed from over 3 billion base pairs of four nucleotides (adenine, thymine, cytosine and guanine). The human genome constitutes 23 chromosome pairs, collectively housing around 25,000 genes that 'direct the process of development by programming the formation of protein molecules' (Toates, 2011, p. 71). Our genes influence not only physical characteristics, but psychological outcomes too. Research using twins (detailed in the box below) indicates that around 40–50% of the variance in SWB may be due to genetic factors (Lykken & Tellegen, 1996; see Hefferon & Pluess, 2013). Moreover, increasingly sophisticated technology means we are able to develop an ever-greater understanding of the specific factors at a molecular level that influence such outcomes. For example, the neurotransmitter serotonin plays a key role in our emotions – e.g., depletion of serotonin is associated with depression (Ferguson, 2001). Crucially, for our purposes here, there may be a genetic element to serotonin activity. For instance, polymorphism (i.e., variation) in the serotonin transporter gene 5-HTTLPR means that its two alleles (i.e., gene variants that produce different phenotypic traits) can either be long or short in length (Lesch et al., 1994). Research suggests that short alleles may be associated with susceptibility to depression (Caspi et al., 2003), whereas long alleles are linked to life satisfaction (de Neve et al., 2012).

RESEARCH AND PRACTICE CASE STUDIES . . .

Much of our understanding of the impact of genetic factors on psychological outcomes derives from twin studies. In PP, one of the most influential studies is Lykken and Tellegen's (1996) analysis of the heritability of SWB, comparing monozygotic 'identical' twins (from the same embryo, with matching chromosomes) with dizygotic 'fraternal' twins (siblings who share a womb). Of twins reared together – who thus shared a similar upbringing – the correlation in SWB between dizygotic twins ($n = 733$) was negligible ($r = .08$), whereas the correlation between monozygotic twins ($n = 647$) was strong ($r = .44$). The results for twins reared *apart* were even more striking. While there was essentially no correlation in SWB between dizygotic twins ($r = -.02$; $n = 36$), the correlation between monozygotic twins ($n = 75$) was even stronger ($r = .52$). Overall, the researchers concluded that around 44–52% of the variance in SWB is associated with genetic variation. To put that into context, in the same sample, socio-economic status and income each accounted for just 2% of the variance in SWB, and marital status a mere 1%. Moreover, based on longitudinal testing of a smaller sample, the researchers argued that SWB heritability may be as high as *80%*, provocatively concluding that 'trying to be happier is as futile as trying to be taller' (Lykken & Tellegen, 1996, p. 189). Similar figures have been obtained more recently by Nes and colleagues (2005) in studies on Norwegian twins. Nevertheless, in an influential paper, Lyubomirsky et al. (2005) argued that even if 50% of the variance in SWB may be due to genetic factors, we can still influence the remaining 50%, with around 10% arguably shaped by circumstances and 40% by our activities. However, this paper is often misunderstood, and we must be careful in interpreting it: even if these percentages are correct – which is contestable – they apply to whole populations; to assume that they hold true for individuals is to commit what is known as the 'ecological fallacy'. What is your view? Is our level of happiness written in our genes, or can we shape our own destiny?

Although the links between genetic factors – such as polymorphism in the serotonin transporter gene 5-HTTLPR – and wellbeing are intriguing, we must be wary of seeming to espouse genetic determinism. The causal chain from alleles to psychological processes is so bewilderingly complex and little understood that we cannot speak simplistically of a gene *for* particular outcomes such as depression (Hefferon & Pluess, 2013). Gene expression and subsequent psychological outcomes are strongly influenced by environmental factors. In the diathesis-stress model of psychopathology, individuals are viewed as being genetically either vulnerable or resilient to particular disorders. However, this genetic risk-factor only becomes operative in conditions of adversity (Monroe & Simons, 1991). Likewise, the differential susceptibility hypothesis suggests that some people have greater 'developmental plasticity' than others, being more malleable to both adversity *and* positive environments (Belsky et al., 2007). Nevertheless, while researchers remain cognisant of the complex interaction between genes and environment, efforts to understand the genetic basis of mental health outcomes are advancing rapidly. Moreover, from an APP perspective, this research is not only theoretical, but may potentially have future practical applications, such as gene therapy, as outlined in the box below. However, such applications are currently highly problematic, being both ethically contentious and technically challenging. As such, although one day we may see the emergence of fields such as 'applied positive biochemistry', this rather science-fiction possibility is some way off yet, if it happens at all!

REFLECTION . . .

Gene therapy involves 'correcting inherited diseases by inserting a normal copy of the relevant gene into somatic cells' (Kohn & Candotti, 2009, p. 518). So far this technology has mainly been explored only in relation to illnesses which are 'well understood at the molecular level', like blood diseases (e.g., sickle cell anemia). However, pioneering animal studies hint at the potential for gene therapy in relation to mental health and illness. Alexander et al. (2010) found that 'depression-like behaviours' in mice were linked to the absence of a serotonin receptor binding protein, and that restoration of this protein corrected the behaviours. While such research is clearly at a very early stage, it is possible that humans will one day be able to harness gene therapy to alter psychological outcomes. How do you feel about the notion of gene therapy? This is a contentious ethical area (Evans, 2002). Some people recoil from the idea of 'tampering' with genetics, accusing researchers of 'playing God', or warning of a slippery slope leading to the creation of 'designer babies'. Other people argue that humans have a right and even a responsibility to harness science to improve wellbeing, and as such technologies like gene therapy should be vigorously pursued. Where do you stand on these issues?

Finally, we can briefly mention an aspect of physiology which arguably pertains to biochemistry: nutrition. Our health is affected by what we consume, which, ultimately, provides the material our bodies are formed from and the 'fuel' our bodies run on (Blanchflower et al., 2013, p. 1). There is increasing understanding of the components of a healthy diet, as reflected in guidance given by public health bodies, such as the advice to eat five (or possibly even more) portions of fruit and vegetables per day (NHS, 2014a). However, nutrition is a complex field and our concern here is not to dispense dietary recommendations, but simply to point out that eating habits affect wellbeing, and so fall within the purview of PP. Diet not only indirectly impacts on mental wellbeing (i.e., a good diet improves health, which then affects outcomes like SWB), but may even directly influence mental health. Controlling for other relevant health factors, Ford et al. (2013) found a correlation between positive affect (PA) and consumption of a 'Mediterranean' diet (e.g., non-starchy fresh vegetables, olive oil, nuts, fish and legumes). Likewise, Blanchflower et al. (2013) observed an association between PWB and intake of fruit and vegetables; moreover, dose–response analysis indicated that there was an optimal daily dose of seven pieces/portions. These findings were corroborated by White et al. (2013), who employed a micro-longitudinal, correlational design to assess the impact of dietary intake on PA and NA (negative affect) in young adults. In addition to finding a similar optimal dosage (seven to eight portions), White et al. observed that self-reported PA was higher on days when participants ate more fruit and vegetables, and moreover this intake predicted their mood the following day.

From an APP perspective, we can not only make recommendations relating to diet, but construct PPIs to promote healthy eating. McMillan et al. (2011) designed a ten-day nutrition intervention in which participants were given an 'eating plan' detailing foods which should (and should not) be consumed during that time period, such as increasing their intake of fruits, vegetables and wholegrain cereals. Relative to a control group (who continued with their regular diet), there were significant self-rated improvements in vigour, alertness and contentment among the participants. However, in considering diet, it is important to appreciate that eating habits are not simply a matter of physiology, but are guided by factors from the other domains of the LIFE model. Eating can fulfil psychological functions (e.g., regulating mood), and so some dietary interventions work on helping people control their eating behaviour, such as 'Mindful eating and living', a treatment for eating disorders that encourages mindfulness in relation to food intake (Dalen et al., 2010). Contextual factors matter too. Williamson et al. (2007) describe a school-based obesity prevention programme that involved interobjective structural aspects (e.g., provision of healthy food) and also intersubjective strategies (e.g., educating teachers and parents in promoting healthy eating).

Neurons

Moving up the strata of the objective domain, we turn our attention to neurons, i.e., cells specific to the nervous system that are advanced in delivering and processing information (Toates, 2011). The neuron comprises three components: the cell body (housing the principle biochemical machinery of the cell); dendrites (tree-like branches that receive information from other neurons); and the axon (which sends electrical impulses to other cells). The average brain comprises approximately 100 billion neurons, each connected by its dendrites to as many as 200,000 other neurons (Liu et al., 2013). To simplify an incredibly complex process, brain activity is generated by communication between neurons via neurotransmitters (NTs), i.e., 'chemical substances that carry messages' (Holt et al., 2012, p. 104). The neuron is stimulated by NTs from other neurons, which allows charged particles (e.g., sodium ions) to enter the cell body, thus altering the electrical polarity of the cell. If the neuron is sufficiently stimulated, a threshold is reached and the neuron 'fires', sending an electrical impulse (an 'action potential') down the axon. As the electrical signal reaches the axon terminals, it releases the neuron's own NTs (by opening the vesicles in which they are stored), which then pass across the synaptic cleft (where the terminal meets the dendrite of another neuron) to impinge on other neurons. Although the brain is arguably the 'most complex object in the universe' (Killeen & Glenberg, 2010, p. 66), the NCC paradigm is beginning to shed light onto 'neural systems and properties of those systems' (Fell, 2004, p. 709). We will briefly look at three aspects of neural functioning – NTs, brain regions and brain waves – highlighting the 'neural correlates of wellbeing' (Urry et al., 2004).

First, we can consider NTs, which play a central role in emotional experiences (and indeed all aspects of brain functioning). As noted above, serotonin (5-hydroxy-tryptamine) is implicated in affective disorders, as well as in perception, appetite, temperature regulation and sleep induction (Tortora & Derrickson, 2009). Noradrenaline (or norepinephrine) is central to the 'fight or flight' response – the stimulation of the sympathetic nervous system in stressful situations – producing an 'adrenaline rush' that leads to physiological changes like increased heart rate and blood pressure (Curtis & O'Keefe, 2002). Dopamine is the 'reward currency' of the brain: it plays a key motivational and gratificatory role in shaping behaviour by generating sensations of pleasure when desirables like food or sex are obtained; as such, dysfunction of the dopamine system is associated with outcomes like depression and drug addiction (Bressan & Crippa, 2005). A special class of NTs are endorphins (a concatenation of the terms endogenous (deriving from the body) and morphine (the pain-relieving analgesic)). These peptides (short chains of amino acids) are known as the body's own 'natural painkillers' (Tortora & Derrickson, 2009, p. 482). Endorphins are associated with pleasurable states arising from certain activities, like the 'runner's high' brought on by exercise (Boecker et al., 2008). However, elevated endorphin activity is also implicated in disorders such as schizophrenia (Lindström et al., 1986). From an applied perspective, the study of NTs has generated a proliferation of psychopharmacological interventions in psychiatry for the treatment of mental health disorders, which influence mental states by altering NT levels. To return to the case of serotonin, selective serotonin re-uptake inhibitors (SSRIs) treat depression by effectively increasing serotonin transmission in the brain (by preventing re-uptake by the pre-synaptic neuron) (Ferguson, 2001).

REFLECTION . . .

In addition to the regulated psychoactive drugs of psychiatry, many people take illicit substances to similarly alter their mood. In the UK, 36% of adults have taken illicit drugs at least once in their life, and 9% have used within the past 12 months (NHS, 2011). Keeping with the example of serotonin, the drug MDMA (methylenedioxymeth-amphetamine) floods the brain with this, producing a state of euphoria (i.e., 'ecstasy'). Used in this uncontrolled way, MDMA can be dangerous, and has even been linked to fatalaties in some instances (Arendt et al., 2011). Moreover, its long-term use is linked to chronic depletion of serotonin levels (Kish et al., 2000). However, some people suggest that careful MDMA use can promote positive outcomes, like a deep sense of meaning and spirituality (Adamson & Metzner, 1988). Sessa (2007) even makes a case for developing 'MDMA-assisted psychotherapy' for psychiatrists to use as an adjunct to more conventional treatments. What do you think? Should people be allowed and even encouraged to take psychoactive drugs to enhance their wellbeing (and not simply to alleviate mental health problems)? Should drugs like MDMA even be legalised and given by medical practitioners in a regulated way, thus enhancing the safety of those who would likely use drugs in any case? What about the risks of addiction? Where do you stand?

Neural networks

We now turn our attention to neural networks, which comprise whole assemblies of neurons (and as such constitute the next level up on the LIFE model). Here we are interested in specific brain regions, and the complex interactions between these. In contrast to the lay perception that different parts of the brain are *for* particular psychological processes, generally speaking such processes are produced by the interaction of areas *distributed* throughout the brain (Fell et al., 2010). From a PP perspective, the NCC paradigm has been deployed to explore the role that neural processes play in underpinning states of wellbeing, work referred to as 'affective neuroscience' (Davidson, 2003) or a 'neural correlates of wellbeing' approach (Urry et al., 2004). For instance, Kringelbach and Berridge (2010, p. 587) have studied the 'functional neuroanatomy of pleasure and happiness'. While Berridge and Kringelbach (2011) differentiate between sensory pleasures (e.g., food) and higher-order pleasures (e.g., spiritual fulfilment), they suggest that both utilise the same neurophysiological pleasure/reward systems. In particular, reflecting the idea of mental activity being distributed across brain regions, they argue that such experiences derive from the interaction of 'pleasure hotspots' that are 'distributed as a chain of "liking"-enhancing islands of brain tissue across several deep structures of the brain' (Berridge & Kringelbach, 2011, p. 7), including the nucleus accumbens and the ventral pallidum. These 'hotspots' are seen as forming a 'functional integrated circuit' that acts 'as a coordinated whole to amplify core pleasure reactions'.

RESEARCH AND PRACTICE CASE STUDIES . . .

Of all the PPIs deployed in APP, meditation has received the most empirical attention from an NCC perspective, driven by collaborations between advanced meditators and eminent neuroscientists (Lutz et al., 2009). While meditation involves the interaction of numerous brain regions, a model proposed by Newberg and Iversen (2003) highlights the role of two principal areas: the prefrontal cortex (PFC) and the anterior cingulate cortex (ACC). Their significance is that both play a key role in the control of attention, which is a defining feature of meditation, as noted in Chapter 2. The PFC is implicated in higher-level cognitive activities like volition, planning and decision making, and is central to complex goal-driven behaviour (Fuster, 2008). The ACC is similarly pivotal in regulating cognitive/emotional processing (Posner & Dehaene, 1994). Brain activity in meditation, analysed via fMRI (functional magnetic resonance imaging, which measures blood flow), shows increased ACC and PFC activation, which forms part of the evidence that meditation develops skills around attention regulation (Hölzel et al., 2007). Moreover, meditation does not only activate areas involved in attention processing; long-term practice is associated with neural growth in these key regions (Lazar et al., 2005), a phenomenon known as neurogenesis. So, how you use your brain over time can actually change its structure!

Finally, in our brief tour of neural functioning, we can touch upon brain waves. The significance of these is that they reflect the large-scale synchronisation of neural networks, and thus are a proposed mechanism allowing communication between spatially distributed brain areas (Basar et al., 2001). So, what are brain waves? As neurons are stimulated by NTs, this alters the neuron's electrical potential; as this happens, neighbouring cells tend to have similarly altered membrane potentials, and the synchronised electrical oscillations combine additively to create larger regional currents, detectable by electrodes (e.g., on the scalp). The waveforms produced by these currents can be analysed in terms of various parameters, a paradigm known as electroencephalography (EEG) (Cacioppo et al., 2007). Amplitude refers to the magnitude of the electrical signal, reflecting the amount of synchronised activity in the underlying tissue. Frequency is the number of oscillatory cycles per second (measured in Hz), and is divided into different bands: Delta (1–4 Hz); Theta (4–8 Hz); Alpha (8–12/13 Hz); Beta (13–30 Hz); and Gamma (36–44 Hz). Coherence is the stability of the relationship between different electrodes, and reflects the functional connectivity between distant brain regions. In the EEG paradigm, these parameters are then linked with particular mental states. To return to our case study of meditation, meditative states are frequently associated with increased amplitude and coherence in alpha and theta bandwidths (Lomas et al., 2013b). Although the *interpretation* of these parameters can be difficult (Shaw, 1996), this pattern is thought to reflect a state of relaxed alertness (Fell et al., 2010). Indeed, in studies using the neurophenomenology paradigm – where physiological assessments are combined with subjective reports – this interpretation is corroborated by meditators themselves (Cahn & Polich, 2006).

RESEARCH AND PRACTICE CASE STUDIES . . .

EEG is not only a methodological paradigm; excitingly, from an APP perspective, it can also serve as a PPI. Neurofeedback involves providing participants with real-time information about their brain activity, often rendered graphically in imaginative ways. Perhaps alpha bandwidth activity might be represented visually as a lake, where the amplitude determines how choppy the water is (i.e., the greater the amplitude, the calmer the water). Strikingly, people can use this information to regulate their brain activity, even if they are not sure how they are doing it! For instance, if a desired goal state is elevated alpha amplitude (i.e., the meditative state of relaxed alertness), simply instructing people to 'make the water calm' can produce the desired effect. Consequently, neurofeedback is beginning to be harnessed as 'an evidence based behavioural therapy' (Moss, 2009, p. 656). For example, Johnston et al. (2010) piloted an fMRI neurofeedback therapy for developing emotional regulation. Similarly, Gruzelier et al. (2013) used neurofeedback with children to enhance music creativity, attention and wellbeing. As a non-invasive intervention that can improve wellbeing and brain functioning, without the side effects of some medications, neurofeedback is a promising area for APP to explore in future.

The nervous system

Moving up through the levels of the LIFE model, encompassing the brain is the broader nervous system, which regulates the interactions between the body and the outside world (e.g., the fight/flight response mentioned above). The nervous system comprises the central nervous system (the brain and spinal cord) and the peripheral nervous system (neurons located throughout the body). Both of these systems can be subdivided further, deconstructed according to their constituent elements. We have already subdivided the brain above (into neurons, etc.). However, the peripheral nervous system has its own stratification: it can be divided into two systems, the autonomic and the somatic, which can in turn be further subdivided. For example, the autonomic system comprises the sympathetic nervous system (linked to the fight/flight stress response) and the parasympathetic nervous system (ongoing processes that keep the body alive, such as breathing, heartbeat and digestion). When under stress, the sympathetic nervous system primes the body for action, increasing heart-rate, dilating the lungs for increased oxygen intake and shutting down unnecessary activity (e.g., salivary production) to redirect blood flow to the muscles that need it. Conversely, the parasympathetic system slows the heartbeat and stimulates organs to return to normal resting levels of functioning. (Incidentally, the fact that the nervous system has its own complex holarchical 'layers' reinforces the point, emphasised in Chapter 1, that our LIFE model is not the only viable way of stratifying the domains. One could choose to 'carve up' the domains in any number of ways, depending on one's priorities and agenda.)

In PP, researchers have begun exploring the intricate links between nervous system functioning and wellbeing. Some of this is from a 'negative' perspective, i.e., exploring the impact of dysphoric states on physiological processes. The fight-flight stress response involves a release of 'stress hormones', such as cortisol and adrenaline. In the short term, these propel the body into action, but, if sustained, can have deleterious consequences (Kemeny, 2003). Over-exposure to stress and subsequent cortisol production can cause dysregulation of the hypothalmic-pituitary-adrenal (HPA) axis – part of the neuroendocrine system that regulates diverse body processes, from immune system functioning to digestion – which can lead to illness (Stratakis & Chrousos, 1995). Conversely, the flip-side of this psychosomatic interaction is that positive emotions potentially have a beneficial impact upon nervous system functioning and subsequent health. Cohen et al. (2006) found that individuals with more positive emotional styles were less likely to become infected with a rhinovirus after being exposed in a controlled environment. Strikingly, studies have even tentatively suggested that positive emotions may influence mortality rates, potentially via their influence on immune system functioning and other physiological processes that influence health and illness. A recent review by Diener and Chan (2011) included prospective longitudinal studies which indicated that, taking into account base-line health and socio-economic status (SES), PP factors like PA can predict health and longevity. However, the evidence for the impact of such factors on outcomes like illness survival rates is highly contentious (Coyne & Tennen, 2010). As such, we need to be careful how we interpret and communicate the results of studies purporting to show a causal link between positive emotions and physical health, as elucidated in the box below.

REFLECTION . . .

Critics have accused PP researchers of making claims concerning the impact of emotional factors (e.g., SWB) on health outcomes (e.g., longevity) that are unsubstantiated or overstated (Coyne & Tennen, 2010). However, in reply, Aspinwall and Tedeschi (2010) argued that such critics often misinterpret or misrepresent the literature in this area, accusing PP theorists of making bold claims (e.g., that 'positive thinking can cure disease') that were never in fact put forward. Moreover, Aspinwall and Tedeschi suggested that even if there were some validity to these criticisms, it would still be 'premature to abandon efforts to understand and promote positive phenomena among people with various life-threatening illnesses' (2010, p. 27). Nevertheless, it is fair to say that while the possibility of psychosomatic influence is intriguing, it is poorly understood, and as such we must tread carefully in this area. Thus, when considering the possibility of psychosomatic interaction (e.g., if we are working with people who have been diagnosed with severe illnesses such as cancer), we need to be careful:

- Not to overgeneralise or over-extrapolate from a small number of promising studies
- To take into account studies which do *not* show any positive psychosomatic interaction
- Not to overstate our understanding of psychosomatic relationships or mechanisms
- Not to allow wishful thinking to colour our interpretation of data
- Not to promote a 'tyranny' of positive thinking (Held, 2002), i.e., compelling or pressurising people to think or feel in a particular way
- To be ethical, cautious and considerate in our dissemination of research findings
- To undertake or utilise rigorous and sophisticated longitudinal psychophysical research

Given the relationship between physiological processes and wellbeing, from an APP perspective we can encourage people to *harness* these processes in order to *promote* flourishing. In terms of 'working with' the nervous system to engender wellbeing, perhaps the most important practice in this regard is physical activity and exercise.[1] Regular exercise has a protective effect on physical health, reducing the risk of diverse health conditions, including type-2 diabetes (Colberg et al., 2010), cardiovascular disease (Vuori, 1998) and some cancers (Thune et al., 1997). Exercise also has a positive impact on mental health, ameliorating the impact of conditions like depression (Hoffman et al., 2011) and anxiety (Herring et al., 2010), as well as promoting other desirable psychological outcomes, including enhanced self-perception and self-esteem (Fox et al., 2001), SWB (Reed & Ones, 2006) and even cognitive functioning (Hillman et al., 2008). The mechanisms by which exercise promotes such effects range from increasing cardiovascular fitness, to increasing the production of beneficial NTs, such as endorphins. There are some caveats: perceptions of the psychological benefits of exercise can sometimes exceed the actual evidence (Ströhle, 2009), and there are attendant physical risks involved, such as musculoskeletal injury (Koplan et al., 1985) or myocardial infarction (Acevedo, 2012). Thus, people must be sensitive to these risks, and take advice from a doctor if worried or in doubt. Moreover, while there are standard guidelines for recommended levels of physical exercise (as outlined in the box below), people must ensure that their exercise programme is tailored to their current fitness levels and physical abilities (Biddle & Mutrie, 2008). Nevertheless, even with such caveats, the American College of Sports Medicine argues that the 'benefits of exercise far outweigh the risks in most adults' (Garber et al., 2011, p. 1334). Thus, the considerable physical and psychological benefits of exercise and general physical activity mean that these constitute 'stellar' PPIs (Hefferon & Mutrie, 2012).

PSYCHOMETRIC SCALES . . .

How much exercise should you do? Current guidelines, issued by the influential American College of Sports Medicine (Garber et al., 2011), recommend that adults undertake regular exercise, including 'cardiorespiratory, resistance, flexibility, and neuromotor exercise training beyond activities of daily living' (p. 1334). More specifically, it is recommended that each week adults engage in the following levels of each type of exercise. Next to each type of exercise, estimate how often you engage in this (i.e., days per week). Compare these estimates with the recommended levels. Could you perhaps be doing more?

---

[1] Physical activity refers to 'any bodily movement produced by skeletal muscles that results in energy expenditure' (Caspersen et al., 1985, p. 126). A subset of such activity is exercise, which is defined as having 'the specific objective of improving or maintaining physical fitness or health' (Acevedo, 2012, p. 4). The positive outcomes noted above are not limited to exercise, but can extend to many forms of physical activity (Colberg et al., 2010). Nevertheless, we will use the generic term 'exercise' here.

	Estimate (days per week)
Moderate-intensity cardiorespiratory exercise training for ≥30 minutes per day, on ≥5 days per week, for a total of ≥150 minutes per week	_____
or	
Vigorous-intensity cardiorespiratory exercise training for ≥20 minutes per day, on ≥3 days per week, for a total of ≥75 minutes per week	_____
or	
A combination of moderate- and vigorous-intensity exercise	_____
plus	
Resistance exercises for each of the major muscle groups, on 2–3 days per week	_____
and	
Neuromotor exercise involving agility and coordination (e.g., yoga), on 2–3 days per week	_____
and	
Flexibility exercises for each of the major muscle-tendon groups (a total of 60 seconds per exercise), on ≥2 days per week	_____

The body

Finally, we turn to the body 'as a whole'. We have already touched upon the idea of embodiment in Chapter 2, focusing on our subjective experience of our body. In this section, our concern is more with what we can *do* with the body to promote wellbeing. Having already considered one such activity in the section above (exercise), here we expand our focus to include behaviours such as art and music. However, before exploring these pastimes, it is worth reflecting for a moment on what it means to *be* a body. In philosophy, this question has been studied most extensively within phenomenology, an approach which involves systematically enquiring into the nature of subjectivity. In this branch of philosophy, although the various *aspects* of embodied experience (i.e., visceral sensations in particular parts of the body) are not especially problematic, the status of the body as a whole is more mysterious. Edmund Husserl (1952), generally considered to be the 'father' of phenomenology, regarded the body as an 'anomaly', neither being a part of a person's consciousness, nor an object alongside other entities, but 'a thing inserted between the rest of the material world and the subjective sphere' (p. 161). Likewise, Merleau-Ponty (1962) felt the body was at once both an elusive phenomenon and yet also the very ground and vehicle for all our perceptions and actions. As Carman (2000, p. 161) articulates it, the body plays a 'constitutive role in experience precisely by grounding, making possible and yet remaining peripheral in the horizon of our perceptual awareness'. Thus, we do not *have* or *own* our bodies, but rather understand ourselves as *being* bodies, with our bodies an integral yet mysterious part of the lived self.

REFLECTION . . .

Critical sociologists argue that our experience of our bodies is also shaped by discourses and practices in society at large. The influential theorist Foucault (1979) held that we are constantly subjected to observation by other people, a phenomenon he referred to as 'the gaze'. Even when we are alone, we perceive ourselves according to how others might see us. More perniciously, he thought that this gaze served to objectify, define and ultimately control us, by compelling us to behave in ways sanctioned by the powers-that-be in society. Thus, the gaze can even deprive us of autonomy over our own body, ceding control to those vested with power. He gives the potent example of a patient being examined by a medical professional whose impersonal jargon around health and illness might serve to objectify and even dehumanise the patient. Frank (1990) refers to this as the 'medicalised body', in contrast to other 'types' of body-experiences, such as the 'disciplined body' (controlled by the person themselves through regimented fasting, extreme work and power). It has further been pointed out that there is often a gendered dimension to the gaze, and that women are especially subjected to this objectifying cultural scrutiny, being pressured to view self-worth in terms of appearance, and thus to monitor and regulate themselves accordingly (Fredrickson & Roberts, 1997). Have you experienced the gaze?

Our experience of the body is further shaped by how we *use* it. We can express ourselves through the body in a multitude of ways. We will touch upon three expressions that have featured in most cultures throughout recorded history – dance, art and music – exploring their impact on wellbeing. First, we can consider dance, since as both a physical activity and a vehicle for self-expression it nicely bridges the section above (on the health benefits of exercise) and our focus here on creative pursuits. Dance refers to 'body movements [that] are organized into spatial patterns' (Brown et al., 2006, p. 1157). The benefits of dance to wellbeing are manifold. Linking back to our discussion on the value of exercise, dance can enhance physical health, e.g., increasing cardiovascular fitness (Burkhardt & Brennan, 2012). Moreover, dance has unique psychological benefits – including a 'fun' factor – which means it can appeal to hard-to-reach or at-risk populations (e.g., adolescent females) who may resist other types of exercise, like competitive sports (Burkhardt & Rhodes, 2012). This appeal means dance can be a particularly effective intervention for at-risk populations, not just in terms of exercise, but as a form of health education/promotion and as a tool for promoting community cohesion. Positive mental states associated with the act of dancing range from flow to stronger emotions like joy (Hefferon & Ollis, 2006). Dance can even engender more rarified states, such as spiritual experiences; indeed, dance has long been an important component of religious rituals in many cultures (Highwater, 1992). Moreover, this cultural usage highlights a further important feature of dance, namely as a vehicle for realising and expressing one's cultural identity (Grau & Jordan, 2002).

RESEARCH AND PRACTICE CASE STUDIES . . .

From an APP perspective, people can of course be encouraged to join dance classes and groups (e.g., in the community) to suit their musical and physical tastes. However, more structured interventions have also been developed in recent years, which may be helpful for people with particular physical or psychological needs, for instance as an adjunctive treatment to conventional mental health therapies. Foremost among such interventions is dance therapy, also known as dance/movement therapy (DMT), defined by the American Dance Therapy Association as 'the psychotherapeutic use of movement as a process which furthers the emotional, cognitive, physical and social integration of the individual' (Loman, 2005, p. 68). By facilitating this integration – which embraces all the domains of our LIFE model – DMT can enhance psychological functioning and general wellbeing (Strassel et al., 2011). DMT has been harnessed in the treatment of both physical and mental health disorders: Bradt et al. (2011) used DMT with cancer patients to help increase body awareness and reconnection to the physical self, while with mental health, DMT has been used to alleviate distress and other symptoms in conditions ranging from depression (Jeong et al., 2005) to schizophrenia (Xia & Grant, 2009).

Turning now to art, we are using this term to cover the multitude of forms of visual expression that people have created over the centuries, from painting and photography to sculpture and ceramics. The urge to express ourselves using art is a constant in human history, with the earliest works of art dating back at least 40,000 years (Than, 2012). Still today, art plays an important role in many people's lives: a comprehensive survey in the USA of art engagement (over the previous year) found that around half the nation's adults created, shared or performed art of some type (National Endowment for the Arts, 2013). In considering the relevance of art to wellbeing and hence to PP, we can approach this from two perspectives: appreciation and practice. First, even if one does not *practise*, wellbeing can be engendered simply through enjoying art (and indeed all forms of expression). There is a whole field of philosophy devoted to beauty and the positive mental states that this can induce, namely aesthetics (Kivy, 2009). The value of aesthetics is beginning to be recognised in PP: 'appreciation of beauty and excellence' is a character strength in the 'values-in-action' (VIA) taxonomy

(Peterson & Seligman, 2004) – detailed in Chapter 6 – where it is a component of the broader virtue of transcendence. Indeed, art can be a powerful route to some of the more elevated states of wellbeing. For example, Keltner and Haidt (2003) discuss the significance of the complex emotional state of awe, in which a person can be moved profoundly by experiences that challenge their understanding of the world. They argue that works of art have the power to induce this state, and can facilitate transformative experiences.

TRY ME! . . .

Even if one does not experience transformative states of awe in response to art, a little art appreciation can certainly reduce one's stress levels! Clow and Fredhoi (2006) asked 28 workers in the financial district of London to spend 35–40 minutes visiting a local art gallery. The researchers took salivary samples before and after the visit to assess participants' cortisol levels (a 'stress hormone', as noted above). They found that cortisol had reduced significantly by the end of the session, as had self-reported levels of stress. Why not find a gallery near you and spend an hour or so looking around. As you do, reflect on your responses to the art, and on what the experience generally does for you.

Beyond simply appreciating art, practising it oneself can be highly conducive to wellbeing. We can understand its impact through the prism of numerous concepts in PP. As anybody who has ever been absorbed in creative acts will attest, artistic pursuits are effective at engendering flow (Swindells et al., 2013). Moreover, the act of self-expression can help satisfy key psychological needs, especially autonomy and competence (Deci & Ryan, 1985). On a deeper level, art is a powerful vehicle for self-exploration, for engaging with and communicating one's intimate thoughts and feelings, which can be particularly helpful in the context of coping with physical or mental illness. Reynolds and Lim (2007) found that artistic expression helped individuals diagnosed with cancer make sense of their illness experience, helping to alleviate distress and even endowing their plight with a sense of meaning, facilitating posttraumatic growth. Given the manifold ways art can engender mental wellbeing, art therapy has been found to be very helpful in the treatment of mental health problems, especially for people who struggle to express themselves verbally, such as children who have been abused or adults with cognitive dysfunction (Pratt, 2004). Art interventions can be beneficial in non-clinical contexts too: Swindells et al. (2013) report that a community art intervention for older adults was highly effective at engendering PWB. Moreover, such interventions can have powerful knock-on effects on other aspects of wellbeing, particularly in at-risk populations. Renton et al. (2012)

found that delivering art interventions with people from lower socio-economic groups, who tend to have less engagement with the arts, produced positive changes in other areas of life (e.g., health behaviours).

Finally, in our brief and selective tour of ways we 'use' our body to promote wellbeing, we turn to music. Its mysterious power to evoke mental states has been known at least as far back as classical Greece: Pythagoras developed an esoteric philosophy of music, connecting harmonic properties to mathematical ratios that structure the universe, and used it in a meditative way to restore his mental equilibrium before sleeping (West, 2000). The idea that music can be used in a curative way still flourishes today. Ruud (2013) observed that people use music strategically to regulate their wellbeing, perhaps listening to particular songs to alleviate distress, and even calls it a 'cultural immunogen' (i.e., a phenomenon with health-related outcomes). Ruud (2008) refers to these curative effects as 'musical self-medication' (p. 50). Beyond emotional regulation, music can form a central part of one's personal and cultural identity, and can even constitute a way of life (Hays & Minichiello, 2005). As with art, we can focus on the value of both appreciating and practising music. The above studies, highlighting the role of music in emotional regulation, point to the fact that simply listening to music can have a powerful positive impact on our emotions. Indeed, an emergent branch of psychobiological research is dedicated to exploring why music can have such potent effects, such as Panksepp and Bernatzky's (2002) analysis of the neuroaffective mechanisms underlying the power of music to elicit 'chills' (shivers down the spine). They suggested that the phenomenon involved a rush of endorphins combined with the type of galvanic skin response that emotional stimuli tend to prompt.

TRY ME! . . .

Which music gives you the chills? In Chapter 2, we recommended the practice of listening mindfully to music. Pick a piece of music that you find has the potential to evoke the chills. Listen mindfully to it, paying particular attention to your physiological sensations as you listen. Try to gain a sense of *why* it has these effects. The chills are a wonderful illustration of the mystery of mind–body interaction.

Practising music oneself can be further conducive to wellbeing, in both clinical and non-clinical contexts. Like art, music has been harnessed as a therapeutic tool in the treatment of physical and mental health problems. Ruud (2008) outlines various types of music therapy (MT), including creative MT (where collaborative improvisation is used to facilitate bonding between therapist and client);

resource-oriented MT (harnessing the clients own 'resources', e.g., helping them write original songs to explore their personal issues); and community MT (music participation as a route to social engagement). MT has been successfully used with diverse patient populations, including those with physical problems ranging from cancer (Magill, 2000) to traumatic brain injury (Nayak et al., 2000), and psychological issues including depression (Maratos et al., 2008), autism (Gold et al., 2006) and Alzheimer's disease (Kumar et al., 1999). As with art and dance therapy, MT is an especially good form of therapy for people who have difficulty verbalising their emotions. Of course, practising music does not only benefit clinical populations. Playing music is associated with wellbeing in the population at large, across the age spectrum, from childhood and adolescence (Trainor et al., 2010) to older age (Hays, 2005). Moreover, one does not even have to play an instrument to benefit from practising music. Choral singing can be a wonderful way to participate musically – one does not even have to consider oneself to be a good singer! – and is very effective at engendering positive emotions, in addition to the social benefits of joining a choir (Sandgren, 2009). Why not join one yourself?

SUMMARY – THIS CHAPTER HAS...

- Outlined the stratified layers of the LIFE model's objective body/brain domain
- Reflected on biochemical processes, focusing in particular on genetics and nutrition
- Explored the neural correlates of the wellbeing paradigm, including the use of neurofeedback
- Analysed the relevance to health of nervous system functioning, and the value of exercise
- Considered artistic ways of using our bodies to enhance wellbeing, e.g., dance, art and music

QUIZ...

1 How many chromosome pairs constitute the human genome?
2 Depression is linked to which type of alleles of the serotonin transporter gene 5-HTTLPR?
3 Approximately how many billions of neurons comprise the average human brain?
4 What specific brain region does the acronym PFC stand for?
5 Which EEG frequency band ranges from 4–8 Hz?
6 The fight/flight stress response is linked to which branch of the nervous system?
7 In the phrase 'HPA axis', what does the acronym HPA stand for?
8 Who is cited in the text as being the 'father' of phenomenology?

9   Which branch of philosophy is concerned with beauty?

10 Which classical Greek philosopher is cited in the text as developing a philosophy of music?

RESOURCES AND SUGGESTIONS...

- For recommendations around nutrition and healthy eating, please visit the NHS Healthy Eating website at www.nhs.uk/livewell/healthy-eating. Helpful advice can also be found on the US government website www.nutrition.gov.
- A good example of the neural correlates of wellbeing paradigm is the 'positive neuroscience' project, which can be found at www.posneuroscience.org.
- More information on the connection between art and wellbeing can be obtained from the Society for the Arts in Healthcare (www.thesah.org). An informative resource for readers in the UK is the London Arts in Health Forum (LAHF), found at www.lahf. org.uk.

CULTURE AND SOCIETY

Never doubt that a small group of thoughtful,
committed citizens can change the world.
Indeed, it is the only thing that ever has.
Margaret Mead

LEARNING OBJECTIVES – AT THE END OF THE CHAPTER YOU WILL BE ABLE TO...

- Differentiate between intersubjective (culture) and interobjective (society) domains
- Think about how to apply PPIs at all levels of Bronfenbrenner's experimental ecology
- Know how to make the microsystem (immediate setting) more conducive to wellbeing
- Articulate the relevance of the mesosystem (links between microsystems) to wellbeing
- Conceive of and plan exosystem (community-level) PPIs
- Appreciate how macrosystems (e.g., political structures) influence wellbeing
- Understand the relevance to PP of progressive social movements (e.g., environmentalism)

LIST OF TOPICS...

- Relationships and social capital
- Theories of gender
- Aesthetic and ergonomic design
- Virtual interaction
- Community wellbeing factors
- Quality of life acts
- Shared spaces and urban planning
- Bhutan and Gross National Happiness
- Libertarian paternalism
- Positive economics
- Progressive social movements
- Environmentalism and ecological wellbeing

So far we have focused on the individual domains of our LIFE model, working with the mind and the body to promote wellbeing. Now we expand our horizons by incorporating the two collective domains into our comprehensive approach, exploring the impact of culture and society on wellbeing. Doing so is a relatively new departure for PP, at least according to its critics. As noted in Chapter 1, PP has been accused of promulgating a rather individualistic conception of wellbeing, where happiness is presented as a question of having the right psychological qualities and strategies (Becker & Marecek, 2008). Although some attention has been paid in PP to social context, this is often limited to 'social in the narrow sense' (Bellah et al., 1996, p. xxv), e.g., observations around the importance of supportive relationships. There has been little critical analysis of the way structural factors impact upon people's ability to flourish. However, critical psychologists argue that wellbeing cannot be separated from issues around social justice and (in)equality, as it is harder to flourish if one is socially disadvantaged (Prilleltensky, 2008). Structural differences arising from social inequalities – related to social class, gender, ethnicity and race – can dramatically affect wellbeing via factors like access to healthcare, educational and economic opportunity, and safe and secure living conditions. These are exactly the kinds of issues and factors that we will address in this chapter.

From an analytic perspective, we can conceptualise these structural differences as being 'contextual determinants' of wellbeing. According to one of the most extensive surveys of such determinants – the World Values Survey (Helliwell & Putnam, 2004) – the most important are relationships, income, work, social capital, and health. These factors allow us to appreciate the way social issues can affect wellbeing, especially the adverse impact of being socially disadvantaged, as reflected in the statistic that men in the lowest socio-economic class in England are almost three times more likely to have depression and/or anxiety than men in the highest (Equality and Human Rights Commission, 2010). This association between poverty and mental health is observed globally (Lund et al., 2010). Theorists have been able interpret this association according to the factors highlighted by the World Values Survey. For example, although the correlation between income and wellbeing tails off after one's basic needs are met, until this point is reached, there is a robust link between the two (Lucas & Schimmack, 2009). So, being poor adversely affects wellbeing; moreover, this is exacerbated by social inequality – the more unequal a society, the worse it is to be poor within that society (Pickett & Wilkinson, 2007). Disadvantaged communities are also characterised by other factors which hinder wellbeing, including greater unemployment and lower social capital (e.g., higher crime rates) (Ross, 2000). So, even this very brief précis shows that contextual determinants play an important role in shaping wellbeing.

From an APP perspective, not only do we recognise that there is a social dimension to wellbeing, we can actually try to change this dimension for the better. Indeed, our efforts to improve wellbeing will be hindered if we *do not* engage with this dimension. This point is made rather forcefully by Becker and Marecek (2008, p. 1771), who argue that 'To suggest that self-help exercises can suffice in the absence of social transformation is not only short sighted but morally repugnant'. This quote does not imply that the kind of PPIs outlined in Chapters 2 and 3 are ineffectual or should not be promoted. However, in themselves, they are not *sufficient* for developing a comprehensive approach to wellbeing, and as such we must also engage with the collective domains of our multidimensional model. Thus, in this chapter, we will examine the intersubjective quadrant (i.e., relationships, and the shared meanings and values that emerge from them), and the interobjective quadrant (i.e., the non-personal structural aspects of our social networks). As befitting the APP focus of the book, we will consider practices and recommendations pertaining to both domains that enhance wellbeing. Moreover, following our LIFE model, we will explore both domains according to the levels of Bronfenbrenner's (1977) experimental ecology (plus our additional level of the ecosystem). As such, the chapter is in five parts, proceeding upwards/outwards through the model, looking in turn at the relevance to wellbeing of micro-, meso-, exo-, macro-, and eco-systems.

PRACTICE ESSAY QUESTIONS . . .

- Critically evaluate the influence of the various levels of Bronfenbrenner's (1977) ecological model on individual wellbeing.
- Progressive social change is beyond the remit of positive psychology. Discuss.

Microsystem

The microsystem is the immediate social setting of the person – the actual location or situation they are in at any point. While at home, this is their microsystem; when at work, this is their microsystem; and so on. When PP *has* taken social dimensions into account, it is usually just at this level. From a PP perspective, the key point about the microsystem is that interpersonal relationships have a strong impact upon wellbeing. Indeed, according to the World Values Survey, close relationships are the *most* important contextual determinant (Helliwell & Putnam, 2004). Partnerships like marriage are highly beneficial, constituting the most potent form of social capital (Nakhaie & Arnold, 2010). Conversely, one of the greatest depressants of wellbeing is separation, then widowhood (Blanchflower & Oswald, 2004). From a romantic perspective, relationships offer the potential of love, a gateway to some of the most elevated states of wellbeing (Becker, 1992). More functionally, arrangements such as marriage offer 'protection' effects which enhance wellbeing, like division of labour, companionship and emotional support (Arrindell & Luteijn, 2000). Of course, the value of relationships is not limited to romantic partnerships. There is a voluminous literature on the importance of friendship and good relationships with others generally, e.g., as sources of social support during stress (Umberson & Montez, 2010).

From an APP perspective, one approach to the microsystem involves interventions to enhance the quality of relationships. We have already touched upon some relevant PPIs in Chapter 2. Exercises to promote pro-social emotions, like LKM, can enhance relational connectedness (Fredrickson et al., 2008). There are also more comprehensive PPIs specifically designed to improve relationships. Kauffman and Silberman (2009) highlight the use of PPIs in couples' therapy. Drawing on the work of Miller (1986), they argue that 'growth-fostering relationships' are characterised by empowerment, knowledge, self-worth, connection and zest. They then outline exercises for promoting these qualities. For instance, all these qualities are served by effective communication strategies, such as responding positively to good news. Responses can be categorised as either active or passive, and constructive or destructive (Gable et al., 2004). Least conducive to relational wellbeing are passive-destructive responses: not merely unenthusiastic, but actively critiquing the news. Conversely, active-constructive responding engenders flourishing. Couples can be taught this model, and encouraged to use active-constructive responding, perhaps committing to doing so once a day for a week on a trial basis (Seligman et al., 2006). Of course, PPIs aimed at enhancing relationships are transferable to other microsystems; e.g., the active-constructive responding model of communication has been promoted in occupational settings as a leadership strategy (Avolio et al., 1999), as discussed in Chapter 6.

71

Beyond just enhancing relationships within micro-settings, an intriguing avenue of exploration for PP is the *creation* of micro-settings that are conducive to wellbeing. We can consider this idea in terms of both intersubjective dynamics (the culture of a micro-setting) and interobjective factors (its structural aspects). We will focus first on the former. To highlight the importance of intersubjective dynamics, as a case study we can explore an area that has not received much attention in PP: gender. There are various ways of conceptualising gender. The biological 'sex-differences' paradigm holds that gender – i.e., the way men and women act – is determined by their physiology (Maccoby & Jacklin, 1974). However, the determinism of this view has been critiqued, including by social-learning theorists who view gendered behaviour as shaped by socialisation, where, influenced by stereotypes, males and females are encouraged/coerced into gender roles (Mischel, 1975). Yet although such theories eschew biological determinism, gender is still often viewed in an essentialist way as rather fixed, with men and women conceptualised as homogeneous groups (e.g., *the* masculine personality). Nevertheless, recent social constructionist theorising has taken a more nuanced view of gender, recognising diversity among people, and among forms of masculinity and femininity (Connell, 1995). Moreover, people are not seen as having a fixed gender; instead gender is viewed dynamically as a *verb*, something which people 'do' (i.e., actively construct) in the context of particular local situations (West & Zimmerman, 1987).

This latter theory means we can think of consciously creating microsystems that have 'salutogenic cultures' (Graeser, 2011), i.e., which promote health/ wellbeing, such as settings which encourage adaptive forms of gendered behaviour. To focus on masculinity, it is argued that societal norms encourage certain toxic behaviours in men, like risk-taking and aggression, that are detrimental to the wellbeing of men *and* those around them (Courtenay, 2000). However, it is possible to find local microsystems that promote *alternative* masculine norms. One such potential microsystem is a community of people meeting to meditate at a Buddhist centre. In one centre, Lomas (2014) observed an alternative system of gender norms (see the box below), which were conducive to wellbeing: men were encouraged to be compassionate, to abstain from alcohol and to pursue spirituality. We can learn from such cases by being critically aware of the intersubjective dynamics of microsystems and consciously reshaping these into cultures that are more salutogenic. For example, schools have been accused of systematic complicity in upholding and promulgating corrosive gender norms, a phenomenon that Kenway and Fitzclarence (1997, p. 117) label powerfully as 'poisonous pedagogy'. Positive psychology could play a role in helping educators address this complicity, e.g., by offering gender-awareness PPIs to students. Even more far-reaching forms of socio-cultural change are possible, as seen with progressive social movements like feminism (such movements are briefly highlighted below in the sections on macro- and eco-systems). By learning from such movements, PP can develop a more sophisticated approach to the collective dimensions of wellbeing.

RESEARCH AND PRACTICE CASE STUDIES. . .

Men in the study by Lomas (2014) were encouraged to be tough as they were growing up as a way of demonstrating their masculinity. One man recalled his mother's sto-ries about his grandfather: *'He was as tough as old boots, he didn't have "emotions." There was a lot of that growing up . . . You don't want to be soft.'* These lessons were influential when he underwent a *'difficult time'* as an adolescent: *'I remember a sense of, "I shouldn't cry.'"* However, he suffered from learning to repress his emotions – he had anger issues, and eventually an emotional breakdown. It was only when he finally entered therapy that he felt *'able to cry'* and explore emotions that had *'stayed buried for so many years'.* He was grateful to eventually find the Buddhist centre, which allowed him to express qualities he felt were seen as unacceptable – for a man – in other social settings: *'In this community, I can be more affectionate and more loving, [because] I feel trusting. [Outside] there's wariness, a critical voice of what other people might think, [like] if I'm too loving or kind to a man people might think I'm gay.'* This quote shows the power of microsystems to regulate behaviour, and the value of social con-texts which promote alternative gender norms that are more conducive to wellbeing.

Lastly, we can briefly consider the interobjective aspects of the microsystem. This means reflecting on how its non-personal features might be reshaped to better promote wellbeing. First, we could consider its aesthetics. Gesler's (1992) work on therapeutic landscapes has shown the double beneficial effects of pleasing environments: rewarding to appreciate *and* create. Natural light and greenery are conducive to emotional wellbeing, as are gardens generally, and as such are often incorporated into healthcare settings (Marcus & Barnes, 1999). Moreover, *creating* such environments constitutes a PPI in itself, with gardening a potent therapeutic activity, being a powerful combination of 'achievement, satisfaction, and aesthetic pleasure', and also social bonding if done collectively (Milligan et al., 2004, p. 1781). While beauty can be subjective, common aesthetic factors include cleanliness and simplicity, as exemplified in Zen landscapes (Hoover, 2010). Again, while providing such an environment for a client to appreciate can be deemed a PPI, involving people in creating this also constitutes a powerful well-being activity (Enns & Kasai, 2003). Other interobjective considerations include the ergonomics of the micro-setting. Ergonomics focuses on enhancing the fit between people and their environments, so as to 'optimize human wellbeing' and improve the functioning of the environment (Wilson, 2000, p. 560). Examples of ergonomic application include designing chairs to encourage healthy postures and promoting their use in settings like classrooms (Linton et al., 1994). From an APP perspective, ideally all microsystems would be designed following ergonomic and aesthetic principles.

TRY ME! . . .

Consider the microsystems in which you spend most of your time, such as your home, classroom or office. What are these like in terms of aesthetic and ergonomic design? How might they be improved? As a task, go and buy a large, attractive plant. Clear a space in a prominent part of the room, and clean this space as if preparing a shrine. Place the plant there, and make an effort to water and care for it each day. As you do so, reflect on how appreciating and caring for the plant makes you feel.

As a final point, it is worth saying that microsystems are not limited to material settings, but extend to virtual realities. We are of course talking about interactions in cyberspace, such as on social media sites. Although a relatively new area for PP to consider, the role the internet plays in our lives will surely only grow in the years ahead. The internet does already have a role in PP in terms of PPIs being delivered online, as in Seligman et al.'s (2005) seminal study. However, here we are referring to the more far-reaching notion that our online existence constitutes participation in a whole intersubjective world-space, involving relationships, and emergent norms and values. In this sense, we are concerned with the impact of this existence on wellbeing and, from an APP perspective, how this existence might be enhanced. Online interaction seems to generate different relationship dynamics compared to 'offline' interaction. In particular, there is greater disinhibition online, generated by factors like anonymity, invisibility, and minimisation of authority (Suler, 2004). Sometimes this can be positive. Freedom relating to such disinhibition, such as the creation of alternative desired identities in the form of avatars, has been linked to wellbeing (Castronova, 2003).

However, it can also give licence to some of our most ignoble qualities, leading to online abuse, which is clearly harmful (Shin, 2008). In future, in terms of APP, we might intervene to make online interaction more conducive to wellbeing. At a more personal level, this could involve delivering PPIs through mobile phone apps and/or embedding them in social media sites. For instance, Munson et al. (2010) used Facebook to engage people in the 'three good things' exercise. We might also intervene at a more structural or systemic level, such as teaching safe internet use in schools, or strengthening privacy laws (Berson et al., 2002).

Mesosystem

The mesosystem refers to the *interaction* between microsystems. This recognises that people 'exist in inter-locking contexts' which together affect functioning (Sheridan et al., 2004, p. 7). For example, Sheridan et al. suggest the two primary microsystems in a child's life are home and school. These have a 'bidirectional, reciprocal influence over each other', and so together constitute a mesosystem (2004, p. 11). This is evident if we consider an outcome such as school performance. We cannot understand the performance of a particular child by looking at the school microsystem in isolation. Success or failure in school is heavily influenced by a child's home environment, including interobjective factors like their family's socio-economic status (Dubow & Ippolito, 1994), and intersubjective factors such as the educational support offered by their parents (Davis-Kean, 2005). However, the mesosystem perspective is often overlooked: 'We typically psychologize children's problems and ignore the social and political context in which their problems occur' (Prilleltensky et al., 2001, p. 157). Needless to say, mesosystem interactions do not only affect children. A meso-level issue familiar to most adults is that of 'role-conflict', i.e., the 'simultaneous occurrence of two (or more) sets of pressures such that compliance with one would make more difficult compliance with the other' (Kahn et al., 1964, p. 19). A common such case is work–family conflict: even if each domain is rewarding in itself, wellbeing can be diminished by imbalance between the two, or from one (or both) impinging on the other.

TRY ME! . . .

How well-balanced are the different aspects of your life? As an exercise, list all the various activities that make up a typical week, such as sleeping, eating, commuting, working, socialising, etc. For one week, keep track of the number of hours you spend on each activity. At the end of the week, reflect on whether the list is as balanced as you would like. How could you make your life more balanced?

From an APP perspective, interventions will be enhanced if they take into account the mesosystems in which people exist. An excellent model of this is family-centred positive psychology (FCPP) (Sheridan et al., 2004). FCPP aims to empower families, supporting them in 'proactively identifying needs, mobilizing resources, and accomplishing goals through the development of personal capacities, strengths, and abilities' (p. 9). One of the desired outcomes of FCPP is the psychological growth of the child. It is recognised that the key microsystems in which this growth occurs are the family and the school. As such, from a mesosystem perspective, the interaction between these contexts is crucial. Thus, FCPP works to establish partnerships between families and schools. This involves a process of 'conjoint behavioural consultation' – 'a structured, indirect form of service delivery in which parents and teachers are joined to work together to address the academic, social, or behavioural needs of an individual for whom both parties bear some responsibility' (p. 10). Parents and teachers, together with an FCPP 'consultant', engage in a structured problem-solving process involving four stages: problem identification, problem analysis, treatment implementation and treatment evaluation. These processes span both home and school settings, thus creating mesosystem collaboration. A case study involving a particular child suggested that the protocol was successful in meeting desired behavioural outcomes – in that case, a strategy for reducing tantrums. Unfortunately, hardly any PPIs currently incorporate a mesosystem perspective; this will be an important area of development for PP.

Exosystem

The exosystem refers to the wider 'social structures' that 'impinge upon or encompass' one's microsystems (Bronfenbrenner, 1977, p. 515). Exosystems can be regarded as the community in which one lives and/or works. Community is an elastic concept – if you live in a city, your community may be primarily your immediate neighbourhood, although the city at large will also to some extent function as your community, albeit in a more distant way. Wellbeing is affected by a panoply of community-level factors. A comprehensive analysis by Burke et al. (2009) identified *120* factors, aggregated into six main categories (listed below, with representative factors included for each). These categories are a blend of interobjective elements, like the first category (necessary human and social services), and intersubjective elements, like the second category (neighbourhood support), which overlaps with the concept of social capital (Bourdieu, 1986). Their analysis revealed intriguing variations according to socio-economic status (SES): those with low SES saw necessary human and social services as the most important factor, while neighbourhood support mattered most to those with high SES. There were also differences according to gender: females rated 'negative community factors' as the most important category, whereas males rated this the least important. Nevertheless, all of the following categories and factors mattered to most people to some extent:

- ***Necessary human and social services***: e.g., places of worship, medical facilities, homeless shelters, libraries, recreation centres, employment services, public transport, disability access.
- ***Neighbourhood support for each other***: e.g., friendly neighbours, safe environment, privacy, neighbourhood watch, neighbourhood pride, social cohesion, sense of community.
- ***Green areas and natural environment***: e.g., air quality, low traffic, good lighting, walkable areas, bike paths, gardens, parks, trees, good road/pavement maintenance.
- ***Social make-up of people in the neighbourhood***: e.g., pets, children, age-diversity, not too many students, well-maintained houses, home owners, good educational levels, low unemployment.
- ***Neighbourhood affordability***: accessible and affordable shops, restaurants, and parking.
- ***Negative community factors*** – low levels of: noise, crimes, pests, police harassment, drug-dealing, graffiti, prostitution, vandalism, substance abuse, violence, impatient bus drivers.

From an APP perspective, any action to enhance any of these factors could loosely be deemed a PPI, as one would have intervened to improve the quality of the neighbourhood. Of course, many of these factors have structural components that are driven by macrosystem processes, such as governmental policy. Thus, to an extent, some factors can only be really affected by macrosystem interventions, as discussed below. In particular, the ability of local authorities to provide many of the above factors is limited by budgetary constraints imposed by central government, especially since the 2008 economic crash (King, 2013). From a critical perspective, such constraints are arguably not inevitable, but result from a neoliberal ideology that seeks to shrink the role of the state (Grimshaw & Rubery, 2012), as explained further below in the section on macrosystems. As such, considerations of the exosystem need to be situated within the larger context of the macrosystem – e.g., politically driven economic policies that impact upon wellbeing (Klein, 2007) – as this chapter endeavours to do. Nevertheless, even within financial constraints, authorities can try to thoughtfully design neighbourhoods according to aesthetic and ergonomic principles. A case in point is the positive impact of preserving/creating open communal spaces where people can meet and interact, particularly if such spaces incorporate natural greenery, as per the concept of therapeutic landscapes above (Chiesura, 2004).

RESEARCH AND PRACTICE CASE STUDIES . . .

The concept of 'shared spaces' was developed by Jacobs (1985) as an approach to urban planning. He observed that many cities had ceded much of their public space to traffic routes, such that these spaces were unwelcoming and even hostile to pedestrians and the general public. He proposed some radical ideas for re-shaping the architecture of these spaces to redress this balance – making these spaces not only more pleasant for non-drivers, but also safer. Based on Jacob's ideas, the village of Makkinga (in the Netherlands) removed *all* traffic signs, signals and markings, compelling drivers and pedestrians to interact more carefully and considerately. Not only did the village become more aesthetically pleasing, there was also a reduction in traffic speeds of over 40% (previous measures achieved only 10% reductions) (Hamilton-Baillie, 2008). This is a great example of creative urban planning that helps promote wellbeing (while remaining cost-effective). The idea is beginning to be implemented more widely, including by the UK government (www.gov.uk/government/publications/shared-space).

Of course, communities are not only improved through centralised top–down local authority planning. Such improvements are potentially far more effective if enacted in a bottom–up way by communities themselves. For example, while a local authority initiative to remove graffiti from a neighbourhood would enhance community wellbeing, as with therapeutic landscapes, the activity of cleaning could itself promote wellbeing, engendering civic togetherness and personal satisfaction. (However, this does not mean local authorities should use such outcomes to justify withdrawing local services.) For instance, Mongkolnchaiarunya (2005) describes a community-based waste management initiative in Thailand: while this addressed the interobjective factor of waste disposal (e.g., exchanges were set up where locals could bring recyclable material and receive eggs in return), it engendered intersubjective benefits beyond the cleanliness, such as 'community empowerment through self-reliance' (p. 27). Less functionally but no less powerfully, community arts initiatives to improve the neighbourhood (e.g., decorating public spaces) not only enhance its aesthetics, but promote social and individual wellbeing, like social cohesion and self-esteem (Dunphy, 2009). Indeed, as noted in Chapter 3, community-arts initiatives generally, from theatre to music, are powerful social bonding tools (Belfiore, 2002), in addition to the numerous individual-level psychological benefits of such artistic activities (e.g., self-expression) (Croom, 2012).

RESEARCH AND PRACTICE CASE STUDIES . . .

The 'broken windows' theory of policing proposes that targeting 'quality of life crimes' (i.e., minor disorders such as vandalism) helps prevent more serious crime (Wilson & Kelling, 1982). The theory is based on the concept of neighbourhood effects, i.e., the idea that 'arrangements in human space may significantly affect human behaviour' (Harcourt, 1998, p. 278), a principle that also informs the notion of shared space, detailed above. In the broken windows theory, signs of social disorder are seen as generating an influx of criminal activity, arising from a perception that law and order controls are not very effective in that area. Consequently, the aggressive prosecution of quality of life misdemeanours was adopted as a policing strategy by some US cities, such as New York, where it arguably contributed to a fall in serious crime (Kelling & Bratton, 1998). While it is evidently not the remit of APP to prosecute quality of life crimes, we can certainly think of engaging in quality of life *acts* that help to promote positive neighbourhood effects, such as fixing vandalism and keeping our community clean.

In addition to initiatives to improve specific aspects of communities, more comprehensive wellbeing interventions have been attempted. We can consider two such initiatives, in quite different contexts, to appreciate the possibilities in this area. A community empowerment initiative – the Family Wellbeing Programme (FWB) – was devised in partnership with Aboriginal residents in Australia (McCalman et al., 2010). Residents had identified violence within the community as a concern. Efforts were thus made at a collective level to identify community strengths and develop strategies for 'personal, family and community healing'. Organisational outcomes included setting up a 'healing centre' (facilitating access to alternative therapists), and delivering the FWB programme to groups such as victims of domestic violence and prisoners. Across the globe in the UK, the Well London project was devised to improve health behaviours among marginalised communities in the most deprived parts of the city (Wall et al., 2009). As this was a collaborative project – working with local communities to identify and meet their needs, not being paternalistically prescriptive (i.e., telling them what is good for them) – the particular constellation of projects used with each community varied (see www.welllondon.org.uk). Projects included: 'Healthy Spaces' (improving public spaces to encourage physical activity and provide a sense of security); 'Active Living' (giving residents maps featuring healthy local resources, such as farmers' markets); 'Be Creative, Be Well' (cultural activities to foster social capital); and 'DIY Happiness' (fun PP-based activities). Although analysis of the project is ongoing, initial appraisals are positive (Phillips et al., 2012).

Macrosystem

The last of Bronfenbrenner's (1977) levels refers to 'overarching institutional patterns' at a national and international scale. These include the 'economic, social, educational, legal, and political systems' of which the other levels are 'concrete manifestations' (p. 515). These systems are all-pervasive: they are the matrices which structure our existence, and their influence permeates all the levels beneath them. A powerful case in point is the way global macro-economic forces have concrete implications for every exosystem community and every microsystem setting, as witnessed in the aftermath of the 2008 financial crash (King, 2013). Given their top–down influence, macrosystems necessarily impact upon wellbeing. Consequently, efforts have been made to conceptualise and assess this impact. Take the case of political systems. The World Bank measures the quality of governance of countries on six indices: voice and accountability (e.g., civil rights); stability (of government); effectiveness (e.g., bureaucratic competency); regulatory framework (e.g., economic policies); rule of law (e.g., efficacy of legal systems); and control of corruption (Kaufmann et al., 1999). It is recognised that a country's performance on these indices influences the wellbeing of its citizens, and that a greater quality of life is enjoyed by communities with 'effective social and political institutions' (Duncan, 2010, p. 165). Moreover, not only are we beginning to appreciate the impact of such macrosystems on wellbeing, from an APP perspective it is possible to redesign and restructure these systems to make them *more* conducive to wellbeing.

When it comes to macrosystems, APP essentially consists of action at the *policy* level. Although macrosystems are huge structural edifices, it is possible to leverage change within these by altering the rules that govern them. The most famous case of this is the Himalayan kingdom of Bhutan (Braun, 2009). In 1972, the fourth King of Bhutan replaced Gross Domestic Product (GDP) as their gauge of societal progress with Gross National Happiness (GNH). Whereas GDP reflects the market value of goods and services produced by a country, GNH is an assessment – made by canvassing its citizens – encompassing nine domains: psychological wellbeing; time use; community vitality; cultural diversity and resilience; ecological diversity and resilience; health; education; living standards; and good governance (Ura, 2008). Crucially, from an APP perspective, GNH is not only measured, but is used by the Gross National Happiness Commission (a planning branch of the government) to inform policy decisions in the kingdom. This Commission is also guided by a 'GNH policy lens', formulated by the Centre for Bhutan Studies, which systematically evaluates all proposed policies according to GNH considerations. Bhutan is more advanced than other countries in terms of incorporating an explicit wellbeing agenda into its system of governance. However, other countries are beginning to at least consider wellbeing as a potential policy issue. For example, in 2011 the UK Office for National Statistics (ONS) began to gather SWB data as part of its Integrated Household Survey, disseminated annually to 200,000 people, thus creating a National Well-being index (ONS, 2011b). Moreover, in 2010, the UK Prime Minister David Cameron announced that this index would help guide policy decisions, and even set up internal policy units geared towards this end (Bache & Reardon, 2013).

In the event, David Cameron's coalition government has been accused of implementing regressive policies that are detrimental to wellbeing, particularly for the poorest in society (Mabbett, 2013). Nevertheless, we can still appreciate the beginnings of a national conversation about wellbeing as a policy driver, and even glimpse what this might look like in practice. One of the policy units established by Cameron was the Behavioural Insights Team, also known as the 'nudge unit'. It is influenced by Thaler and Sunstein's (2003) concept of libertarian paternalism, which reconciled two opposing theories of government. Libertarianism suggests that people should be free to do as they please, providing they do not harm others. Conversely, paternalism implies that governments know what is best for people, and so should be empowered to force people to act accordingly. Libertarian paternalism seeks to encourage people to make healthy choices, crucially, though, without coercion but by arranging the 'choice architecture' in such a way that makes the 'right' choice more likely. For example, it is generally seen as desirable for employees to be enrolled in a pension scheme (Thaler & Sunstein, 2008). A paternalistic policy would automatically enrol people; a libertarian one would mean employees actively having to freely choose it. However, if enrolment were the *default* option – automatic enrolment unless one explicitly asked not to be – most people would just remain enrolled by virtue of inertia. That is, although people still had free choice, most would just go along with the easy option (i.e., not making the effort to opt-out), which importantly was also the 'right' one from a wellbeing perspective. We can perhaps imagine a government extending this policy-level approach to all areas of life pertaining to wellbeing.

REFLECTION . . .

Other policy-level ideas for restructuring the choice architecture of a decision to achieve a desired outcome include the issue of organ donation. In the UK, the present system is opt-in – a person must actively choose to be a donor. However, with a current shortage of donors, it is suggested that people should automatically be considered as donors unless they specifically opt-out (Johnson & Goldstein, 2003). What do you think of this idea, and of the concept of libertarian paternalism generally? In what other areas of life could we alter the default options in order to better promote overall wellbeing?

So, we have been arguing that wellbeing considerations can influence policy-making. However, what role can *we* play in this? Some people sympathetic to PP may be in a position to write policy or advise those who do. Unfortunately, most of us do not wield such power, and it is easy to feel powerless in the face of mac-rosystems that shape our lives. Indeed, politics itself often seems subservient to larger economic forces that limit the scope for politicians to act. It is common to hear politicians plead that particular decisions must be made to appease 'the market', an omniscient and omnipotent force that Cox (1999) argues is treated in the same deferential way as a divine entity. Unfortunately, the current dominant global economic paradigm is arguably neoliberalism (Plehwe et al., 2005), as promulgated by the influential economist Milton Friedman (1951). Neoliberalism advocates laissez-faire capitalism, in which markets should be 'unfettered' by state regulation and companies should be free to maximise profits, regardless – according to critics – of the costs to individuals or the environment. This model is thus potentially harmful to wellbeing. For example, unemployment lowers SWB (Lucas et al., 2004). While capitalism can of course create jobs, from a neoliberal perspective the aim of a company is to *reduce* employee numbers in the name of efficiency. Indeed, as discussed further in Chapter 6, driven by an overriding con-cern with profit-maximisation, many companies are unfortunately run in ways that can be detrimental to its employees, not to mention to the wider society (Winpenny, 1999).

It is possible, however, to imagine and work towards other ways of regulat-ing our macrosystems, advocating for political, social and economic change. In economics, inspired by PP, Haque (2011) has called for a 'positive economic par-adigm' that is concerned not only with profit maximisation, but with fulfilling 'human potential'. Similarly, the New Economics Foundation (NEF) is a UK think-tank whose motto is taken from the subtitle of Schumacher's (2010 (1973)) clas-sic work *Small is Beautiful*: 'Economics as if people mattered.' Its concern is with promoting policy recommendations that can 'transform the economy so that it works for people and the planet' (www.neweconomics.org, website homepage). Moreover, macrosystems can be changed through the bottom–up transforma-tive power of progressive social movements. We have already seen nascent efforts to alter the dominant neoliberal economic model, like the recent Occupy protests in major financial centres (DeLuca et al., 2012). The potential for such movements to impact upon macrosystems is illustrated by previous efforts to engender socio-cultural change (intersubjective shifts in values and interobjec-tive changes to social structures). As an exemplar, we can return to the issue of gender: recent centuries have witnessed a hard-fought struggle across the globe in the direction of greater gender equality, as outlined in the box below. Such causes are relevant to PP, since they aim towards flourishing and wellbeing. However, this is not a limited person-centred view of flourishing, but one that is inextricably tied to just and equitable social arrangements (Becker & Marecek,

2008). From a critical perspective, socio-cultural change is – or certainly should be – a fundamental concern of PP.

RESEARCH AND PRACTICE CASE STUDIES . . .

Throughout history, gender relations have usually been characterised by power imbalances, with women subject to oppressive gender roles limiting their participation in public life (Weedon, 1997). However, following Mary Wollstonecraft's (1990 (1792)) seminal feminist treatise, recent centuries have seen efforts to redress this balance, with a slow but steady progression of victories. For example, in the UK, the National Union of Women's Suffrage (the right to vote) was founded in 1897. After escalating protests, parliament granted the vote to women aged over 30 in 1918 (and extended it to all in 1928). The struggle for gender equality is ongoing: women are still paid less than men for comparable jobs (Tharenou, 2013), and are underrepresented in many professions, particularly at the higher echelons (Dowling & Aribi, 2013). Nonetheless, we can discern an inexorable movement in the direction of gender equality. Such movements can give us heart that genuine socio-cultural change *is* possible.

Ecosystem

Finally, we turn to the global ecosystem. Although not in Bronfenbrenner's original model, we can appreciate that even macrosystems are embedded within a still larger context, namely the biosphere: all levels *ultimately* depend upon the environment for their very existence. Thus, environmental issues are of fundamental concern to PP because, existentially, our wellbeing depends on the wellbeing of the environment: our planet must be capable of supporting life for flourishing to even be conceivable (Smith et al., 2013). Even aside from issues of existential survival, our quality of life depends heavily on the state of the environment, including factors like air quality and access to fresh water (Boyd & Banzhaf, 2007). It is rather appropriate that this section should follow the one on social change, since environmental concern is itself a product of recent social movements. Humans have, of course, cared about nature for millennia, with many pagan religions founded on reverence of the natural world (Taylor, 2005). However, it was really only with the publication of Rachel Carson's *Silent Spring* (2002 (1962)) that ecological damage became a major concern, spurring the emergence of the environmental movement (Griswold, 2012). Since then, driven by ever-increasing awareness of the existential dangers posed by anthropogenic climate change, environmental concerns have risen up the political and cultural agenda, even in the face of climate-change scepticism (frequently driven by ideological resistance from groups with a vested interest in the status quo; McCright et al., 2013). Assessments of societal wellbeing are consequently being developed that take environmental variables into account, such as the 'ecological footprint' of a society in the New Economics Foundation's (2013) 'Happy Planet Index'.

ART LINKS . . .

Social-change movements have often been galvanised by powerful protest songs. The civil rights struggle in America became associated with powerful traditional songs such as *We shall overcome*, *We shall not be moved*, and *Oh freedom*, as well as contemporary classics including Sam Cooke's *A change is gonna come*. Anti-war movements were inspired by anthems like *Blowing in the wind*, by Bob Dylan, and John Lennon's *Imagine* and *Give peace a chance*. Joni Mitchell's *Big yellow taxi* has been a rallying call for the environmental movement. What songs have inspired you to make a difference in the world? Which anthems might capture the spirit of the PP movement?

Ecological wellbeing depends to some extent on human behaviour. As such, from an APP perspective, our remit is to encourage people to act in more environmentally-friendly ways. This could be done at any of the tiers of Bronfenbrenner's model. At a microsystem level, sustainable energy consumption could be encouraged by equipping houses with smart meters that provide feedback about energy expenditure (Fischer, 2008). At the mesosystem level, energy consumption used commuting *between* microsystems might be reduced, e.g., interventions to encourage car-pooling (Kearney & De Young, 1995), or active commuting, involving walking or cycling (Yang et al., 2010). Exosystem PPIs might include attempts to promote recycling, for instance. From an intersubjective perspective, this means attempting to make it a cultural norm, as in Hopper and Nielsen's (1991) intervention which framed it as an altruistic act. From an interobjective perspective, this means establishing/enhancing provision of recycling services (Read, 1999). At a macrosystem level, policy commitments to sustainability need to be established nationally and internationally. Early attempts at such regulatory solutions include carbon trading (Spash, 2010). This brings us back to the importance of environmentalism as a social movement. In the face of such an overwhelming and complex problem as climate change, it can be tempting for politicians and the public to bury their heads in the sand and focus on short-term goals, especially when other concerns seem more pressing, such as economic issues (Scruggs & Benegal, 2012). However, this means PP must help keep environmentalism on the political and cultural agenda, and work towards progressive social change at all socio-cultural levels of the LIFE model.

SUMMARY – THIS CHAPTER HAS…

- Critically highlighted the need for PP to take socio-cultural dimensions into account
- Given detailed descriptions of each of the levels of Bronfenbrenner's ecological model
- Added the ecosystem level to the original model
- Differentiated each of these levels into intersubjective and interobjective aspects
- Provided ideas for PPIs appropriate to each level

QUIZ…

1　According to the World Values Survey, what is the *most* important contextual determinant of wellbeing?
2　Who is credited with developing the concept of therapeutic landscapes?
3　Which two microsystems does Family-Centred Positive Psychology try to connect?
4　How many separate community wellbeing factors were identified by Burke et al. (2009)?
5　Which American city is noted here as adopting the broken windows theory of policing?
6　In which country did the Family Wellbeing Initiative take place?
7　In which year did Bhutan introduce the concept of Gross National Happiness?
8　The Behavioural Insight team established by David Cameron is also known as the '….' unit?
9　Who wrote what is generally considered to be the first feminist work, in 1792?
10　Who wrote the seminal environmental book *Silent Spring*?

RESOURCES AND SUGGESTIONS…

- If you are interested in aesthetics, two useful sources of information are www.british-aesthetics.org (based in the UK) and www.aesthetics-online.org (based in the US).
- For more information about ergonomics, please visit www.ergonomics.org.uk.
- For details about the Behavioural Insight team, see www.gov.uk/government/organi sations/behavioural-insights-team. In 2013 it was announced that President Obama was creating a similar unit in the US (www.decisionsciencenews.com/2013/07/15/us-behavioral-insights-team).
- For progressive economic think-tanks, please check out the New Economics Foundation in the UK (www.neweconomics.org), and the Schumacher Center for a New Economics in the US (www.centerforneweconomics.org). For protest movements related to economics, the Occupy movement is a good place to start (www.occupytogether.org).

CHILDHOOD AND DEVELOPMENT

> If we are fortunate, we will age
> If we are truly fortunate, we will age well.
> Williamson and Christie (2009, p. 165)

LIST OF TOPICS…

- Bronfenbrenner's chronosystem
- Positive parenting and parenting styles
- Pregnancy and the perinatal period
- Attachment theory and interventions
- The parenthood paradox
- Positive education
- The Penn Resilience Program
- Positive youth development
- Working with at-risk youth
- Structural developmental models
- Spiral dynamics
- Positive aging

So far, we have elucidated the four ontological domains of our LIFE model – mind, body, culture and society – providing a comprehensive framework for conceptualising and promoting wellbeing. Now, we consider these four domains collectively through a particular prism: time. Earlier chapters looked at the domains in an essentially static way. Now we introduce a dynamic element to the model by exploring the idea of development over time. This is in keeping with Bronfenbrenner's (1977) theory, which influenced the stratification of the LIFE model: Bronfenbrenner's original paper is entitled 'Toward an experimental ecology of human development'. In fact, the main point about his model was to explore how the various systems, from micro- to macro-, impacted on development through the life course. Bronfenbrenner (1993, p. 40) referred to this dynamic, developmental aspect of his model as the *chronosystem*, defined as 'change or consistency over time not only in the characteristics of the person but also of the environment in which that person lives'. There are two main ways of approaching the chronosystem: a narrower focus on particular life transitions (e.g., adolescence), and a more encompassing examination of the whole life course – the 'entire sequence of developmental transition' (Bronfenbrenner, 1986, p. 724). Here, we shall do both. The chapter looks at particular developmental stages in turn, beginning in infancy and culminating in old age. Furthermore, in doing so, we aim to give a sense of the existential folding of the entire life course, from birth to death.

Of course, in considering the life course, we seek to do so from a *positive* perspective, exploring the factors that enable people to flourish at each life stage. Moreover, given the applied emphasis of the book, we consider PPIs and recommendations to promote wellbeing and development throughout the lifespan. We begin *before* life starts, exploring pregnancy and childbirth. At this early stage, the focus is more on the parents/caregivers upon whom the infant depends, than on the infant *per se*. As such, a key thread through these early sections is the idea of positive parenting. While there is currently not a positive parenting sub-discipline within PP as such, the term has been in use for some time (e.g., Latham, 1994), and we deploy it here to cover all aspects of PP that *approach children's wellbeing by focusing on parents and caregivers*. As we move into infancy and childhood, we begin to explore the relationships between children and parents/caregivers, looking particularly at relational dynamics at home. Progressing further, we follow the child into school, examining the burgeoning field of positive education (Seligman et al., 2009). As we enter into adolescence, the focus moves beyond education *per se* to the broader notion of positive youth development (Larson, 2000). From there, the chapter explores the idea of positive development across the lifespan (Beck & Cowan, 1996). Finally, as we reach the culmination of the life journey, we consider the notion of positive aging (Tornstam, 2005), showing that APP can potentially play a role in promoting wellbeing throughout the entire lifespan.

Pregnancy and birth

We begin our story at the moment of conception, the start of an intricate pre-natal developmental process that lasts around 266 days (Holt et al., 2012). During all the prenatal phases – germinal (0–2 weeks), embryonic (2–8 weeks) and foetal (9–36 weeks), and the general perinatal period (5 months pre-birth to 1 month post-birth) – the baby's wellbeing is 'inextricably linked' to the health of the mother (Darmstadt et al., 2013, p. 1). Medical advancements have enabled us to understand the importance of healthy antenatal practices for subsequent positive development. In terms of the LIFE model, some recommendations pertain to the objective domain (i.e., the body), where pregnant mothers are advised to curtail or cease negative health behaviours such as smoking, excessive alcohol consumption and drug use (NHS, 2014b). Expectant mothers are further exhorted to engage in health behaviours such as healthy eating, including the use of supplements like folic acid (NHS, 2014c). They must also avoid teratogens (chemicals or diseases in the environment which can harm foetal development), like mercury, lead and radiation (Holt et al., 2012). From the perspective of the subjective domain (i.e., the mind), the mother's antenatal emotional state may also affect the wellbeing of the child. High levels of chronic stress are a risk factor for poorer birth outcomes, e.g., preterm birth and low birthweight (Hobel & Culhane, 2003), as well as subsequent cognitive, emotional and behavioural problems in the child (van den Bergh et al., 2005).

As such, in terms of promoting the wellbeing of the child, our focus at this stage is more on the health and wellbeing of the *mother*, upon whom the infant's wellbeing depends. Thus, although the child has not yet been born, following our definition above, this nevertheless falls under the remit of positive parenting. From an APP perspective, emphasising the above considerations is certainly not a question of placing pressure or burdens on women to act in the 'right' way, but about giving help and support to enable expectant mothers to flourish and have a successful pregnancy. Some support takes the form of interventions and services to help encourage health behaviour, e.g., programmes for smoking cessation (Lumley et al., 2009) and alcohol reduction (O'Connor & Whaley, 2007) during pregnancy. In keeping with the multidimensional perspective of the LIFE model, it is essential to appreciate that health behaviours are set in the context of wider socio-cultural factors. People in more deprived social situations are far more likely to drink and smoke for a complex of reasons, including a poorer level of education and greater exposure to stress (Lynch et al., 1997). Indeed, Penn and Owen (2002) found that the number of women who continued to smoke during pregnancy was ten times higher in the most deprived group than the least deprived. As such, they stress the importance of strategies that 'address pregnant women's life circumstances and broader inequalities as well as those that focus on individual smoking behaviour' (Penn & Owen, 2002, p. 17). PP is often guilty of overlooking such contextual factors (Prilleltensky & Prilleltensky, 2005), as emphasised in Chapter 4. Consequently, it will be important that we keep this critical perspective in mind throughout the chapter, and indeed the book generally.

RESEARCH AND PRACTICE CASE STUDIES . . .

In Chapter 2, we touched upon the astonishing proliferation of PPIs based on mindfulness. It may not be a surprise to find that mindfulness interventions have been developed in the context of pregnancy. Some cover the antenatal period. Vieten and Astin (2008) observed that expectant mothers taking part in an eight-week intervention had lower stress and anxiety levels than wait-list controls. Other interventions adapt mindfulness specifically for the process of childbirth – 'mindful yoga paired with deep relaxation' is described as 'an excellent body-centered preparation for labor and delivery' (Sale, 2008, p. 7). A more encompassing PPI covering the entire perinatal period is a Mindfulness-Based Childbirth and Parenting program (Duncan & Bardacke, 2010). A mindfulness yoga intervention (M-Yoga) has even been used as an alternative to pharmacological treatment for psychiatrically high-risk pregnant women, reducing symptoms of depression and increasing maternal–foetal attachment (Muzik et al., 2012). The value of mindfulness is not limited to the perinatal period, but can extend throughout parenthood. Duncan et al. (2009) have developed a 'mindful parenting' model, involving five domains: '(a) listening with full attention; (b) nonjudgmental acceptance of self and child; (c) emotional awareness of self and child; (d) self-regulation in the parenting relationship; and (e) compassion for self and child'. Such parenting is conducive to the wellbeing of parent and child, for reasons including reduced parental stress and consequent reactivity, which enhances family interactions (Bögels et al., 2010).

Infancy

We now move on to the first few years of a child's life. In the months following the birth, perhaps the most important interaction between infant and parent/caregiver for positive development – aside from obvious childrearing duties, such as ensuring the baby is warm, well-fed and clean – is **touch**, arguably the most important sense in early childhood (Gallace, 2012; Hertenstein, 2010). In child psychology, one very influential theory – Piaget's (1971) framework of cognitive development – describes a universal invariant sequence of stages: sensorimotor (0–2 years; integration of physical and sensory capacities); pre-operational (2–7 years; symbolic thought); operational (7–11 years; logical thought); and formal-operational (11+ years; abstract thought). In the sensorimotor stage, learning and development occur primarily through tactile exploration of the external world. This is illustrated by studies showing that low birthweight babies whose mothers are more tactile have greater gross motor development and visual-motor skills at one year of age (Weiss et al., 2004). Touch is especially important for such a population, as low birthweight is a risk factor for later cognitive, emotional and social development (Werner, 1996). From an APP perspective, touch interventions like massage (moderate pressure) have been utilised to help low birthweight and pre-term babies gain weight and return home from hospital faster. Among the outcomes associated with such interventions are reduced stress responses, increased vagal tone, and enhanced responsiveness and alertness (Field et al., 2010).

Beyond just facilitating cognitive and motor development, touch plays a vital role in perhaps the most important relational aspect of infancy: emotional **attachment** between parent/caregiver and child. The pioneering theorist John Bowlby (1969) proposed that attachment develops through five behavioural stages: *indiscriminate attachment* (neonates cry and elicit support from any caregiver); *discriminant attachment* (at around 3 months old, infants differentiate strangers from stable caregivers and begin to attach to the latter); *specific attachment* (at around 7 months of age a solid attachment is made with the caregiver, who becomes their secure base to explore the world); *goal-corrected attachment* (at around 3 years old the child becomes aware of the caregiver's needs, enters into a 'partnership' with them, and is able to be left alone); and a *lessening of attachment* (at around school age, the child is able to spend longer periods alone, and has created a sense of trust with the caregiver). Returning to the topic of touch, this is vital in establishing close connections, particularly during the early stages of discriminant and specific attachment. Indeed, physical and emotional problems in childhood have been linked to 'maternal deprivation and difficulties in maintaining physical closeness' (Feldman et al., 2004, p. 1089). Of course, establishing attachment is not only about touch, but general affection from caregivers, as well as such figures being 'available and responsive in times of need', providing for needs such as food or comfort when required (Mikulincer & Shaver, 2013, p. 835).

RESEARCH AND PRACTICE CASE STUDIES . . .

Bowlby (1969) suggested that caregiver–infant relationships generally fall into three main attachment styles: two insecure types (anxious-avoidant and anxious-resistant) and secure attachment. These types were observed empirically via the 'strange situation' paradigm developed by Mary Ainsworth and colleagues (1979). It involves several stages of interaction and 'abandonment' between child and parent. First, the mother, baby and an observer are all present in a room containing toys. The observer then leaves, and the mother and infant are free to play. After three minutes, a new stranger enters, and proceeds through a three-minute sequence of silence, interaction with the mother, then interaction with the baby. The mother then leaves the infant with the stranger for another three minutes. After this, the mother re-enters and engages with the baby. The behaviour of the child is documented upon this reunion, with the reaction seen as indicative of attachment style. *Anxious-avoidant* infants ignore the mother upon their return and do not engage in communication. *Anxious-resistant* children exhibit the need for closeness, but are unable to obtain it, engaging in anger or resisting soothing from parents. In contrast, *securely attached* infants display some distress when the mother leaves, but are happy to be reunited and are easily soothed. In addition to these, Ainsworth et al. added the style of *disorganised attachment*, featuring behavioural contradictions and disorientation when the parent returns. Secure attachments are most common, exhibited by as many as three-quarters of all infants (Holt et al., 2012).

Attachment has traditionally been examined in a 'negative' way to assess the adverse effects of absent parenting during early childhood on later normative development (Mikulincer & Shaver, 2013). However, attachment theory has experienced a surge of interest in PP, particularly as it is thought that early attachments affect lifespan development, including 'interpersonal functioning and mental health' (Shorey, 2009, p. 64). For instance, Mikulincer and Shaver (2013) demonstrated the importance of secure attachments on later adult experiences of positive emotions, emotional regulation, PWB and relational wellbeing. Conversely, early insecure attachment can later inhibit the 'broaden-and-build' (Fredrickson, 2005) benefits of positive emotions. So, from an APP perspective, what can be done to help engender secure attachments? One effective approach involves making caregivers *aware* of their attachment style, and giving them support to help develop more secure attachments with their child. One such intervention, for mothers with insecure attachments, was devised by Klein Velderman et al. (2006). Over the course of four home visits (when infants were aged 7–10 months old), the mothers were videoed interacting with their child, and given detailed feedback. They were also provided with brochures to enhance sensitive parenting, and were invited to engage in discussions centred on their *own* childhood attachment experiences (in relation to their present caregiving style). The intervention had the desired effect of enhancing maternal sensitivity, thus reducing insecure attachment patterns.

Early childhood

As the child moves into early childhood, the importance of **parenting styles** comes to the fore. These are theorised as falling across two main dimensions – *warmth versus hostility* and *restrictiveness versus permissiveness* – thus generating four main styles (Baumrind, 1967). The first is *authoritative*, which combines warmth and acceptance with restrictive practices, offering children a stable, consistent and controlled environment imbued with love, affection and care. Overall, this style has been associated with the most positive outcomes, including higher self-esteem and life satisfaction in adolescence, and lower levels of depression (Milevsky et al., 2007). Second is *authoritarian*, combining *hostility* and *restrictiveness*. This involves the control of authoritative parenting, but lacks its care/warmth, and can engender negative affect and low self-esteem (Rudy & Grusec, 2006). *Indulgent* parenting offers children *warmth* and *acceptance*, but in a permissive, unstructured manner. These parents tend not to set limits/rules, which can impact on children's ability to develop responsibility and self-control, and is even implicated as a risk factor in obesity (via poor eating habits) (Rhee et al., 2006). Finally, *neglectful* parenting combines *hostility* and *permissiveness*, providing neither care nor structure. Unsurprisingly, this style is associated with the worst developmental outcomes: children subjected to this type of parenting tend to exhibit signs of insecure attachment, difficulties with peer relationships, poor goal-motivation, and elevated impulsivity and aggression (Holt et al., 2012).

REFLECTION . . .

Being supportive and encouraging of children can be a tricky business. Carol Dweck and colleagues suggest that certain types of praise can adversely affect subsequent performance (Mueller & Dweck, 1998). Dweck (2006) argues that if parents praise outcomes (like grades), as opposed to effort, these messages can be internalised by children to create a *fixed* mindset; the child thus adopts an essentialist '*entity theory*', in which abilities/qualities are seen as set from birth. Ultimately, this type of mindset can hinder us from taking risks and advancing in a given area. Conversely, praising *effort* creates a *growth* mindset; the child internalises an '*incremental theory*', which holds that, with effort, people can grow and develop (Dweck et al., 1995). Moreover, this type of praise enables children to become more motivated in the face of setbacks, and ultimately more resilient. How do *you* encourage others?

So, we have suggested that an authoritative parenting style is perhaps most conducive to the wellbeing of the child (Milevsky et al., 2007). Can we be more specific about the elements of good parenting? Based on their work with children in care, Cameron and Maginn (2011) created eight **Positive Pillars of Parenting**, designed to facilitate good parenting in foster homes. They argued that 'professional parenting' by foster parents should not be left to 'trial and error'. Parents are encouraged to choose one or two pillars to work on – various activities are recommended for each pillar – as suited to the child's specific needs. The pillars were created through research and consultation with knowledgeable individuals (including psychologists, social workers and parents) on 'what good parents do' (Cameron & Maginn, 2011, p. 49). While originally developed for foster parents who face the challenging task of caring for vulnerable children, the pillars identify what could be regarded as universally important components of good parenting, and so are valid more generally. As such, all parents might be encouraged to develop their parenting in ways suggested by the pillars, which are:

- **Primary care and protection**: meeting the child's basic needs; showing they are cared for.
- **Making close relationships**: fostering secure attachments; acting as a buffer to risks.
- **Positive self-perception**: helping create a positive self-image via encouragement.
- **Emotional competence**: supporting/encouraging relationships outside the home.
- **Self-management**: teaching the child to self-regulate their behaviours.
- **Resilience:** facilitating the development of insight and empathy, thus helping the child understand their experiences.
- **Sense of belonging**: helping children feel part of a social structure.
- **Personal and social responsibility**: teaching children to act in a considerate and just way.

Other similar programmes have been created to help parents build relationships with their children and foster healthy development, some of which draw on PP theory. For example, the Penn Resilience Program (PRP) is a school-based PPI, one of the most researched and well-validated interventions in positive education (Gillham et al., 1990), as explained below. PRP comprises 12 sessions, centred on what the authors propose are the seven learnable skills of resilience, teaching children: (a) how to identify feelings; (b) tolerance of ambiguity; (c) an optimistic explanatory style; (d) how to analyse causes of problems; (e) empathy; (f) self-efficacy; and (g) how to reach out and try new things. Its use in an educational context is detailed below. Of relevance here is that Gillham et al. (2006) adapted the original curriculum for a parental context as part of the 'Resilience Project'. This involved parent-focused interventions implemented alongside the child's educational activities. Parents were taught PRP skills and urged to use them in their own life, as well as supporting their child's use of these at home. By fostering development at school through attending to circumstances at home, the Resilience Project may be thought of as a mesosystem intervention, comparable to family-centred positive psychology, introduced in Chapter 4 (Sheridan et al., 2004). In the pilot, Gillham et al. (2006) found that this adapted PRP (i.e., involving a parenting component) significantly reduced depression and anxiety symptoms relative to a control group, with these effects observed longitudinally (one year later).

A particularly comprehensive intervention is the Triple-P Positive Parenting Program, a multi-levelled parenting and family support strategy created to 'reduce the prevalence of behavioural and emotional problems in preadolescent children' (Sanders, 1999, p. 71). It has five levels of increasing strength. Level 1 (Universal Triple P) is a universal information strategy, providing guidance (e.g., via booklets) to all interested parents. Level 2 (Selective Triple P) is for parents with specific concerns about their child, and involves giving tailored advice to parents (e.g., via face-to-face clinician contact). Level 3 (Primary Care Triple P) is for parents who require specific skills training, comprising a brief therapy programme (one to four sessions), to help them manage their child's particular issues. Level 4 (Standard Triple P) is for children with more severe behaviour problems, and involves close scrutiny of parent–child interaction, with intensive teaching of positive parenting skills. Finally, level 5 (Enhanced Triple P) is deployed when child behavioural problems are compounded by family dysfunction, and involves an intensive behavioural intervention programme, including teaching stress management strategies. The Triple-P has been used and studied extensively (mainly in Australia, where it originated) with very good results. A meta-analysis of 55 studies concluded that it generated 'positive changes in parenting skills, child problem behavior and parental well-being' (Nowak & Heinrichs, 2008, p. 114).

REFLECTION . . .

What about the parents?! What effect does parenting have on *their* wellbeing? Kahneman et al. (2004) found that mothers rated taking care of their children as less enjoyable than watching TV or preparing food, and only just better than chores and commuting! However, despite such findings, parenthood is considered one of the most fulfilling experiences a person can have. Baumeister (1991) described this disjunction as the '*parenthood paradox*'. However, scholars have begun to develop a more nuanced appreciation of the kind of wellbeing found in parenthood. Using the experiencing sampling method, Nelson et al. (2013) found that parents reported higher overall life satisfaction and meaning than non-parents, and had more moment-to-moment positive emotional experiences. Based on such findings, Nelson et al. (2014) created the 'parent well-being model', which identifies mechanisms mediating the relationship between parenthood and wellbeing: parenthood is a potent source of meaning in life; having children fulfils our higher-level human needs (Deci & Ryan, 2000); children can be a source of positive emotions and variety in life; and children can provide parents with additional social roles, which can be beneficial to wellbeing. Weighed against these, however, are other factors associated with parenthood that might reduce wellbeing, including an increase in negative affect (e.g., frustration and anxiety); less fulfilment of basic biological needs (e.g., sleep); financial worries; and marital strain. Thus, as readers who are parents might attest, the link between parenthood and wellbeing is complex!

Education

As infants move through childhood, school plays an increasingly prominent role in their lives, with a concomitantly powerful impact upon their wellbeing. As such, positive education has fast established itself as one of the biggest and most widely researched areas within PP. Positive education is defined as 'education for both traditional skills and for happiness' (Seligman et al., 2009, p. 293); it aims to develop 'skills of wellbeing, flourishing and optimal functioning in children, teenagers and students, as well as parents and educational institutions' (Hefferon & Boniwell, 2011, p. 210). There is a focus on developmental approaches that are both *preventative* (protective against mental health problems) and *enabling* (helping people to positively flourish). Positive education is seen as important for three key reasons: to alleviate mental health issues; to promote SWB and PWB; and to enhance learning and creative thinking (Seligman et al., 2009). Furthermore, given that most children and adolescents spend the majority of their day in school, it is the perfect medium for reaching young people and working with them to facilitate wellbeing. Many schools across the globe have taken on a wellbeing curriculum and/or have been influenced by PP. Positive education has mostly been incorporated into late primary and early adolescent educational settings; however, its remit is beginning to expand in both directions, with emergent research into its application in early primary and higher educational contexts (Gokcen et al., 2012).

Although many social and emotional education programmes have been implemented over the years worldwide, few have been evaluated empirically through randomised controlled studies (Hefferon & Boniwell, 2011). However, we are beginning to see more rigorous assessment of such interventions, including several that teach/promote topics related to PP. The most widely implemented of these is the PRP, introduced above, which has been running for over 20 years and has been assessed by over 20 studies ($n > 3,000$), involving participants from diverse populations and various implementation formats (Gillham et al., 1990). Originating in the USA, the PRP is mainly used with school grades 5 to 8 (ages 10 to 14) and consists of 12 sessions, lasting 90 to 120 minutes, structured around the seven learnable skills of resilience elucidated above. Findings suggest that the PRP can prevent as well as alleviate depression and anxiety; ameliorate conduct issues; increase optimism; and improve health behaviours (Seligman, 2012). Brunwasser et al. (2009) conducted the first meta-analysis on the PRP, analysing 17 studies (n = 2,498). The PRP was found to be significantly better at reducing depressive symptoms than no-intervention control groups (a modest effect size). However, this significance did not remain when compared with active controls. Consequently, the authors urge further research into the PRP's causal mechanisms, cost-effectiveness and transferability to real-world settings.

RESEARCH AND PRACTICE CASE STUDIES . . .

Geelong Grammar is a well-known, fee-charging Australian boarding school which redesigned its entire curriculum according to PP principles, guided by prominent PP scholars and Penn MAPP graduates (Norrish et al., 2013). The project involved several phases, including instructing Geelong staff in the PRP, embedding US high school PP teachers in the classes, and visits from PP scholars to give talks and stay on campus to help support the venture. The motto of the project, which took around a year, was 'teaching it, embedding it, living it' (Seligman, 2012). The project has rightly been hailed as an excellent instance of positive education. However, from a critical perspective, one must note that its budget was several million Australian dollars. Not many schools have this kind of money to facilitate such an intricate and well-staffed redesign of an entire curriculum. It is vital to find feasible ways to implement positive education into schools generally, especially those that lack access to funding.

In addition to the PRP there are a number of other positive education programmes. These come in a variety of modes of delivery, including time-limited approaches (from 3 months to 1 year), curriculum embedment (in subject-specific classes) and school-wide programmes (involving all staff and pupils) (Wells et al., 2003). Prominent programmes include:

- **Bounce Back!** (McGrath & Noble, 2003). A practical, teacher-friendly programme, developed in Australia, for primary and secondary schools.
- **Wisdom curriculum** (Reznitskaya & Sternberg, 2004). Focuses on the intellectual and moral development of children in the context of mainstream subjects. Students are encouraged to formulate their own ideas about wise

thinking (i.e., *how* to think, not what to think), promoted through 16 pedagogical principles (including reflective thinking and dialectical thinking).

- **Making hope happen for kids** (Lopez et al., 2004). A five-session programme, including creating a story about navigating obstacles; playing the Hope Game (multiple goal pursuits); designing hope cartoons; emphasising hopeful language; and writing hope stories about goals.
- **Strengths Gym** (Proctor & Fox-Eades, 2009). A strengths-based programme, involving age-appropriate strength-based exercises in class and for homework. It uses the 'Strengths builder' to engage students, with the aim of applying strengths concepts to real life.

Broadly speaking, these programmes have been found to be effective at promoting wellbeing, with school-wide programmes generally being more effective than class-based interventions (Wells et al., 2003). A positive psychological climate/ ethos in the school as a whole is linked to increased teacher and student satisfaction, lower stress levels and better academic results (Sangsue & Vorpe, 2004). So, what constitutes a good psychological climate? Peterson (2006a) argues that 'good schools' have five characteristics: (1) they encourage students to be engaged with and enthusiastic about learning; (2) they provide a safe environment; (3) they have an articulated, shared vision of the school's purpose; (4) they offer explicit goals for students; and (5) they place an emphasis on the individual student, rewarding their efforts and improvements. Overall, social and emotional learning (SEL) programmes in schools – whether PP-based or not – have a beneficial impact on wellbeing. A meta-analysis of 213 studies assessing the impact of SEL programmes ($n = 270,034$) found that these were generally successful in enhancing SEL and academic skills, and in reducing conduct problems and emotional issues (Durlak et al., 2010). Assessments of such programmes are often conducted using psychometric tools specifically tailored for use with young people. One of the most prominent is the Brief Multidimensional Students' Life Satisfaction Scale (Seligson et al., 2003), featured in the box below. Readers working with children might like to try it.

PSYCHOMETRIC SCALES . . .

Huebner's (1994) Multidimensional Students' Life Satisfaction Scale (MSLSS) provides an index of 'global' life satisfaction (i.e., all aspects of life considered together), as well as satisfaction in five key domains of a young person's life: family, friends, school, self, and one's living environment. Initially comprising 76 items, the scale was refined to 40 questions (Huebner, 2001). Recently, a brief version, the BMSLSS, has been introduced

(Continued)

(Continued)

(Seligson et al., 2003). This has the advantage of comprising only six questions (one for each domain and a general one), which helps in encouraging children to complete it! Despite its brevity, the scale has good reliability and validity, and is recommended for people aged 8–18 (Proctor et al., 2009). The scale involves six statements. Next to each statement, participants are encouraged to write down one of seven possible answers: *terrible, unhappy, mostly dissatisfied, mixed (equally satisfied and dissatisfied), mostly satisfied, pleased,* and *delighted.* (For an alternative format, all seven options can be written next to each statement, with pupils asked to circle the one that applies.)

Answer

1. I would describe my satisfaction with my *family life* as:　　＿＿＿＿＿
2. I would describe my satisfaction with my *friends* as:　　＿＿＿＿＿
3. I would describe my satisfaction with my *school* as:　　＿＿＿＿＿
4. I would describe my satisfaction with my *self* as:　　＿＿＿＿＿
5. I would describe my satisfaction with my *living environment* as:　　＿＿＿＿＿
6. I would describe my satisfaction with my *life* as:　　＿＿＿＿＿

The participant's response to each item is given a score, based on the following scoring: 1 = *terrible*, 2 = *unhappy*, 3 = *mostly dissatisfied*, 4 = *mixed (equally satisfied and dissatisfied)*, 5 = *mostly satisfied*, 6 = *pleased*, 7 = *delighted*. The total score is derived by adding all the scores, with higher overall scores seen as indicative of greater life satisfaction.

Youth development

As children move into adolescence (i.e., 12–18 years old), in addition to positive education we can consider the overlapping notion of positive youth development. Though some critical psychologists suggest that adolescence is a socially constructed ideological concept that emerged in the nineteenth century (Griffin, 1997), others argue that it is found universally across cultures, though the form it takes varies greatly (Dasen, 2000). From the perspective of each of the domains of the LIFE model, adolescence is a period of rapid development. In subjective terms, it is a time of dynamic, often turbulent, emotional change and identity formation (Lerner, 2009). From a physiological perspective, while neural growth has slowed relative to childhood, the brain still engages in a complex process of strengthening and reducing neural networks, with particular restructuring in the prefrontal cortex and the limbic system (involved in the regulation of emotions as well as pleasure and reward) (Casey et al., 2008). In socio-cultural terms, adolescence involves a period of dis-embedding from the family nexus, and exploring new social worlds. Typically, research into adolescent development has taken a relatively pathological approach, focusing on the 'storm and stress' of cognitive, emotional and physical changes (Lerner, 2009). Such concern is understandable: despite maturational development relative to the 'frailties' of childhood, over-all morbidity and mortality increase 200% in adolescence (compared to early school age). This is mainly due to 'difficulties in the control of behaviour and emotion', leading to high rates of accidents, suicide, homicide, depression, alcohol/drug abuse, etc. (Dahl, 2004, p. 3).

ART LINKS . . .

A powerful and poignant real-life depiction of our existential journey from childhood through to older ages is provided by the ground-breaking UK TV series *7 Up*. In 1964, Michael Apted interviewed a group of school children, aged 7, hailing from a range of different backgrounds. He asked them about their lives, and their hopes and fears for the future. He then returned every seven years to interview the same people, following the way their lives unfolded in often unexpected ways. For example, one of the children, Neil Hughes from Liverpool, dreamed of being an astronaut at age 7. Tragically, aged 28, Neil was homeless and suffering from mental health problems. However, in a heart-ening twist, when viewers later encountered Neil aged 42, he had turned his life around and had become a politician in London. The latest instalment, *56 Up*, was released in 2012. A beautiful fictional rendering of adolescence is provided in a new film by Richard Linklater, entitled *Boyhood*, which was filmed over the course of 12 years, using the same actors. It follows the journey of a boy, aged 7 to begin with, as he navigates the difficult waters of adolescence and gradually becomes a man.

However, more recently, a Positive Youth Development (PYD) paradigm has emerged (Larson, 2000). Augmenting the more common problem-focused approaches, PYD involves programmes designed to help foster positive qualities and skills (Catalano & Toumbourou, 2012). These programmes take a mesosys-temic approach, recognising the multiple contextual influences that affect youth behaviour and wellbeing, including home, school, neighbourhood, peer groups and society generally. The ethos is that youth are 'resources to be developed, and not problems to be managed' (Roth & Brooks-Gunn, 2003, as cited in Lerner, 2009, p. 155). Lerner, one of the leading researchers in PYD, has developed a '5C model of PYD': (1) *competence*; (2) *confidence*; (3) *connection*; (4) *character*; and (5) *caring*; with a possible sixth 'C', *contribution*, where individuals contrib-ute to the community as a result of the other five Cs. Structured PYD programmes provide environments in which young people can learn and exhibit these five Cs, as well as other positive physical and psychological outcomes (Larson et al.,

2004). By way of illustration, one activity promoted by such programmes is volunteering, which can have such a powerful impact on wellbeing that Jenkinson et al. (2013, p. 1) call it a 'public health intervention'. One can clearly see how such an activity could effectively inculcate all of the five Cs.

TRY ME! . . .

Are you or have you ever been a volunteer? If so, why do/did you do it? Take a moment to reflect on what it means/meant to you, and its impact on your wellbeing. If you do not currently volunteer, perhaps you could find something to give your time to, even if only for an hour or so each week. Why not find an activity, cause or charity that personally resonates with you, and give it a try!

In terms of designing/implementing such programmes, Larson et al. (2004) offer recommendations for the adult leaders of these, including: (i) follow the youth's lead, thus increasing their autonomy and ownership; (ii) create a culture of youth input; (iii) monitor the balance between youth lead and adult guidance; (iv) develop intermediate structures between the leaders and the youth (e.g., use organising calendars for the activities); and (v) stretch the participants to try out different roles and tasks (pp. 553–556). Overall, those working to promote PYD need to balance young people's autonomy and ownership with structure and guidance when appropriate. Further modifications may be needed with specific groups, such as at-risk youth, i.e., 'adolescents who face disadvantage or adversity narrowly or broadly defined' (Swahn & Bossarte, 2009, p. 225). At-risk factors include living in areas of high crime and poverty, involvement in the juvenile justice system, and exclusion from school. Almost by definition, there are poorer wellbeing outcomes for at-risk youth (Alicea et al., 2012). With such populations, extra effort is needed across the board, including reaching out to them to begin with, accommodating the often complex and challenging nature of their lives, and supporting/encouraging them in the face of the greater psychosocial burdens that they are likely to be suffering under (Mendelson et al., 2010).

RESEARCH AND PRACTICE CASE STUDIES . . .

A prominent construct in PP is resilience, i.e., 'the ability to withstand hardship and rebound from adversity, becoming more strengthened and resourceful' (Bayat, 2007, p. 702). The resilience concept stemmed initially from studies of at-risk children, and the fact that some flourished *despite* being at-risk. One of the most widely cited is the

Kauai longitudinal study, which followed a cohort of babies on the Hawaiian island from 1955 to 1995 to identify factors that facilitate resilience into adulthood among at-risk populations (Werner, 1992, 1993). Initially, 30% ($n = 201$) of the cohort were identified as high-risk, based on factors including perinatal stress, poverty, and parents with various difficulties (e.g., alcoholism or mental health problems). The researchers were interested in who among the at-risk population went on to live 'normal lives', defined as having good relationships with significant others, healthy personalities and stable careers. At the longitudinal follow-ups, while two-thirds of the original cohort who were at-risk had social, academic and emotional issues, one-third of these high-risk individuals ($n = 72$) enjoyed successful lives. So, what was different for these 72? The key factors in children who were resilient throughout their life included:

- positive childhood temperaments (e.g., active, affectionate)
- good relationships with classmates
- good communication, reading and reasoning skills
- a bond with at least one caregiver, and being close to someone for the first year of life
- having a good role model (this was especially important for boys)
- a strong support network outside the home (e.g., friends, grandparents, community)
- continuing into further education
- a positive self-concept and internal locus of control

These factors touch upon many of the concepts explored above in this chapter, such as having a strong bond with a caregiver (which pertains to attachment). Indeed, one of the strongest elements to creating a resilient adult was having a supportive role model (either within or outside the home) in childhood.

Development throughout adulthood

It is important to appreciate that psychological development does not necessarily stop when people reach adulthood, but can continue through the lifespan. Here we are indebted to pioneering theorists who drew attention to this possibility of life-long growth. Perhaps the most famous is Maslow (1987 (1954)), whose hierarchy of needs – a theory of motivation – proposed that as particular innate needs are met, people become aware of and driven by 'higher level' needs. Common conceptualisations of the model describe the following sequence of needs: biological/physiological (e.g., food); safety (e.g., security); belongingness/love (e.g., affection); esteem (e.g., achievement); cognitive (e.g., meaning); aesthetic (e.g., beauty); and self-actualisation (e.g., self-fulfilment). Over 50 years on, psychologists continue to find his model useful (Koltko-Rivera, 2006). Another prominent theory is Erikson's (1963 (1950)) model of psychosocial stages. This suggested that one's sense of self developed through eight stages, each revolving around a certain psychosocial crisis, the successful resolution of which propelled a person smoothly on to the next stage (unsuccessful resolution would lead to ongoing psychological problems relating to the crisis). The sequence is: trust versus mistrust (around age 0–2); autonomy versus shame/doubt (2–4); initiative versus guilt (4–5); industry versus inferiority (5–12); identity versus role-confusion (12–19); intimacy versus isolation (20–24); generation versus stagnation (24–64); and ego-integrity versus despair (64+). These models are joined by schemas describing the development of other qualities throughout the lifespan, including values (Graves, 1970), worldviews (Gebser, 1985) and morals (Kohlberg, 1981).

RESEARCH AND PRACTICE CASE STUDIES . . .

Kohlberg (1981) developed his theory of moral development by posing the following scenario:

> A woman was dying from illness. There was a drug that could save her. However, the only chemist in town was charging $2,000 for it, 10 times what it cost to make. The woman's husband borrowed money from everyone he knew, but only raised $1,000. He pleaded with the chemist to sell it cheaper, or let him pay the rest later, but the chemist refused. In desperation, the husband stole the drug.

Kohlberg asked people whether they thought the husband was right or wrong to steal it. Crucially, he asked people of different ages, and found that the answers they gave revealed a pattern, involving a number of stages. People in early stages of life (e.g., childhood) said that the husband was right to steal, simply because he wanted/needed the drug. Kohlberg called this the 'pre-conventional' stage, where morality is determined by hedonic needs and consequences (i.e., what one wants). In contrast, people who were slightly older (e.g., early teens) tended to suggest that the husband was wrong to steal it, because it was against the law. Kohlberg called this the 'conventional' stage, where morality is a question of obedience to societal conventions (i.e., rules/laws). However, with increasing age, people again usually said that the husband was right, not for hedonistic reasons, but because higher moral values (e.g., the right to life) trumped the narrower societal rules. This stage was labelled 'post-conventional', because people had transcended the conventional social laws.

Given this profusion of developmental schemas, theorists have attempted to look for commonalities between the models, with the aim of constructing an overarching synthesising framework. One such framework is Spiral Dynamics (Beck & Cowan, 1996), which proposes eight levels of development. These levels are called vMemes (value-systems), and are labelled with a colour name. Each level is a mode of being, encompassing attitudes, values and worldviews. The levels can be aggregated into the stages identified by Kohlberg. There are three pre-conventional levels. First, *beige* is the 'instinctual' consciousness of neonates, a primal concern with physiological needs (cf. Maslow). Second, *purple* is the kind of animistic thinking of infants, where the world is seen as centred on and responsive to their needs. Third, *red* is the emergence of a distinct ego-identity (as separate from the world) in childhood, with concomitant self-assertive behaviours. Next emerges the *blue* conventional vMeme, as people are socialised into group norms and taught particular cultural worldviews. *Orange* then straddles the conventional and post-conventional: people are educated into a 'scientific' mindset that causes them to question their inherited *blue* assumptions. Then follow various post-conventional levels. *Green* is characterised by post-modern 'pluralistic-relativism': one recognises a plurality of worldviews, but sees all of these, including the prior scientific-rationalist *orange* vMeme, as cultural constructions with no particular claim to superiority. *Yellow* is then integrative: while still valuing all worldviews and prior vMemes, these are assembled into an integrative structure that *does* differentiate between them. Spiral Dynamics is itself seen as a reflection of *yellow* thinking. Beyond yellow is *turquoise*, and even higher potential levels, reflecting future hypothesised developmental capacities.

People are seen as progressing up the spiral, moving gradually from level to level. However, the model does not simply categorise people as being rigidly 'at' a particular level, for various reasons. First, we can think of vMemes being inherent potentials in people. Even if a particular level has been transcended, it remains as a psychological structure that can be activated in certain circumstances. For example, a person may generally espouse *'green'* tolerance, but if they feel threatened, they are likely to protect themselves with *'red'* aggression. A second argument against rigid categorisation of people is that development is not seen as unitary. Spiral Dynamics derived from theories which emphasised different developmental capacities, from morals (Kohlberg, 1981) to values (Graves, 1970). As such, people are seen as comprising numerous developmental 'strands'. This has parallels with Gardner's (1985) idea of multiple intelligences (musical, visual-spatial, verbal-linguistic, logical-mathematical, bodily-kinaesthetic, interpersonal, intrapersonal and naturalistic). In Gardner's model, people excel at some intelligences more than others. Similarly, advocates of Spiral Dynamics suggest that people can be more advanced in some areas than others. Thus, Wilber (2000) proposes that development is best conceptualised using a psychograph model: people progress along the various developmental lines – which are 'quasi-independent' (i.e., distinct, but usually interrelated) – in a staggered, idiosyncratic fashion.

Spiral Dynamics is not without its critics, who argue it reflects an ethnocentric 'Western' conception of development (Taylor, 2003). (Advocates for Spiral Dynamics in turn accuse such critics of being stuck at the *green* pluralistic-relativism stage.) Moreover, it must be emphasised that it cannot yet be regarded as fully empirically substantiated; it is more a tentative model. Nevertheless, it is helpful to articulate the potential details of psychological development. While development is a key component of PP theories, like Ryff's (1989) model of PWB, its precise nature is rarely made explicit. Even if the details of Spiral Dynamics prove incorrect, it offers a useful theoretical starting point. Moreover, from an APP perspective, it has been found to be *pragmatically* useful: it has been used in the treatment of alcoholism/addiction (Dupuy, 2013); it has been deployed as a conflict-resolution/reconciliation tool to promote systemic change in situations like the former Yugoslavia (Stambolovic, 2002); and it has proved popular in the fields of business and leadership (as discussed further in the next chapter), being embraced as a way of understanding organisational dynamics, fostering social integration and managing people (Cacioppe & Edwards, 2005). More broadly, Wilber (1995) suggests that simply teaching people the concept of 'levels' (vMemes) and 'lines' (developmental capacities) can help foster development, since people can hone their strengths while also working on capacities that are weaker.

Aging

As we reach the end of our journey through the life stages, we shall briefly touch upon the idea of positive aging. Modern Western culture is often seen as being fixated on the brightness and vigour of youth. In contrast to some other cultures, which afford respect and even reverence to old age (e.g., as a source of wisdom), there is a common view of old age simply as a period of decline and decay (Löckenhoff et al., 2009). Moreover, our perceptions of what aging is like are often misjudged. Without minimising the real hardships faced by older people – from the loneliness of social isolation to the burden of physical problems – Tornstam (2005, p. 2) suggests there are 'severe mismatches between the nuisances and miseries we tend to project on old age and what those who have reached advanced age tell themselves'. Indeed, longitudinal studies indicate that wellbeing is 'U-shaped' through life: analysing data on 500,000 Americans and Europeans, Blanchflower and Oswald (2008) found that wellbeing declined from youth into middle age, but then rose again as people entered older ages. In light of such findings, gerontologists (those who study aging) are beginning to understand the nature of and factors contributing to, successful/positive aging. Such research aims to 'add more life to years, not just more years to life' (Vaillant, 2004, p. 561).

RESEARCH AND PRACTICE CASE STUDIES . . .

From an APP perspective, one way we can promote positive aging is to help older people maintain autonomy. In a famous study, Rodin and Langer (1977) designed an intervention to 'increase feelings of choice and personal responsibility over daily events' among elderly residents of a nursing home (p. 897). Some residents (the experimental group) were given a plant to take care of, while others (the comparison group) were also given a plant, but were told *the staff* would take care of it. After three weeks, the experimental group had significantly higher wellbeing levels, including sociability, vigour and self-initiative. Most strikingly, the intervention even appeared to influence mortality. Before the study, the average death rate in the home was 25%. In the 18 months afterwards, just *15%* of the experimental group had died (7 of 47), against 30% of the comparison group (13 of 44). These results, which the researchers describe as 'startling', suggest that although many factors relating to aging may not be controllable, there are ways we *can* help people live better for longer. What is your view of aging, and what would constitute successful aging for you?

There are many components of 'successful aging', including avoiding disease, experiencing loving relationships, engaging in continual learning and staying active (Williamson & Christie, 2009). It is helpful to put these factors in place *before* reaching old age. For example, Vaillant (2004) conducted a landmark longitudinal study, comparing Harvard sophomores with non-delinquent inner-city boys. He found that controllable lifestyle components before the age of 50 predicted healthy aging (even after taking into account the very different life challenges faced by the two groups). Some variables *did not* predict healthy aging, including ancestral longevity, cholesterol, temperament, or stress levels. Factors that *did* predict healthy aging included not smoking, adaptive coping styles, absence of alcohol abuse, healthy weight (BMI between 21 and 29), stable marriage, exercise (500 kilocalories per week) and years of education (independent of social class and IQ). Moreover, when people *do* enter old age, there are ways to promote wellbeing, like helping people maintain autonomy, as demonstrated in the box above. Positive aging is also facilitated through the careful choice of goals: taking on fewer goals (to reduce strain), but crucially making these select goals more meaningful (Baltes & Carstensen, 2003). People can then put more resources into these goals, and compensate for age-related barriers. While we have only touched briefly upon the idea of positive aging, it is sufficient to make us appreciate that positive development is not only about giving people the best start in life, but helping ensure that their existential journey ends well too.

SUMMARY – THIS CHAPTER HAS...

- Articulated a lifespan chronosystem approach to positive development
- Outlined factors around pregnancy, birth and early infancy relating to wellbeing
- Reviewed the important role of parenting and attachment for later adjustment and wellbeing
- Discussed the burgeoning field of positive education
- Offered suggestions for interventions to promote positive youth development
- Considered models of development throughout the lifespan
- Touched upon the idea of successful/positive aging

QUIZ...

1   The perinatal phase of pregnancy is defined as covering which time period?
2   According to Piaget (1971), what is the first stage of cognitive development?
3   Who pioneered the theory of attachment, and who investigated it using the strange situation?
4   What are the four attachment styles?
5   Parenting styles are categorised according to which two dimensions?
6   In which country did the Triple-P Positive Parenting Program originate?
7   What is the most widely used PP programme in education?
8   What are the five Cs of Positive Youth Development?
9   Who formulated the theory of Spiral Dynamics?
10 In Vaillant's (2004) Harvard study, name any two factors which predicted positive aging.

RESOURCES AND SUGGESTIONS...

- For details on the PRP for schools, please visit www.ppc.sas.upenn.edu/prpsum. htm. This contains details of the curriculum, lists of references, and past and present projects.
- Another innovative programme for fostering positive child development is Families and Schools Together (FAST) (www.familiesandschools.org). This is a multifamily mesosystem group intervention designed to build protective factors for children, and is endorsed by bodies ranging from Save the Children in the UK, to the United Nations Office on Drugs and Crime.
- You can find more information about youth development at the Tufts Institute for Applied Research in Youth Development (http://ase.tufts.edu/iaryd/default.htm).
- For the most updated review of Vaillant's Harvard study of positive aging, please check out *Triumphs of Experience: The Men of the Harvard Grant Study* (Vaillant, 2012).

OCCUPATIONS AND ORGANISATIONS

Work is love made visible…
And what is it to work with love?
It is to sow seeds with tenderness and reap the harvest with joy,
even as if your beloved were to eat the fruit.
Kahlil Gibran

LEARNING OBJECTIVES – AT THE END OF THE CHAPTER YOU WILL BE ABLE TO…

- Differentiate positive organisational behaviour and positive organisational scholarship
- Conceptualise and approach occupations and organisations using the LIFE model
- Understand the impact of occupations, workplaces and organisations on wellbeing
- Appreciate the factors that contribute to work engagement
- Identify different PPIs to apply in the workplace and occupational situations

LIST OF TOPICS…

- The Job Demands-Resources (J D-R) model
- Engagement, and its psychological drivers
- Strengths (including the VIA and the Realise2 models)
- Coaching, career counselling and mentoring
- Psychological capital (PsyCap)
- Meaning and purpose at work

- Health and safety
- Job content and control
- Leadership and 'climate engineering'
- Organisational-level values/ strengths
- Appreciative Inquiry
- Political and economic work-related factors

Although utopian visions of society have dreamed of an existence in which people are liberated from having to work (Guest, 2002), work remains central to human life. Simply from a quantitative perspective, work can consume a significant portion of our waking hours (Office for National Statistics, 2011a). More centrally, in an existential sense, our work can come to define us, structuring our days, generating the bulk of our interactions and providing us with crucial components of our identities (Ryan, 1995). In speaking of work, we do not only mean paid employment. As the title suggests, our focus here encompasses any of the ways people substantively and productively 'occupy' their time, from studying to raising children to volunteering. Similarly, 'organisations' refers not only to companies, but to any functional group of people, from families to political parties. Thus, although most of the concepts and activities in this chapter have traditionally been discussed in relation to paid work, readers are encouraged to freely apply these to their own circumstances (e.g., the section on leadership can easily be transposed to domains such as parenting). Given this centrality of work to our lives, it understandably has a considerable impact on our wellbeing. In academia, this impact has traditionally been explored by applied disciplines like occupational psychology (Lewis & Zibarras, 2013). More recently though, it has been examined by emergent PP paradigms, most notably positive organizational behaviour (POB) (Luthans, 2002) and positive organizational scholarship (POS) (Cameron et al., 2003).

There is considerable overlap between POB and POS. However, Bakker and Schaufeli (2008) suggest that POB is more 'organization-driven' (i.e., getting the best out of employees for the benefit of the organisation), while POS is more 'employee-driven' (getting the best out of the organisation for the benefit of employees). Luthans (2002, p. 59) defines POB as 'the study and application of positively oriented human resource strengths and psychological capacities that can be measured, developed and managed for performance improvement in today's workplace'. Bakker and Schaufeli warn that this emphasis on performance risks a utilitarian concern with maximising employee output. Echoing this, Wright (2003) argues that employee wellbeing must be an end in itself. Reflecting this latter concern, POS is 'the study of that which is positive, flourishing, and life-giving in organizations', i.e., aspects of the organisation that help employees thrive (Cameron & Caza, 2004, p. 731). Being psychologists, we naturally lean more towards POS than POB, which in APP terms means trying to improve the wellbeing of workers (as opposed to prioritising business success). However, these two perspectives are not necessarily oppositional, but can be synergistic – as discussed in the final section – since companies that care for their employees are arguably more likely to prosper (Zwetsloot & Pot, 2004).

In terms of a theoretical model to help ground the chapter, perhaps the most well-researched relating to work and wellbeing is the Job Demands-Resources (J D-R) model (Demerouti et al., 2001, p. 501). Job demands are 'physical, social or organisational aspects of the job that require sustained physical or mental effort and are therefore associated with certain physiological or psychological costs (e.g., exhaustion)'. Conversely, job resources are 'physical, psychological, social or organisational aspects of the job that may do one of the following: (a) be functional in achieving work goals; (b) reduce job demands and the associated physiological and psychological costs; (c) stimulate personal growth and development'. Broadly speaking, wellbeing at work is a function of the trade-off between demands and resources (Bakker et al., 2005). If demands exceed resources, the result is work-related stress and, eventually, burnout; conversely, if resources surpass demands, one ideally attains the positive work-related state of *engagement* (Schaufeli et al., 2009). Thus, from an APP stance, we can endeavour to ameliorate job demands and/or enhance job resources. Moreover, we can seek to do so across all four domains of the LIFE model. Indeed, this multi-dimensional approach is reflected in the definition of the J D-R model above. There are clear parallels to the four domains in Demerouti et al.'s description of job resources being 'physical [i.e., objective body], psychological [i.e., subjective mind], social [i.e., intersubjective culture] or organisational [i.e., interobjective society] aspects of the job'. As such, this chapter is in four parts, focusing on each of the domains in turn: mind, body, culture and society.

PRACTICE ESSAY QUESTIONS . . .

- Critically evaluate the differences between positive organizational behaviour and positive organizational scholarship.
- Outline the various occupational factors associated with employee wellbeing, and discuss their relative importance.

The mind

This first section focuses on psychological resources that facilitate engagement, and PPIs/activities to enhance these resources. The construct of engagement encompasses a range of outcomes relevant to PP. For Schaufeli et al. (2006), engagement comprises vigour, dedication and absorption. Somewhat differently, Fine et al. (2010) conceptualise it as an amalgamation of commitment, satisfaction and discretionary effort. Given this conceptual indeterminacy, we shall simply use engagement to refer to the whole spectrum of positive work-related outcomes, from absorption to satisfaction to meaning. The question is, what resources are the 'drivers' of engagement? Crabb (2011) distinguishes between drivers at an organisational level and an individual psychological level.

Organisational-level drivers (e.g., leadership) are discussed below in the sections on culture and society. In this first section we will examine the three psychological drivers identified by Crabb: focusing strengths, managing emotions and aligning purpose. However, before discussing these, let us contextualise our thinking by reflecting on our own work situation (or comparable activity, such as studying). Schaufeli et al. (2006) have devised a widely-used questionnaire. Try this out in the box below!

PSYCHOMETRIC SCALES . . .

The Utrecht Work Engagement Scale – 9 is a series of statements about how you feel at work. If you have never had this feeling, write '0' (zero) next to the statement. If you have had this feeling, indicate how often you felt it by writing down the number (from 1 to 6) that best describes how frequently you feel this way. 0 = *never*, 1 = *almost never (a few times a year or less)*, 2 = *rarely (once a month or less)*, 3 = *sometimes (a few times a month)*, 4 = *often (once a week)*, 5 = *very often (a few times a week)*, 6 = *always (every day)*.

                                                                              Answer

1. At my work, I feel bursting with energy.   _____
2. At my job, I feel strong and vigorous.   _____
3. I am enthusiastic about my job.   _____
4. When I get up in the morning, I feel like going to work.   _____
5. My job inspires me.   _____
6. I feel happy when I am working intensely.   _____
7. I am proud of the work that I do.   _____
8. I am immersed in my work.   _____
9. I get carried away when I am working.   _____

                                                    Total = _____

Add the numbers you wrote for each item: the higher your score, the greater your work engagement!

Focusing strengths

The first psychological driver of engagement is using one's strengths at work. A focus on strengths was an initial defining feature of the PP movement. A drive was initiated to generate a taxonomy of strengths, mirroring the American Psychiatric Association's (1994) classification of psychological disorders (Peterson & Seligman, 2004). Researchers studied classic texts of the world's great religious and philosophical traditions, looking for universal virtues valued across all cultures throughout history (Dahlsgaard et al., 2005). This search generated 24 distinct strengths, aggregated into six larger virtues, set out in the box below. This schema, known as the 'Values in Action' (VIA) framework (Peterson, 2006b), is assessed using the 'VIA inventory of strengths' (VIA-IS), a 240-item self-report questionnaire. Although there are other taxonomies and classification tools, such as Realise2 (Linley et al., 2009), the VIA is arguably the most widely used (Linley et al., 2010). A key message of the strengths paradigm is that people benefit more from cultivating their strengths than working on weaknesses, with the use of self-perceived strengths over time linked to longitudinal increases in wellbeing (Wood et al., 2011).

REFLECTION . . . WHAT ARE YOUR 'TOP 5' STRENGTHS?

Wisdom and knowledge

- Creativity
- Judgement
- Perspective
- Curiosity
- Love of learning

Courage

- Bravery
- Perseverance
- Honesty
- Zest

Humanity

- Love
- Kindness
- Social intelligence

Justice

- Teamwork
- Fairness
- Leadership

Temperance

- Forgiveness
- Humility
- Prudence
- Self-regulation

Transcendence

- Appreciation of beauty and excellence
- Gratitude
- Hope
- Humour
- Spirituality

The notion of strengths has been embraced within business, particularly in the field of coaching. As discussed in Chapter 1, we can arguably conceptualise coaching as a subset of APP, one involving the cultivation of a 'professional relationship' between a coach and client, and which generally operates 'in the context of working toward specific goals' relating to work (Biswas-Diener, 2009, p. 544). The benefit of a coaching relationship is that it can facilitate *skilful* cultivation of strengths. The strengths concept has been critiqued for often being deployed in an *essentialist* way. (Essentialism is the idea that people possess relatively fixed sets of characteristics, and is the conceptual basis of psychometric classification, such as trait theories of personality (Costa & McCrae, 1992).) However, embracing a more dynamic social constructionist perspective, Biswas-Diener et al. (2011a) argue that strengths are 'potentials for excellence' that people can strive to cultivate. Framing the construct in this way affects strength development: asking people to *identify* their strengths increases their belief that strengths are fixed (i.e., engenders a fixed mindset), decreasing motivation to work on these; conversely, exhorting people to *develop* their strengths fosters belief in the possibility of improvement (i.e., facilitates a growth mindset) (Louis, 2011). This is where the value of coaching asserts itself. Tools like the VIA should ideally not be used in a crude prescriptive way ('Here's your strengths – go and use them!'). Rather, as explained by Lucy Ryan (2013), a successful executive coach (www.mindspring.uk.com), identifying strengths in coaching is just the means to a 'deeper, broader coaching conversation' about how the client can develop in their work role and as a person. Similarly, Roche and Hefferon (2013) emphasise the importance of people being debriefed following a strengths assessment to enable them to understand and utilise this assessment more effectively.

ART LINKS . . .

An imaginative and novel approach to exploring strengths is offered in Wedding and Niemiec's (2008) book *Positive Psychology at the Movies*. This uses films to illustrate and enrich our understanding of strengths, as well as other PP concepts, such as resilience and flourishing. With over 1,500 films included and reviewed, readers are invited to watch these and identify when strengths (and other PP concepts) are being practised and applied. Do you have a favourite film in which the protagonist(s) is using their strengths in a particularly memorable, enlightening or inspiring way?

Thus, in a work setting, the strengths construct means helping people make better use of their talents and develop their potential. This need not only occur in the context of coaching; it can be adopted more generally as a management strategy (e.g., managers could utilise the construct in appraising their employees and delegate tasks accordingly) (Clifton & Harter, 2003). As a management strategy, perhaps a more nuanced tool than the VIA is Realise2 (Linley et al., 2009). This identifies three areas: strengths, learned behaviours (skills we may be good at, but which are not fulfilling) and weaknesses. Moreover, these areas can be broken down further: strengths can be either realised (identified and used regularly) or unrealised (dormant potentials); learned behaviours may be regular (habitually used) or infrequent; and weaknesses can be exposed (in the open) or unexposed (the current situation is concealing flaws that would be exposed if circumstances changed). With the Realise2, rather than the arguably unrealistic aim of eradicating people's weaknesses, a more manageable goal is rendering such weaknesses *irrelevant*. From an APP perspective, strategies for implementing the Realise2 model in practice include: role-shaping (tailoring a role so it plays to people's strengths); complementary partnering (working with someone whose strengths compensate for your weaknesses, and vice versa); and strengths-based teamwork (the complementary partnership principle applied to a whole group); and, if it is not possible to render weaknesses irrelevant, general skill training for such weaknesses.

Managing emotions

The second driver of engagement is 'managing emotions'. This is essentially a catch-all term for all one's psychological resources, including many of the psychological skills outlined in Chapter 2. Many studies attest to the value of such skills in the workplace, and the utility of workplace PPIs to cultivate these. Take mindfulness, for instance. Trait mindfulness is associated with employee wellbeing and job performance, with one explanation being that mindfulness enhances engagement by enabling people to become more absorbed in their work (Reid, 2009). Moreover, meditation-based PPIs help promote mental health in occupational settings, with successful interventions delivered to workers ranging from school teachers (Gold et al., 2010) to therapists (Shapiro et al., 2007) to call centre staff (Walach et al., 2007). Likewise, Fredrickson et al.'s (2008) LKM intervention (introduced in Chapter 2) corroborated Fredrickson's (2005) 'broaden-and-build' theory in the context of a software company. In terms of managing emotions, Mayer and Salovey's (1997) EI construct is particularly relevant, associated with positive outcomes in work settings, such as coping with challenging occupations, e.g., nurses engaging in end-of-life care (Bailey et al., 2011). Moreover, from an APP stance, work-based EI training can enhance wellbeing, as seen cross-culturally in interventions with workers in diverse sectors, from intensive care nurses in Iran (Sharif et al., 2013) to business managers in India (Ganpat & Nagendra, 2011).

Another prominent psychological resource in POS and POB is 'PsyCap', i.e., psychological capital (Luthans et al., 2007). PsyCap comprises four qualities: self-efficacy (Bandura, 1977); optimism (Carver & Scheier, 2003); hope (Snyder, 2000); and resilience (Masten, 2001). PsyCap links these in an interesting way, being defined as 'an individual positive state of development that is characterised by: (1) having confidence (self-efficacy) to take on and put in the necessary effort to succeed at challenging tasks; (2) making a positive attribution about succeeding now and in the future; (3) persevering towards goals and, when necessary, redirecting paths to goals (hope) in order to succeed; and (4) even when beset by problems and adversity, sustaining and bouncing back and even beyond (resilience) to attain success' (Luthans et al., 2007, p. 3). PsyCap is linked to employee wellbeing (Avey et al., 2010a) and, from an organisational perspective, desirable employee attitudes, behaviours and performance (Avey et al., 2010b). Moreover, various PsyCap interventions are being developed. Luthans et al.'s (2010) two-hour training programme involves exercises to engender all four qualities. Hope (i.e., positive expectations for the future) is cultivated by generating personally-meaningful work-related goals. Self-efficacy is promoted by identifying concrete plans to help achieve these goals. Optimism is facilitated by conceiving of multiple pathways towards the goals, and by 'obstacle planning' (i.e., working out how to overcome challenges). Finally, resilience is inculcated by reflecting on 'personal assets' that will help in the pursuit of these goals, such as one's strengths.

RESEARCH AND PRACTICE CASE STUDIES . . .

A wonderful case of PsyCap in action is demonstrated by the astronaut Chris Hadfield, who found a global audience with an incredible series of videos recorded aboard the International Space Station, including a rendition of David Bowie's 'Space Oddity'. In his account of his experiences (Hadfield, 2013), while he does not use the term 'PsyCap', he demonstrates its qualities in abundance. Optimism (belief in future success) and hope (persevering towards goals) were both necessary in the extremely selective and challenging career path towards being an astronaut. While such qualities were arguably inherent features of Hadfield's character, a useful lesson for us here is the striking way in which his astronaut training programme instilled resilience and self-efficacy, namely, the 'power of negative thinking'! (Hadfield, 2013, p. 51). The trainers helped the astronauts overcome fear by devising elaborate simulations of 'bad-news scenarios', covering every possible mishap or malfunction (which in space could easily be fatal). In an extreme example of 'obstacle planning', the astronauts would act out these scenarios again and again so that, if the worst did occur, they had the resilience and self-efficacy to handle it. Hadfield writes: 'Being forced to confront the problem of failure head-on – to study it, dissect it, tease apart all its components and consequences – really works. After a few years of doing that pretty much daily you've forged the strongest possible armor to defend against fear: hard-won competence' (p. 54). This case highlights the complexities of emotions, and the difficulty of associating PP just with 'the positive' (discussed in Chapter 1), as here 'positive' outcomes arose from focusing on the 'negative'.

There are also work-based interventions to develop individual PsyCap components, such as Reivich et al.'s (2011) Master Resilience Training (MRT) programme, an adaptation of the Penn Resilience Program (outlined in Chapter 5). MRT is based on the ABC model of explanatory styles (Ellis, 1987): the potential for a negative *Activating event* to have adverse emotional *Consequences* depends on the intervening factor of a person's *Beliefs* about that event. Disorders like depression can be the result of a dysfunctional attribution style (Abramson et al., 1978), which cognitive behaviour therapy thus aims to alter, as discussed in Chapter 2. One method of changing an explanatory/attribution style was proposed by Seligman (1990), who augmented ABC with *Disputation* and *Energisation*. Clients are helped to dispute dysfunctional beliefs – perhaps challenging the idea that one is a failure by recalling previous successes, for example – and are ideally energised as a result. MRT has been used in the US army to help personnel identify maladaptive beliefs that are hindering their work performance. These beliefs are referred to as 'icebergs', reflecting the way surface-level thoughts are connected to vast unacknowledged belief structures. Once icebergs are identified, participants are taught to ask: (a) is it still meaningful?, (b) is it accurate?, (c) is it overly rigid?, and (d) is it useful? A particularly salient iceberg in an army context might be the belief that 'Asking for help shows weakness', which could undermine work performance and even harm wellbeing (e.g., one might not seek support for health issues). Once acknowledged, people can be helped to develop more adaptive beliefs. For example, 'Asking for help' could be re-interpreted as a sign of responsibility and courage.

Aligning purpose

Finally, there is the importance of one's work being meaningful. From a theoretical perspective, there are overlapping models concerning meaning in work (Rosso et al., 2010). We can touch upon three here: value, orientation and identity. With value, Persson et al. (2001) differentiate between: concrete value (tangible positive outcomes); self-reward value (work being intrinsically fulfilling); and symbolic value (the significance a person and/or their culture attributes to an occupation). A similar schema differentiates between three types of 'work orientation' (Bellah et al., 1996): a job (a means to an end, i.e., earning money); a career (a route to achievement); or a calling (an intrinsically fulfilling vocation). Whereas in Persson et al.'s model the different types of value offered by work can all be conducive to meaning, in this orientation schema there is a definite hierarchy, with a calling being the most meaningful. Finally, we can differentiate between different positive work identities (Dutton et al., 2010): the virtue perspective (when work identities are suffused with virtuous qualities, e.g., wisdom); the evaluative perspective (feelings of self-regard linked to one's work identity); the developmental perspective (psychological growth over time linked to one's work); and the structural perspective (a harmonious relationship between one's work identity and other identities in life).

In an ideal world, everyone would feel a sense of calling, and would moreover have the talents and opportunities to pursue their vocation. However, in the real world, many people are not so fortunate, ending up in jobs by necessity or chance. That said, the diverse models highlighted above mean there are many different ways people can be *helped to construe* their work as meaningful (Wrzesniewski, 2003). This could begin even before people have entered work. For instance, Dik et al. (2011) developed a school-based 'career education intervention' that was found to be successful in giving students a 'clearer sense of career direction; a greater understanding of their interests, strengths, and weaknesses; and a greater sense of preparedness for the future' (p. 59). If people are already in work, there are numerous strategies to help work become more meaningful, including encouraging people to engage in active 'job crafting', involving physical and/or cognitive changes in the way they approach their job (Wrzesniewski, 2003). Job crafting may be further facilitated by career counselling (Dik et al., 2009), involving quasi-therapeutic activities and conversations to help people construe their work as more meaningful. This may involve perspective-shifting (Wrzesniewski, 2003), such as connecting one's work activities to larger narratives of meaning (e.g., 'providing for one's family', or serving a particular ideal).

So, the three main psychological resources of engagement are using one's strengths, managing one's emotions, and finding one's work meaningful. The crucial question now is how can we structure work so that people have the *opportunity* to develop these resources? We will address this question over the remaining sections, beginning with 'the body', i.e., the physical conditions of work.

The body

Wellbeing at work isn't simply a question of having the right psychological resources; the physical conditions of work matter too. In terms of the LIFE model, here we are concerned with the domain of the body, i.e., the material demands made on one's body, and the physical environment it is in. In the J

D-R model, engagement is the result of a favourable balance of resources and demands, whereas if demands exceed resources, the outcome is work-related stress. The three psychological drivers detailed above constitute resources. Now we consider the other side of the equation, i.e., demands/stressors. From an APP perspective, while in the first section our prerogative was enhancing resources, here our concern is with ameliorating demands. Sauter et al. (1990) outline six categories of stressors: (1) workload and work pace; (2) role stressors (e.g., task-conflict); (3) career concerns; (4) scheduling; (5) interpersonal relationships; and (6) job content and control. Three of these pertain to the body, namely (1), (4) and (6). Additionally, there is the issue of health and safety, which a meta-analysis found to be the most consistent job-demand across different industries (Nahrgang et al., 2011). So, we will look in turn at health and safety, workload and scheduling, and job content and control.

Health and safety

Health and safety provision is a crucial factor in work wellbeing (Kelloway & Day, 2005), and a core component of the American Psychological Association's (APA) (1999) definition of a psychologically healthy workplace (see box below). Workplace hazards are a major concern, being a risk-factor for psychological issues such as burnout (Nahrgang et al., 2011) and physical problems up to and including mortality (approximately 2 million work-related deaths occurred worldwide in 2000 alone; World Health Organisation, 2008). Health and safety issues can be addressed at both an individual level (helping people to work safely) and an organisational level (establishing protocols to ensure safety). For example, among the most prevalent work-related issues is musculoskeletal disorders (Kennedy et al., 2010). Individual-level interventions addressing this include exercise programmes (e.g., stretching; da Costa & Vieira, 2008) and education interventions (e.g., safe handling of objects; Daltroy et al., 1997). Sedentary jobs carry health and safety risks too, addressed by initiatives around the ergonomic design of work stations, e.g., adaptive chair/keyboard postures (Brewer et al., 2006). At a more organisational level, health and safety is addressed through measures like the systematic regulation and inspection of work premises (Tompa et al., 2007).

RESEARCH AND PRACTICE CASE STUDIES . . .

There are various initiatives to recognise good work practices, like the APA's (1999) Psychologically Healthy Workplace Program (PHWP). The PHWP identifies good work practices according to five categories: work–life balance; health and safety; employee

(Continued)

(Continued)

involvement (e.g., in decision making); employee development; and employee recognition. The first two of these pertain to this section on the body. Regarding work–life balance, good practice includes flexible work arrangements (e.g., flexi-time and telecommuting) and assistance with childcare and eldercare. In terms of health and safety, good practice includes health and safety training, initiatives to help employees lead healthy lifestyles (e.g., stress management, weight loss and smoking cessation programmes) and access to fitness facilities. Since 1999, the PHWP has been running an award programme to highlight 'exemplary organizations'. In the four winning organisations for 2013, 84% of employees were satisfied with their jobs (vs. 67% across the USA generally), and less than 19% experienced chronic work stress (vs. 35% nationally). If you work for an organisation, how would it fare on these metrics, and how might it be improved?

Health and safety also encompasses the quality of the work environment. The physical conditions in which we work affect not only wellbeing (Salonen et al., 2013), but also performance, with 15% of employees reporting that building-related issues impede their productivity (Bergs, 2002). One factor is light: regular exposure to daylight enhances mental and physical health; if artificial light is used it must be sufficient, and adjustable by employees (Ulrich et al., 2008). A second issue is temperature: extremes can impair physical and mental health; the aim should be to set levels within a 'thermal comfort' range (sufficient to protect health) of 18–24°C (Ormandy & Ezratty, 2012). A third concern is noise: excessive levels – i.e., above 85 decibels (equivalent to a hairdryer) – impede wellbeing, with around 22 million workers in the USA exposed to hazardous levels at work (Basner et al., 2014). Another factor is air quality: while breathing problems usually only occur above 20,000 ppm (parts per million), deterioration in cognitive performance can happen from 600 ppm (Satish et al., 2012). It is thus recommended that levels ideally be kept below 1,000 ppm via effective ventilation (Steskens & Loomans, 2010). Finally, while not strictly a health and safety issue, the aesthetics of the environment also contributes to wellbeing. This is nicely conveyed by Dalke et al. (2006), who outline the impact of the thoughtful use of colour in hospitals, which affects both the occupational wellbeing of staff and the clinical wellbeing of patients. In designing workplaces from an APP perspective, all these factors would ideally be taken into account.

Workload and scheduling

A second key stressor, which could also be deemed a health and safety issue, is workload (Sauter et al., 1990). Excessive working hours are a problem across different industries, from haulage to higher education (e.g., 80% of lecturers report being overworked!; Sparks et al., 2013). Sparks et al.'s meta-analysis found that excessive working hours were linked to multiple physical and mental health issues, including heart disease, exhaustion and anxiety. Excessive hours also have a detrimental social and relational impact. For example, 75% of UK politicians report that their work causes/exacerbates family problems (Weinberg et al., 2013). From an APP perspective, regulations that limit excessive hours are desirable. In the UK, in 1998 the Health and Safety Executive implemented the European Working Time Directive into law, imposing a maximum weekly working time of not more than 48 hours over seven days, with extra precautions for night work, e.g., conducting health assessments on workers. (That said, the current UK government is seeking to remove this protection, which shows the impact of societal factors like political legislation on work environments, as discussed further below.) A related issue is work scheduling (the fourth of Sauter et al.'s six stressors). Circadian rhythms are disrupted by shift rotation of night work, impeding mental and physical health (Ettner & Grzywacz, 2001). Recommendations for minimising these effects include having eight-hour shifts with later changeovers (7am rather than 6am), and not rotating the shift pattern too rapidly, thus allowing people to acclimatise to shifts changes (Tucker et al., 1998).

TRY ME! . . .

What is your own workload like? Whether you are working, studying or occupied in other ways (e.g., volunteering), how much of your time is taken up with these activities? In Chapter 4, we encouraged you to keep a record for one week of the number of hours spent on various activities. Focus here on the number of hours you recorded for work activities (however you choose to define this), including time spent commuting. Do you exceed the European Working Time Directive of 48 hours per week? If so, are there ways you could possibly reduce your workload? Try to come up with five practical ideas for how you might do so. Over the next five weeks, try out each of these ideas for one week at a time.

Job content and control

A third key stressor is job content and control. Repetitive content with little control over one's activity is a major barrier to two of the psychological drivers of engagement, i.e., using strengths and aligning purpose. As Sauter et al. (1990, p. 1153) put it, 'narrow, fragmented, invariant and shortcycle tasks . . . provide little stimulation, allow little use of skills or expression of creativity and have little intrinsic meaning for workers'. Such work is detrimental to wellbeing and even physical health (Steptoe et al., 1997). Conversely, engagement is promoted by giving people opportunities to use and develop their skills, and autonomy to shape their job content. It is under such conditions that people are more likely to experience flow in their work activities (Bakker, 2005). Such conditions also allow people to invest their work with care and even love, as expressed beautifully in Robert Pirsig's (1974) philosophical autobiography (in which he describes finding value and meaning in technical activities such as fixing motorcycles). Unfortunately, many employees do not enjoy such freedom. Particular occupations are especially liable to job content and control issues, such as call centre work, which employs 3.5% of the UK workforce (Hudson, 2011). Call centres can often have dehumanising features, such as repetitive, de-personalised actions (e.g., pre-determined scripts), and intrusive monitoring (e.g., of toilet breaks). Unsurprisingly, such work is emotionally exhausting, since from a J D-R perspective, demands greatly outweigh resources (Lewig & Dollard, 2003). As such, we can see that the material conditions of work are to an extent dependent on the cultural and structural nature of the work environment, as the next two sections explore.

Culture

We now turn to the intersubjective aspects of work. Essentially, here we are focusing on the value of good work relationships. From a J D-R perspective, relationships are a key work resource (Schaufeli & Bakker, 2004), conducive to mental (Simon et al., 2010) and physical health (Heaphy & Dutton, 2008). Conversely poor relationships, one of Sauter et al.'s (1990) six stressors, hinder wellbeing. While we are interested in good relationships, in a broader sense, we can appreciate that interactions are embedded within a wider organisational *culture* of norms and values, which Parker et al. (2003) call the 'psychological climate'. Kets de Vries (2001) describes workplaces with a positive climate as *authentizotic* organisations (combining the Greek words *authentekos* and *zoteekos*, meaning authentic and vital to life, respectively). Rego and Pinae Cunha (2008) argue that such organisations are characterised by six factors: a spirit of camaraderie; trust in/of the leader; open communication; opportunities for personal development; fairness (a sense of justice); and the facilitation of a good work–life balance. These factors represent 'meta-values' that allow employees to experience the psychological drivers of engagement discussed above, from using one's strengths to finding meaning/purpose in work.

RESEARCH AND PRACTICE CASE STUDIES . . .

There are initiatives to recognise companies that foster a positive work climate. These have parallels with the APA's (1999) PHWP, except the emphasis is on the *relational culture* of an organisation. For example, Levering's (1988) *A Great Place to Work* initiative assesses workplaces on five key qualities (which overlap with Rego and Cunha's (2008) criteria for authentizotic organisations): camaraderie, respect, credibility, fairness and pride. Since 1997, Levering's institute has produced a list of the '100 best companies to work for', surveying over 10 million employees across 45 countries, published annually by the business magazine *Fortune* (Moskowitz et al., 2013). The top company in 2013 was Google, whose stated philosophy is 'to create the happiest, most productive workplace in the world' (Stewart, 2013). Bulygo (2013) suggests that Google's 'unique culture' is the result of detailed data analysis by its 'People Analytics' (HR) team, with continual 'testing to find ways to optimize their people, both in terms of happiness and performance'. An illustration of Google's attention to detail is in its approach to food! Not only are employees treated to free, healthy meals, the eating environment is deliberately structured to foster positive interactions. For example, queuing time is maintained at an optimal three to four minutes: minimal enough to ensure employees do not get frustrated at wasting time, yet sufficient to create opportunities for interaction. How do you feel about interaction being calibrated in this way?

From an APP perspective, the crucial question is how to *create* good organisational climates. We can briefly consider three ways: promoting positive **relationships**; effective **leadership**; and **values**-driven enquiry. First, we can engender good **relationships** in various ways. We could approach this issue from a structural perspective (i.e., in interobjective terms) by creating systems and processes that facilitate interaction. An illustration of this is Google's catering, outlined above; another might be the creation of mentoring programmes, where systematic attention is paid to the creation of nurturing relationships (Ragins & Cotton, 1999). Similarly, from a remedial perspective, if relationships are failing, a good climate can be restored through supportive mediation services (Ridley-Duff & Bennett, 2011). More generally, social capital can be promoted structurally through enhancing the quality of 'network ties' between employees, with systems in place to encourage interconnection, collaboration and effective communication, rather than people being isolated in silos (Bolino et al., 2002). Other interventions can be more intersubjective, such as activities to engender the desired type of positive and supportive interactions. People might be coached or otherwise encouraged to use good communication strategies, like active-constructive responding with colleagues (Avolio et al., 1999), as introduced in Chapter 4. PPIs like LKM also serve to improve workplace relationships (Fredrickson et al., 2008).

In the creation of a work culture, a crucial role is played by the *leadership*, who Linley et al. (2009) call 'climate engineers'. Around two-thirds of the variance in work fulfilment is attributable to the quality of leadership (van Marrewijk, 2004). Beyond just managing people (e.g., delegating work), leadership involves 'mobilizing others to want to struggle for shared aspirations' (Kouzes & Pozner, 1987, p. 30). High-quality leadership is captured in overlapping constructs, including transformational (Bass, 1991), charismatic (House, 1977) and spiritual leadership (Fry, 2003). So, what makes a high-quality leader? Arnold et al. (2007) outline four dimensions: idealised influence (exemplary conduct that engenders respect/trust), inspirational motivation (encouraging people to exceed their own expectations), intellectual stimulation (enabling autonomy of thought and action), and individualised consideration (humanistic regard/care for employees). Moreover, in a top–down way, leaders' values can percolate through an organisation, creating a climate in which employees are encouraged to also adopt such values (Peterson & Park, 2006). Given the importance of leaders, good leadership selection processes are vital. It is also important to have systems in place so that leaders themselves can be managed and supported, with checks/balances that can prevent coercive power hierarchies from developing (Vanderslice, 1988), as destructive leadership can occur if unchecked power degenerates into a cult of personality, with adverse outcomes for those out of favour with the leadership (Padilla et al., 2007). Leaders can also turn to executive coaches to improve their leadership skills (Grant et al., 2009).

REFLECTION . . .

Have you ever been guided by a leader who you felt was particularly impressive? This does not have to be in a work context – leadership matters in all areas of life, from the lofty heights of a politician leading a country, to the micro-case of a person making decisions in any given social situation. What particular qualities did the leader possess that made that person stand out for you? Now reflect on whether there are any situations in your life in which you yourself have, or could have, a leadership role? How could you bring Arnold et al.'s (2007) qualities to bear on this situation, providing idealised influence, inspirational motivation, intellectual stimulation and individualised consideration?

Finally, we can examine *values*, which are not only the property of individuals, but can be embodied in organisations, both intersubjectively (e.g., held conjointly by its members) and interobjectively (e.g., enshrined in governance charters). For example, from a strengths perspective, we can identify 'organisational-level virtues' (Peterson & Park, 2006, p. 1152). One approach to the *development* of organisational values is Spiral Dynamics (Beck & Cowan, 1996), introduced in the last chapter. In Spiral Dynamics, the developmental stages apply not only to people, but to cultures, which can also be encouraged to progress up the spiral. Van Marrewijk (2004) suggests that many companies operate at the intersection of *'blue'* (order) and *'orange'* (success) values; the result is a 'shareholder approach', where the overriding concern is with short-term financial profits (*orange*), achieved through employee obedience and organisational discipline (*blue*). However, organisations can be encouraged to evolve to a more progressive 'stakeholder approach', involving greater consideration of their wider social responsibilities (*'green'* values), and long-term strategising about how to foster the healthy, sustainable development of the organisation itself (*'yellow'* values). This evolution can be promoted by teaching the Spiral Dynamics model to leaders, helping them understand how value systems affect employee wellbeing and the success of the company, and how as climate engineers they themselves can play a key role in fostering organisational development (Robinson & Harvey, 2008). Spiral Dynamics does not only apply to business contexts, but can promote cultural change more generally, and as such has been deployed as a conflict resolution strategy in the Middle East (Volckmann & Maalouf, 2013) and the former Yugoslavia (Stambolovic, 2002).

TRY ME! . . .

A popular value-driven approach to organisational change is Appreciative Inquiry (AI). AI originated in the work of Cooperrider and Srivastva (1987), who explored ways to help organisations fulfil their potential. AI is a strengths-based approach: it involves recognising aspects of an organisation that are *already* good, and then cultivating these. Whitney and Cooperrider (2000) developed an AI protocol involving four stages (the 4D model): *Discovery* (reflecting on the organisation's signature strengths); *Dream* (identifying aspirations and imagining the organisation at its best); *Design* (developing concrete plans for achieving desired goals); and *Delivery/ destiny* (putting these plans into action). One strength of the AI model is that it is non-prescriptive and flexible, and practitioners have latitude in how they apply it in practice (Bushe, 2011). AI interventions can range from a brief one-hour session with a few leaders, to a comprehensive exercise lasting months, involving the entirety of a workforce. Perhaps you could try conducting an AI session with an organisation that you are part of. What might you achieve?

This section has discussed how the cultural values of an organisation impact upon the wellbeing of its members. However, these values are not only manifested in the nebulous form of a psychological climate, but can be instantiated in the actual structure and operation of organisations, as we explore next.

Society

Finally, we turn to the structural aspects of organisations: the overarching systems and processes that govern their operation. From a critical perspective, workplaces are not simply aggregations of people, but are hierarchical institutions, structured by power relations (Becker & Marecek, 2008). Thus, as Foucault (1973) recognised, we must be sensitive to issues around coercive power, like compulsory conformity. To understand these issues, we need to appreciate the inherent *insecurity* of modern work. For a start, there are not enough jobs to go round. In the UK in 2013, for example, 7.8% of the labour force was unemployed, with 2.5 million people looking for but unable to find work. Moreover, those *in* work are often insecure. This is partly due to the perilous economic climate since the 2008 financial crash. It is also due to dominant values in the corporate world, particularly the influence of a doctrine of 'shareholder primacy', which sees the main duty of a corporation as being to maximise shareholder returns, with the wellbeing of employees or stakeholders a secondary consideration (Jacobson, 2012). This doctrine has led to the 'financialization' of the labour market (Phillips, 1993), in which corporate downsizing and declining wages for workers are considered expedient ways to raise corporate profits (Winpenny, 1999). Financialization is aided by political actions, including labour market deregulation, which erode workers' rights (Benería, 2001). Indeed, the current UK government aims to make its workforce the 'most flexible in Europe' (HM Treasury, 2011, p. 5) – flexibility being a euphemism for deregulation – achieved through 'the lowest burdens from employment regulation in the EU' (p. 6).

These structural factors (i.e., the insecure nature of modern work) adversely affect the wellbeing factors above, such as Sauter et al.'s (1990) work stressors. For instance, deregulation proposed by the UK's Department for Business, Innovation and Skills (2013) includes 'relaxing' rules around health and safety, such as opting out of the working time directive (a regulation which alleviates workload issues). The threat of redundancy, a major stressor, has increased sharply in recent years: in the UK in 2011, 40% of the UK workforce reported feeling insecure in their jobs, up from 33% in 2004 (van Wanrooy et al., 2013). Issues around job content and lack of job control are also common in many occupations, with call centres being a paradigm case, as discussed above (Lewig & Dollard, 2003). From a J D-R perspective, such stressors can hinder the psychological drivers of engagement. For instance, job insecurity undermines PsyCap qualities such as optimism and hope. Alternatively, these structural stressors can skew the psychological drivers in pernicious ways. For instance, in light of issues around coercive power, a troubling aspect of 'aligning values' – one of Crabb's (2011) three psychological drivers – is the compulsion workers may feel to align *their* values to fit in with a corporate ethos (rather than choosing work that is consonant with their values), or else risk unemployment (Ehrenreich, 2009). For example, some workers in the financial sector are reported as being pressured to engage in practices they would not voluntarily assent to, like (mis)selling financial products (Chakrabortty, 2013). Aside from the wider social harm caused by such practices, coercion into behaviours contrary to one's values can be detrimental to the wellbeing of the workers themselves (Giacalone & Promislo, 2010). Thus, in many ways, structural aspects of work, including political/economic macrosystems, affect work conditions and employee wellbeing.

RESEARCH AND PRACTICE CASE STUDIES . . .

The recognition that structural aspects of work impact upon wellbeing is not new. Indeed, the struggle for better working conditions has been ongoing for centuries, most notably in the form of the trade union movement (Laybourn, 1997). Historically, the movement has faced considerable opposition. In 1799–1800, fearful of a civil uprising, the UK government criminalised trade unionism: anyone who 'combined with another to gain an increase in wages or a decrease in hours' faced three months in prison. However, public unrest saw the laws repealed in 1824, and the trade union movement began to develop rapidly. However, with political power still much in the hands of a wealthy aristocracy, it faced considerable opposition. For example, in 1834, six agricultural workers from the village of Tolpuddle, the so-called Tolpuddle Martyrs, were arrested for joining a union and were deported to Australia. Since then, the movement has had its successes and its defeats. In 1900 the Labour Party was created in the UK – known initially as the Labour Representation Committee – to represent the interests of workers in parliament, and in 1924 took power for the first time, with six periods in office since. The movement endured a difficult time during Margaret Thatcher's premierships as her Conservative government sought to reduce union power, with the miners' strike from 1983 to 1984 being a particularly bitter and protracted confrontation (Mclaughlin, 2005). Today, around 6.5 million people belong to a trade union in the UK, and although this is a decline from 13.5 million in 1979, it shows the continuing relevance of trade unions to many workers (Musafer, 2012).

Given these macro-level structural factors (e.g., the insecurity of the labour market), what role can PP play in this context? The distinction above between POS and POB appears to suggest two alternatives. From a POB perspective, PP is mainly about helping people deal with the realities of modern work, e.g., fostering resilience towards job insecurity. However, with this approach, there is a danger of PP being used to uphold and even justify structural aspects of work that are detrimental to wellbeing. For instance, rather than challenging a culture of downsizing, one could imagine PP being used to help companies downsize more efficiently. Indeed, Chris Peterson, one of the founders of PP, is reported as saying that 'hard-headed corporate culture' is 'leading the way' in using PP to 'get more out of fewer workers' (cited in Ehrenreich, 2009, p. 170). Such remarks give ammunition to critical theorists like Ehrenreich, who argue that PP pays insufficient attention to social context, and, more perniciously, is even used to justify the status quo, e.g., encouraging people to be resilient to their social situation, rather than helping them to *change* this situation. However, Ehrenreich (2009) suggests that we could imagine a 'more liberal' version of PP being 'a movement to alter social arrangements in the direction of greater happiness', such as 'advocating more democratically organized workplaces' (p. 170). This 'more liberal' version is reflected in the employee-driven POS, which is concerned with helping organisations promote the wellbeing of its employees, not as a means to greater productivity, but as a valuable end in itself (Cameron & Caza, 2004).

Employee wellbeing and organisational productivity are not necessarily oppositional, however, but can be synergistic. As such, perhaps the most persuasive message PP can offer organisations is that the organisation itself will do better if it takes care of its employees. It is no accident that Google, the No. 1 'Great Place to Work' in 2013, is also one of the world's most successful companies. A positive work culture is a key factor in attracting and retaining the best applicants (Smith, 2013). Indeed, this culture can matter even more to people than remuneration: cost–benefit analyses reveal that workers make a trade-off between trust and wages – an increase in social capital of one-third is 'equivalent' to a one-third increase in wages (Helliwell & Huang, 2010). Moreover, engaged employees are more productive, which of course impacts upon business outcomes (Harter et al., 2003). Furthermore, ethical behaviour by organisations – including but not limited to treatment of employees – can be rewarded via ethical consumer decision making: the ethical market in the UK is worth £47.2 billion (up from £13.5 billion in 1999), with 50% of consumers avoiding products based on a company's responsible reputation (up from 44% in 2000) (The Cooperative, 2012). Of course we would argue that employee wellbeing is an important and worthy goal in its own right. However, we are realistic in recognising that the chances of organisations taking an interest in APP depends on PP helping to promote the success of the *organisation*. In that sense, even if only for their own success, we urge all organisations to take a close interest in the wellbeing of their members.

SUMMARY – THIS CHAPTER HAS...

- Differentiated positive organizational behaviour and positive organizational scholarship
- Introduced the Job Demands-Resources (J D-R) model
- Discussed the psychological drivers of engagement: focusing strengths, managing emotions and aligning purpose
- Identified work stressors, including health and safety, workload and scheduling, and job content and control
- Introduced the notion of authentizotic organisations and psychological climate
- Articulated the importance of leadership in creating organisational-level values
- Contextualised the discussion around work in terms of broader political and economic factors

QUIZ...

1   What are the three components of Schaufeli et al.'s (2006) engagement construct?
2   How many distinct strengths are identified in the VIA taxonomy?
3   What four qualities comprise the PsyCap construct?
4   Which song did Chris Hadfield sing aboard the International Space Station?
5   What does the acronym ABCDE stand for?
6   What is the maximum number of working hours per week permitted by The European Working Time Directive?
7   In 2013, which organisation was judged by the Great Place to Work institute as the best company to work for?
8   What are the four stages of Whitney and Cooperrider's (2000) 4D AI model?
9   In 2011, what percentage of the UK workforce reported feeling insecure in their jobs?
10 How many people currently belong to a trade union in the UK?

RESOURCES AND SUGGESTIONS...

- Regarding strengths, for the VIA approach visit www.viacharacter.org, and for the Realise2 model visit www.cappeu.com/realise2.aspx.
- For information on health and safety at work in the UK, including regulations and rights, see the Health and Safety Executive website (www.hse.gov.uk). For the US equivalent, see the National Institute for Occupational Safety and Health (www.cdc.gov/niosh).

- In terms of recognising good workplace practices, the APA's Psychologically Healthy Workplace Program can be found at www.apaexcellence.org, and the Great Place to Work initiative at www.greatplacetowork.com.
- If you are interested in the trade union movement, and even in joining one, in the UK most trade unions are affiliated to the Trades Union Congress (see www.tuc.org.uk for details). For readers outside the UK, see the International Trade Union Confederation (www.ituc-csi.org).

RELIGION AND SPIRITUALITY

If the only prayer you ever say in your life
is thank you,
it will be enough.
Meister Eckhart

LIST OF TOPICS...

- Religion and spirituality
- The religion–health connection
- Self-transcendence
- The sacred
- Buddhism and Hinduism
- Acceptance and impermanence

- The four universal virtues
- The Buddhist precepts
- The five branches of yoga
- Patañjali's eight limbs of yoga
- Christianity, Islam and Judaism
- Developing PPIs from religion

In this penultimate chapter, we shift into a slightly different dimension of experience as we consider the relevance of religion and spirituality to PP. These are tricky concepts to grasp, particularly in today's globalised world, an age of dynamic change and cultural flux that Bauman (2005) refers to as 'liquid modernity'. Religion has been integral to human existence throughout recorded history, and still today, around 90% of people worldwide are thought to engage in some kind of religious or spiritual practice (Koenig, 2009). However, there are massive variations across cultures: asked 'Is religion an important part of your daily life?', the percentages of people agreeing range from 100% in Egypt to just 14% in Estonia (Crabtree & Pelham, 2009). Moreover, it is frequently asserted that religiosity is declining, particularly in ostensibly secular Western countries. For instance, in the UK, the percentage of non-religious people rose from 15.7% to 25.1% between 2005 and 2011 (Office for National Statistics, 2012). However, this so-called 'decline' is not a new phenomenon: in 1867 the poet Matthew Arnold lamented the 'melancholy, long, withdrawing roar' of the 'sea of faith'. Moreover, it is too simplistic to assert that religiosity is fading. When we consider religiosity and spirituality together, a clear majority of people in the West describe themselves as religious and/or spiritual (with even higher numbers of adherents in non-Western countries). The recent American Religious Identification Survey found that 32% of the surveyed population identified with a religious worldview, and a further 32% defined themselves as spiritual (Kosmin & Keysar, 2013). Furthermore, even if people do not currently experience life as religious or spiritual, this does not mean they do not *want* to: a survey in the US revealed that an astonishing 69% of those surveyed had a pressing need/urge to experience spiritual growth in their lives (Gallup & Johnson, 2003).

As such, even if traditional forms of religion are losing relevance for some people, having a religious and/or spiritual dimension to life is clearly important to the majority of humankind. In this chapter, we shall explore these dimensions, and examine their potential relevance to PP. The chapter is in four parts. First, we consider the link between religion/spirituality and wellbeing, often referred to as the 'religion–health connection' (Ellison & Levin, 1998). We also explore what religion and spirituality *mean*. These are conceptually ambiguous terms, and so can hold relevance for people who may not usually define themselves as religious or spiritual. In the second and third parts, we look at two phenomena that have begun to attract considerable attention in PP, and indeed in Western society at large: meditation and yoga. Through the prism of these two phenomena, by considering the religious contexts in which they were initially developed – i.e., Buddhism and Hinduism – we will explore the potential role religion and spirituality can play in our lives, and in our approach to APP. However, in focusing on meditation and yoga, this does not mean that these are the *only* ways in which people can engage with religion/spirituality in the context of PP. The message of this chapter is that *all* religious and spiritual traditions contain ideas and practices that are relevant to PP. As such, in the fourth section, we will very briefly touch on potential contributions that other religious traditions might make to PP. Thus, it bears emphasising that we are simply using meditation and yoga as *case studies* to demonstrate the broader relevance of religion/spirituality to PP. One certainly does not have to practise meditation or yoga, or identify with Buddhism or Hinduism, or even consider oneself to be religious or spiritual, to engage with this chapter, or to explore the possible value of religious/spiritual practices to PP.

PRACTICE ESSAY QUESTIONS . . .

- Critically evaluate the difference between religion and spirituality, and discuss the impact of both on wellbeing.
- How might we utilise our knowledge of religion and spirituality to create contemporary PPIs?

The religion–health connection

In this first section, we examine the link between religion/spirituality and wellbeing. However, first we need to consider what these terms mean. Throughout much of history, religion and spirituality have been inextricably linked (Sheldrake, 2007). Etymologically, the Latin term *spiritualis* is derived from the Greek *pneumatikós*, an adjective referring to the 'spirit of God'. A 'spiritual person' was thus one in whom this spirit dwelt, and often referred specifically to a particularly devout subset of the religious community (e.g., the clergy). However, in the wake of secularising trends over recent centuries, in the twentieth century the terms became increasingly differentiated. Some people found that traditional religious belief systems had lost their relevance or appeal, and yet still felt that the concept of 'spirituality' had some meaning for them. Before differentiating spirituality and religion, we need to examine a concept that bridges both of them: the sacred. This concept is particularly associated with the French sociologist Emile Durkheim (2001 (1912), p. 47), who argued for a distinction between the sacred and the profane: the latter pertained to ordinary everyday life; the former concerned 'things set apart and forbidden'. The sacred is often used to refer to divine beings (e.g., God), and places (e.g., churches) and objects (e.g., relics) connected to such beings (Hill et al., 2000). Importantly, though, it does not necessarily imply theism: it can denote 'numinous' phenomena (mystical, supernatural or sublime); in Eastern philosophies it can concern 'Ultimate Truth or Reality' (Koenig, 2009, p. 284); and it can even be simply an 'emotional state' that occurs whenever 'social actors come together in unified attention to something that is larger than themselves' (Peifer, 2012, p. 122).

REFLECTION . . .

Do you have any objects or places that are 'sacred' to you? For example, you might have a treasured possession given to you by a person who has passed away. It is likely that the subjective value of this to you far exceeds its 'objective' monetary worth or practical use – it is intimately bound up with deep personal meaning and significance, and is thus perhaps literally priceless. Reflect now on this object or place, and why it means so much to you. In doing so, even if you do not normally consider yourself as religious or spiritual, you nevertheless can understand or tap into a sense of the sacred.

Broadly speaking, then, spirituality and religion can be seen as describing different approaches to the sacred (however we define this): the former is more a personal engagement or search, whereas the latter describes a collective or institutional response. As Koenig (2009) articulates it, religion refers to a 'tradition that arises out of a group of people with common beliefs and practices concerning the sacred' (p. 284), whereas spirituality is 'something individuals define for themselves that is largely free of the rules, regulations and responsibilities associated with religion' (p. 281). Thus, religion and spirituality both involve a search for the sacred. Religion involves group-validated and group-organised *means and methods* for this search, including specific theological beliefs and prescribed forms of worship (Miller & Thoresen, 2003). Moreover, religions usually tend to be theistic, involving belief in a divine being(s), accompanied by rituals directed at that being (Argyle & Beit-Hallahmi, 1975). In contrast, spirituality is more a personal, contemplative, subjective pursuit of the sacred (Ellens, 2008). The distinction between spirituality and religion to some extent maps onto the individual–collective dichotomy that underpins the LIFE model. Spirituality is more of an individual response to the sacred, with personal beliefs and patterns of worship that can change fluidly as a person progresses on a spiritual journey. Conversely, religion is inherently social, involving cultural (e.g., relationships and shared meanings) and societal aspects (e.g., places of worship).

RESEARCH AND PRACTICE CASE STUDIES . . .

Although religion and spirituality are often intertwined – many religious people have a deep sense of spirituality – they are not necessarily so. Spirituality can appeal to people for whom traditional religious frameworks have lost their appeal, including atheists (Emmons & Paloutzian, 2003). Conversely, one might 'adopt the outward forms of religious worship' without being particularly spiritual (Fetzer Institute, 1999, p. 2), perhaps engaging more out of duty and tradition, or for its social aspects. The idea that people can be spiritual but not religious, and vice versa, was neatly demonstrated in a study by Ivtzan et al. (2011). Participants were recruited from worship services at religious centres, spiritual group meetings, lectures on spirituality, secular groups, and meetings held by religious students at a university in London. Participants were assessed on their level of spirituality and on their involvement with religious activities. Based on this assessment, participants were divided into four groups:

1 High religious involvement and high spirituality
2 Low religious involvement and high spirituality
3 High religious involvement and low spirituality
4 Low religious involvement and low spirituality

Data were also collected on three wellbeing indices: meaning in life, self-actualisation, and personal growth initiative (see below). The findings were revealing. Groups 1 and 2 scored highest on all three measures of wellbeing. Conversely, group 3 had by far the lowest wellbeing. This group was referred to as 'empty religion': participants followed the rules of their religion by implementing the obligatory means and methods, but lacked the core of the experience, i.e., the spiritual search for the sacred. Intriguingly, members of this group even had lower levels of wellbeing than people with low religious involvement *and* low spirituality (group 4). A possible explanation here is that people in the 'empty religion' group experienced a greater sense of *missing out*: involvement with religion may have thrown their own lack of spirituality into even sharper relief; in contrast, religion did not figure centrally for people in group 4, and so their lack of spirituality may have felt less aberrant or problematic. The study thus identified spirituality as a key intermediary between religious engagement and wellbeing.

As indicated in the study by Ivtzan et al. (2011), there is a strong link between religion/spirituality and wellbeing (although if one engages with religion without necessarily having a sense of spirituality, the link is less clear). We can examine this connection using the LIFE model, exploring the impact of being religious and/ or spiritual on its four domains. In terms of the subjective domain (the mind), two key outcomes are a sense of meaning/purpose in life, and the development of adaptive psychological qualities. First, religion/spirituality can provide a sense of meaning, providing comprehensibility (understanding existence) and significance (endowing one's own life with purpose) (Steger & Frazier, 2005). It is notable that Peifer's (2012) definition of the sacred, cited above, mirrors Seligman et al.'s (2006, p. 777) contention that meaning is found through serving and belonging to 'something that one believes is bigger than the self'. Having a religious/spiritual framework of meaning can then facilitate other positive psychological outcomes, including providing a clear and coherent identity, which can engender self-worth and confidence (Elliott & Hayward, 2007); helping allay existential fears, lifting the burden of mortality (Kramer, 1988); and providing a 'buffer' against trauma, e.g., giving solace in bereavement through belief in the afterlife (Ando et al., 2010). Second, religious/spiritual frameworks often promote positive psychological qualities. This is not always the case: religions can also foster corrosive outcomes like pathological guilt (Faiver et al., 2000), homophobia (Finlay & Walther, 2003) or violent fanaticism (Stern, 2006). However, religions more commonly engender qualities that are conducive to wellbeing, such as forgiveness (McCullough & Worthington, 1999), gratitude (Krause, 2009), compassion (Steffen & Masters, 2005) and hope (Moadel et al., 1999). A particularly valuable quality is self-transcendence (Piedmont, 1999), which is explored in the box below.

PSYCHOMETRIC SCALES . . .

Transcendence is at the heart of spiritual experience. What is it that we transcend? We transcend the narrow, confining constructs of our limited self-identity – e.g., the belief we are an isolated individual, perhaps defined by our personality or our occupation – to identify with something that is 'bigger than the self' (Seligman et al., 2006, p. 777). In religious/spiritual experience, this 'something bigger' is the sacred, whether we define this as God, Ultimate Truth, universal consciousness, or just a powerful, inchoate sense that the universe is a meaningful mystery that is beyond our comprehension. The Spiritual Transcendence Scale (Piedmont, 2004) assesses one's ability to disengage from one's immediate sense of time and place, and experience life from a larger, more objective perspective. This transcendent outlook invites and enables the individual to experience the unity underlying the different aspects of nature. Using the scale below, write down the extent to which you agree or disagree with each statement, choosing from: *strongly agree*, *agree*, *neutral*, *disagree* and *strongly disagree*.

	Answer	Score
1 In the quiet of my prayers and /or meditations, I find a sense of wholeness.	_____	____
2 In my life I have done things because I believed it would please a parent, relative, or friend that had died.	_____	____
3 Though dead, memories and thoughts of some of my relatives continue to influence my current life.	_____	____
4 I find inner strength and/or peace from my prayers and/or meditations.	_____	____

5 I do not have any strong emotional ties to someone
   who has died.   _____ _____

6 There is no higher plane of consciousness or spirituality
   that binds all people.   _____ _____

7 Although individual people may be difficult, I feel an emotional
   bond with all of humanity.   _____ _____

8 My prayers and/or meditations provide me with a sense of
   emotional support.   _____ _____

9 I feel that on a higher level all of us share a
   common bond.   _____ _____

                                                       Total = _____

To score the scale, points are assigned to your responses for each item. For items 1, 2, 3, 4, 7, 8 and 9, assign 5 points for each *strongly agree* response, 4 for *agree*, 3 for *neutral*, 2 for *disagree* and 1 for *strongly disagree*. For items 5 and 6, the opposite applies: give 1 point for each *strongly agree*, 2 for *agree*, 3 for *neutral*, 4 for *disagree* and 5 for *strongly disagree*. Add together your scores for all nine items. Higher scores are interpreted as being indicative of greater levels of spiritual transcendence.

Religion/spirituality can also engender wellbeing via the other domains of the LIFE model. First, in terms of the body, religious participation is associated with health behaviours, generally mediated by prescriptions/proscriptions associated with religious ethical frameworks. For example, many religions place prohibitions on alcohol consumption, with religiosity thus linked to reduced alcohol use (Burris et al., 2011). Second, religion and spirituality are effective vehicles at promoting the social aspects of wellbeing. Religious involvement is almost by definition a collective act, both in intersubjective terms (sharing beliefs and practices with fellow adherents) and in interobjective terms (attending common places of worship). Religions are thus highly effective at providing cultural and structural support for the cultivation of social capital, as they encourage 'long-term investments of time and energy and exchange relations, within contexts governed by norms of trust, reciprocity and mutual obligation' (Sherkat & Ellison, 1999, p. 375). Even if one is not part of a religious tradition or community, but is more spiritually independent, such spirituality is nevertheless usually associated with the cultivation of prosocial qualities like compassion, and consequently with enhanced interpersonal connectedness (Hollingsworth, 2008).

So, we have elucidated the conceptual links between religion/spirituality and wellbeing. However, as emphasised throughout the book, our concern here is not only at the theoretical level. Praxis is crucial to our vision of PP; thus our task here is to explore how we might harness religious and spiritual ideas and practices in

PP to better promote wellbeing. To this end, we shall explore two phenomena which promise to broaden the scope of PP, and enhance wellbeing by introducing a sacred dimension into our lives: meditation and yoga. It is important to emphasise that these two phenomena are not the only religious/spiritual practices of relevance to PP. All great religious/spiritual traditions have a venerable history of engaging with issues around wellbeing and the nature of the good life, and have developed theoretical and practical approaches to engender happiness and personal growth. As such, we contend that PP has much to learn from all these traditions. However, other traditions have hitherto not received the kind of attention or appreciation that PP, and psychology generally, have bestowed upon meditation and yoga. Consequently, we submit that one of the tasks for PP going forward is to explore these traditions, harnessing their ideas and practices to develop PPIs and therapies in the same way that Kabat-Zinn (1982) did so successfully with mindfulness and Buddhism. Thus, we are focusing here on meditation and yoga precisely because these are the religious/spiritual practices that have received the most attention in psychology, and so constitute useful case studies for the adoption of such practices into PP. Therefore, while in future PP will hopefully engage with other traditions to further our understanding of how to promote wellbeing, meditation and yoga are a good place to start!

Meditation and Buddhism

In Chapter 2, we introduced various meditation-based practices, highlighting mindfulness in particular as one that has been enthusiatically embraced in PP, and psychology more generally. Indeed, from a wider perspective, it is remarkable the rate at which meditation has become a prominent feature of the cultural landscape of the West, discussed widely in the media (e.g., CNN, 2013), used in commercials (even for beer!; Advertising and Commercial Archives, 2012), recommended for expectant/new mothers (Vieten, 2009), taught to elite athletes (Bertollo et al., 2009), deployed in rehabilitating prisoners (Bowen et al., 2006), given to schoolchildren (Erricker & Erricker, 2001) and harnessed in business settings (Schmidt-Wilk et al., 1996). However, in this process of cultural transmission to the West, meditation has to some extent been 'de-contextualised', i.e., shorn of its antecedent roots in Hindu and Buddhist religions (Shapiro, 1994). Many people practise meditation in a secular way, e.g., using mindfulness simply as a stress-reduction technique. Indeed, King (1999) suggests that it is precisely the ease with which meditation *can* be shorn of its religious connections and packaged as a relaxation tool that has enabled it to take root and flourish in secular Western societies. One may further argue that this de-contextualisation was *necessary* for meditation to cease to be seen in academia as an esoteric 'occult' religious activity and to be accepted as a legitimate topic for scientific enquiry and clinical application. However, now that meditation *has* attained this acceptance, we might benefit from *re*-contextualising it, exploring the religious context in which it was originally developed, and considering the role that meditation (and its deeper religious context) might play in engendering spiritual engagement.

Many meditation practices derive from Buddhism, a tradition built around the teachings of Siddhartha Gautama, better known by the honorific *Buddha*, meaning 'Enlightened one'. Gautama is believed to have been born in Lumbini, in present-day Nepal, around 480 BCE (Cousins, 1996), although this date is disputed (Coningham et al., 2013). Our understanding of the origins of Buddhism is coloured by the lack of historicity of the source documents (Harvey, 2012). However, the mythologised narrative of Gautama's life describes him living a sheltered existence until age 29, when a series of encounters with people who were ill or dying compelled him to pursue a religious path dedicated to exploring the 'human condition' (Kumar, 2002). After five years of undertaking austere yogic practices – his cultural context was one informed by Hinduism – he felt that self-mortification was unhelpful and decided to pursue a 'middle path' (between indulgence and asceticism). He resolved to meditate until he gained enlightenment, and sat beneath a tree for 49 days until, aged 35, it was attained. He then spent the next 45 years formulating and propagating his insights, known by the Sanskrit term *Dharma*, meaning 'laws' or 'how things are' (Kabat-Zinn, 2003). A key teaching is the Four Noble Truths, a remedy akin to a medical diagnosis for alleviating suffering: suffering is universal; it has a cause; cessation is possible; it can be achieved by following the Noble Eightfold Path. This path is a prescription for 'right living', including wisdom (right vision and conception), ethical conduct (right speech, conduct and livelihood) and meditation (right effort, mindfulness and concentration) (Thrangu, 1993).

ART LINKS . . .

Films can be powerful artistic vehicles, combining narrative, character, music and visual aesthetics to convey messages with the potential to move us deeply. A particularly beautiful and poignant film that pertains to religion and spirituality is the 2003 Korean classic 'Spring, summer, autumn, winter… and spring'. Living in a hut in the middle of a lake in the mountainous wilderness, an old Buddhist master raises a young boy, instructing him in the ways of wisdom and compassion. The film movingly charts the seasons of the boy's life until, turning full circle, he becomes an old man. It is a deeply affecting spiritual meditation on the cycle of life. Please do watch the film, and see what impact it has on you. What films or artworks have you encountered that move you deeply on a religious or spiritual level?

Over the centuries, Buddhism has flowered into a vast and comprehensive system of interconnected ideas and practices, with divergent traditions developing the original teachings in varied ways. While in this chapter we can but scratch the surface of Buddhism, we will briefly touch upon three particular aspects – wisdom, compassion and ethics – and explore their relevance to PP. Regarding wisdom, the first two components of the Eightfold Path, right vision and conception, emphasise the importance of attaining insight into the nature of existence. Buddhism teaches that all phenomena are fundamentally impermanent, subject to change – objects decay, bodies age, people pass away. More fundamentally, this includes one's own self: we have no independent, enduring existence, but are simply a temporary constellation of fleeting components. Crucially, people generally do not appreciate this impermanent nature of existence, and instead become attached to phenomena. This attachment is seen as being primarily responsible for suffering. In particular, attachment to the idea of a 'self' generates negative emotions like greed (coveting desirables for the self) and hatred (for that which threatens the self). Based on these insights, Buddhism holds that alleviation of suffering can be found through deep *acceptance* of impermanence. So, what relevance might this philosophy hold for PP? Buddhist ideas on acceptance have begun to influence contemporary therapies, notably acceptance and commitment therapy (Hayes, 2002). Moreover, we can develop PPIs to engender acceptance, perhaps drawing on various beautiful meditations composed by the renowned Buddhist teacher Thich Naht Hanh (Hanh, 1993), which Hamilton et al. (2006, p. 128) suggest combine 'the best traditions' of cognitive behavioural therapy and PP.

A second key facet of Buddhism is its promotion of four universal virtues: benevolence, compassion, joy and equanimity. This has already influenced PP: the creation of the VIA ('values-in-action') strengths framework was a result of exploring Buddhist and other religious texts, looking for universal virtues (Dahlsgaard et al., 2005). Let us here focus on compassion, as this is arguably the most important: the Dalai Lama (His Holiness the Dalai Lama, 1997, p. 64) calls this the 'essence' of Buddhism, which indeed is often referred to as a 'religion of compassion' (Price, 2010). Of course, compassion is not only advocated by Buddhism but by most religions. In Christianity, St Paul's three theological virtues are faith, hope and charity. Charity, arguably better translated as love (Dahlsgaard et al., 2005) and viewed as equivalent to compassion (Barad, 2007), was declared by St Thomas Aquinas (1981 (1273)) to be the most important. This emphasis on compassion in Christianity serves to reinforce the point that all religious/spiritual traditions have valuable lessons to offer PP – one certainly does not have to practise or identify with Buddhism to be persuaded by the value of developing qualities like compassion and acceptance. Indeed, the significance of compassion is beginning to be recognised in PP, where it is seen as a crucial component of wellbeing (Neff, 2003). So, what is compassion? Etymologically, it means 'to suffer with'. Neff defines it as 'opening one's awareness to others' pain . . . so that feelings of kindness toward others and the desire to alleviate their suffering emerge' (p. 87). The Dalai Lama (p. 49) suggests it involves two key components: wisdom ('one must understand the nature of the suffering from which we wish to free others') and loving kindness ('deep intimacy and empathy with other sentient beings'). PP has begun to develop PPIs to develop compassion, notably loving-kindness meditation (LKM), introduced in Chapter 2.

TRY ME! . . .

LKM is a technique used to increase feelings of warmth and care for the self and for others (Salzberg, 1995). Whereas mindfulness meditation invites you to focus your attention on the present in an open-minded, accepting and non-judgemental way, LKM encourages you to open-heartedly contemplate and generate warm and tender feelings. In Fredrickson et al.'s (2008) classic study, a seven-week LKM intervention was given to employees of a software company. Corroborating Fredrickson's (2005) 'broaden-and-build' theory, participants experienced increases in positive emotions, which in turn built up their personal resources (e.g., purpose in life, social support and mindfulness), subsequently enhancing life satisfaction. If you would like to try LKM for yourselves, please follow our guidelines below. This version of LKM involves five stages. Try to spend a few minutes on each stage.

- **Sit comfortably. Any position will do.** Close your eyes and take a few deep breaths. Inhale and exhale slowly, consciously relax your muscles, and prepare your body and mind for deep awareness of love and compassion.
- *Stage 1 – choose a person you love.* Choose someone who you love easily and naturally, rather than someone for whom you feel an emotionally complicated love.
- **Focus on the area around your heart.** Put your hand over your heart. Once you are able to focus on it, imagine breathing in and out through your heart. Take several deep breaths and feel your heart breathing.
- **Turn your attention to feelings of gratitude and love**, dwelling on any warm and tender feelings that you have for your chosen person.
- *Stage 2 – send loving kindness and compassion to yourself.* Imagine that the warm glow of love and compassion coming from your heart is moving throughout your body. Send these feelings up and down your body. If verbal content is easier for you to connect to, you can repeat these words as you breathe in and out: '*May I be happy*' (breathing in), '*may I be well*' (breathing out), '*may I be safe*' (breathing in), '*may I be peaceful and at ease*' (breathing out).

(Continued)

(Continued)

- ***Stage 3*** **– send loving kindness and compassion to family and friends.** Picture friends and family as vividly as you can, and imagine the warm glow of love and compassion that comes from your heart moving into their hearts. Again, if it helps to articulate your feelings, repeat the phrases above, switching 'you' for 'I': '*May you be happy … may you be well … may you be safe … may you be peaceful and at ease*'.
- ***Stage 4*** **– expand the circle** by sending your loving kindness and compassion to neighbours, acquaintances, strangers, animals, and finally people with whom you have difficulties.
- ***Stage 5*** **– imagine planet earth, with all of its inhabitants**, and send loving kindness and compassion to all living beings.

A third important contribution Buddhism might make to PP is its system of morals/ethics. Morals are 'notions of right and wrong' (Hazard, 1994, p. 451), while ethics refers to communal recognition and promotion of these notions as 'norms shared by a group' (p. 453). Moral/ethical behaviour is central to Buddhism, constituting three facets of the Eightfold Path (right speech, conduct and livelihood). Like most religions, Buddhism has a codified system of prescriptions/proscriptions, encouraging particular forms of behaviour and discouraging others (Dahlsgaard et al., 2005). Specifically, Buddhism has five precepts, which encourage abstinence from harming living beings, taking the not given (i.e., theft), misconduct concerning sense pleasures (e.g., sexual misconduct), false speech (i.e., lying) and un-mindful states related to consumption of alcohol or drugs. So, why are these relevant to PP? It is not the case in Buddhism that contravening these prescriptions is met with any divine retribution. Rather, they are encouraged because following them is thought to be *beneficial to wellbeing*. Acting ethically not only benefits others – although this is an important aspect of ethics, particularly given the standing Buddhism gives to compassion – but affects the actor themselves. Buddhism teaches that if one acts unethically, adverse consequences are liable to occur as a result, internally (one will likely experience negative thoughts) and externally (people may harm you in return) (Harvey, 2012). Unfortunately, although analysis of religious ethics informed the idea of signature strengths (Peterson & Seligman, 2004), there has generally been little consideration of the importance of moral/ethical behaviour in PP (Sundararajan, 2005). However, we can redress this lacuna in future, not only through a consideration of religious precepts, but by exploring other ethical frameworks, as discussed in Chapter 8.

RESEARCH AND PRACTICE CASE STUDIES . . .

In this chapter we are seeking to 're-contextualise' meditation, connecting it to its Buddhist roots, and exploring what relevance these roots might have for PP. Interestingly, studies suggest that people who take up meditation often also go on their own personal journey of re-contextualisation. In Chapter 4, we highlighted research by Lomas (2014) exploring the experiences of male meditators who became involved with a Buddhist centre. Many of these men only took up meditation in the hope of finding better ways to cope with stress (Lomas et al., 2013a). However, over time, most men came to find a deeper sense of wellbeing through engaging with a broader Buddhist path – the *dharma* – of which meditation was only one component (Lomas et al., 2014a). As one said: '*The Dharma is a much broader thing than merely practising meditation. … It includes ethical behaviour, developing friendship, study, ritual, reflection*.' The appeal of Buddhism was manifold. Having lacked a moral framework to guide them previously, some men found meaning in following the precepts. One man said: '*It's all about non-violence and generosity really, and that seems a pretty good way to live.*' Most men found the Buddhist community – the *sangha* – a great source of friendship and support, which contrasted with the loneliness many had previously experienced. Others appreciated taking on values, like compassion, which some felt that *as men* had been closed off to them before, as detailed in Chapter 4. These men's journeys of re-contextualisation can be seen as adventures of self-discovery and development (Lomas et al., 2014b). Perhaps PP is also on a similar path?

As a final consideration in our 're-contextualisation' of meditation, let us return to the concept which we identified above as being central to religion and spirituality: the sacred. Fundamentally, in their deepest and most profound aspects, religious and/or spiritual engagement are not about following ethical rules or cultivating particular attitudinal states, but aiming for something far more radical – union with the sacred. We are straying into esoteric territory here, and so we shall tread carefully and not become wrapped up in complex and abstruse discussions around the metaphysical nature of this union. We shall just say that, through meditation, Buddhism seeks to engender the kind of self-transcendence which we introduced above. (Likewise, other religious/spiritual traditions have their own vehicles for attaining self-transcendence.) Indeed, a revealing longitudinal study examining the evolving motivations of experienced meditators found that these motives progressed from an initial concern with self-regulation (control over self), moved on to self-exploration (knowledge of self) and finally reached self-liberation (transcendence of self) (Shapiro, 1992). Although ideas such as self-liberation are tricky to conceptualise, we might view this as the development of meta-consciousness capacities, represented in our LIFE model as the level awareness+. As noted in Chapter 2, theorists argue that conscious awareness can be superseded by advanced developmental capacities such as non-dual awareness, the ability to experience a bare field of awareness (Josipovic, 2010). Some religious texts suggest that this 'unitive state', in which one does not experience oneself existing as a separate individual, represents union with the sacred, with the divine 'ground of being' (Wilber, 2007). While we are not in a position to comment on the validity of this interpretation, it does give an indication of the way in which PPIs like meditation might intersect with religious/spiritual teachings.

RESEARCH AND PRACTICE CASE STUDIES . . .

Goldstein (2007) has developed an innovative five-day intervention to help people cultivate 'sacred moments'. On the first three days, participants are taught mindfulness. On the third day, they select an object that is precious and meaningful to them, such as a childhood possession, or even a special memory. Then, on the fourth day, participants engage in 'sanctification of the object'. Sanctification refers to a psycho-spiritual process through which 'aspects of life are perceived as having divine character and significance' (Pargament & Mahoney, 2005, p. 180). Participants are encouraged to reflect mindfully on the object, paying special attention to what makes that object so personally meaningful, imbuing it with a sense of being blessed and holy (not in a theological sense, but in the sense of being sacred to oneself). On the fifth day (and onwards), participants are exhorted to spend at least five minutes a day contemplating the object, being 'open to what [is] sacred in the moment'. In the study, compared to a control group (who wrote about daily events), participants enjoyed significant increases in SWB, PWB and spiritual experiences, effects which, moreover, persisted at the six-week follow-up assessment.

Buddhism is of course not the only religion with useful lessons for PP, nor do meditation-based PPIs exhaust the types of intervention we can adopt from existing religious traditions. To illustrate this point, we shall focus on another spiritual practice, yoga, and on the Hindu religion that engendered it.

Yoga and Hinduism

In contemporary Western culture, yoga is perhaps as pervasive and popular as meditation. In the US, an estimated 16 million adults maintain a regular practice (Quilty et al., 2013), spending almost $6 billion a year on yoga classes and products in the process (Macy, 2008). However, as with meditation, yoga has arguably become de-contextualised from the deeper religious/spiritual context in which it was developed. Frequently, when people think of yoga what comes to mind is a somewhat athletic discipline involving various more or less difficult physical postures, being 'often thought of as the headstand, the lotus posture, or another pretzel-like pose' (Chauhan, 1992, p. 21). Moreover, Chauhan suggests that these postures are often conceptualised as 'ends in themselves merely to heal an illness, reduce stress, or look better'. As we shall see, this conceptualisation overlooks the great potential for yoga as a comprehensive system of personal development. Chauhan continues: 'The fact that these postures are a foundation for self-realization is generally ignored.' Similarly, when yoga has been studied in clinical settings, it has largely been analysed simply as a beneficial exercise activity for medical conditions, whether psychopathological disorders (e.g. depression), cardiovascular issues (e.g. hypertension and heart disease), respiratory problems (e.g. asthma) or illnesses like diabetes or cancer. A review by Khalsa (2007) showed that one-third of all yoga studies examined depression, followed by – in descending order – anxiety, addictive disorders, and various other psychopathological conditions. So far, the notion that yoga might be a path to personal development and higher levels of psychological functioning – i.e., the PP prerogative – has effectively been overlooked.

TRY ME! . . .

Go online to Google Scholar (or any other literature search engine). Search for the phrases 'yoga and depression', 'yoga and anxiety', 'yoga and cancer', or 'yoga and stress'. Now search for 'yoga and happiness', 'yoga and meaning', or 'yoga and flow'. Do you see a difference? Consider the fact that in a discipline like yoga, which aims at wellbeing and spirituality, research has mostly been conducted in relation to illness and psychopathology. Exploring its 'positive' potential is a future task for PP.

So, what is the deeper religious/spiritual context of yoga? As with meditation, its origins are shrouded in the mists of history. Yoga refers collectively to a system of physical, mental and spiritual teachings originating in India around the sixth century BCE (Feuerstein, 2002). However, its origins may stretch back much farther: excavations in the Indus valley revealed earthenware seals dated to the second millennia BCE which depict figures seated in a cross-legged meditation posture (Varenne, 1977). (These discoveries show yoga to be the historical progenitor of meditation. Indeed, the religious/spiritual culture that developed in that part of the world, which we now refer to as Hinduism, was the context in which the Buddha lived, with Hindu philosophy suffused throughout his teachings.) The textual origins of Hinduism are the *Vedas*, composed between 1500 and 500 BCE (Kramer, 1986). Their contents were initially chanted and memorised, and were later recorded in Sanskrit. The Vedas comprise four main texts: *Rig-veda* (mantras); *Sama-veda* (songs); *Yajur-veda* (rituals); and *Atharva-veda* (spells). The concluding sections of the four Vedas – the *Vedanta* – are known as the *Upanishads*, composed between 800 and 500 BCE. The Upanishads are esoteric spiritual teachings on the divine origins of the universe and the transcendent dimensions of life. The oldest Upanishad, the *Brihad Aranyaka*, elucidates the idea of *Brahman* as the sacred absolute power and creator of the universe (Dahlsgaard et al., 2005). Expounding on this idea, the Upanishads argue for the interconnectedness of existence, with all things ultimately leading back to Brahman in a cycle of death–rebirth. Self-transcendence and liberation are found through realising that the essence of the self – the soul or *atman* – ultimately *is* Brahman, i.e., the self is a manifestation of the eternal, universal, sacred Ultimate Reality (Firth, 2005).

It was in this Hindu context that yoga was developed. The Sanskrit word *yoga* has various meanings and is derived from the root *yuj*, which is translated as 'to unite' or 'to yoke' (harness). That is, yoga is used to unite or yoke together the different aspects of our being – i.e., the various levels and domains of the LIFE model, including mind, body and 'spirit' (which we are referring to here as awareness+) – so that we experience unity. In contrast to the general Western perception of yoga as a sequence of physical postures, yogic philosophy and practice involves different branches, of which the postures are but one aspect (Feuerstein, 2002). While there are many branches of yoga – as many as 12 in some taxonomies – five of the most prominent are:

- **Rāja Yoga**: The path of meditation. This branch was systematised by the renowned historical figure of Patañjali, who authored the canonical Yoga Sutras (Satchidananda, 2012), possibly in the second century BCE (Brown & Gerberg, 2009). Rāja yoga is discussed further below.
- **Karma Yoga**: The path of service. The philosophical doctrine of *karma* is a metaphysical principle of cause and effect: whatever happens to us is related to our past actions, while our current actions influence future experiences (Mulla & Krishnan, 2006). Karma yoga focuses on selflessness and serving others (partly as a way to cultivate favourable future outcomes).
- **Bhakti Yoga**: The path of devotion. This branch is the yoga of the heart, a spiritual practice of cultivating love (Halstead & Mickley, 1997). Every thought, word and deed is seen as an opportunity to express love, thereby embodying the sacred. One might view the caring actions of a figure like Mother Theresa as an example of bhakti yoga (Coffey, 2012).
- **Jnana Yoga**: The path of study and knowledge. If bhakti is the yoga of the heart, jnana is the yoga of the mind. Spiritual development is pursued primarily through the cultivation of the intellect, involving devoted study of yogic philosophy and Hindu scripture.

- **Hatha Yoga**: The practice of *asanas* (postures). This branch refers to physical postures, often undertaken in specific sequences, accompanied by breathing techniques, that 'unify body and mind' by training one's attention on the body (Sawni & Breuner, 2012). As suggested above, in the West our understanding of yoga is often limited to this one branch (Chauhan, 1992).

In terms of our LIFE model of wellbeing, if we were to limit our understanding of yoga to the hatha branch, we might simply view yoga as a practice pertaining to the individual-objective domain of the body/brain. Or, if we focus on the meditative aspects of yoga, we might place it within the individual-subjective domain of the mind. Then again, if we consider the etymology of yoga as being to 'unite' body and mind, we might situate yoga at the intersection of these two individual domains, subjective and objective. However, when we consider karma and bhakti yoga, we can see that we are touching upon the collective domains too, since our concern in these is with the interconnected nature of existence and with cultivating loving relationships. Thus, we can regard yoga as a comprehensive system of *praxis* that touches upon all aspects of wellbeing. Moreover, the various branches of yoga have parallels with the PP concept of signature strengths. We all have different ways of expressing ourselves, our unique path. As with signature strengths, we can engage with the branch of yoga that resonates most with us, and use this as a path to personal growth. So, as a form of praxis, yoga is a perfect example of APP. It is not just an abstract intellectual exercise, but a thoroughly practical methodology, involving a life-changing engagement with practices that can easily be defined as PPIs. As Ospina et al. (2007, p. 38, our italics) put it, 'the rules or precepts set down in the first systematic work on Yoga, Patañjali's Yoga Sutras, do not set forth a philosophy, but are *practical instructions* for attaining certain psychological states'. So, we can now consider various yogic practices, which can be regarded as PPIs, to explore what yoga has to offer PP in terms of enhancing wellbeing.

RESEARCH AND PRACTICE CASE STUDIES . . .

Ivtzan and Papantoniou (2014) recently examined the intersection of yoga and PP in a paper entitled 'Yoga meets positive psychology: Examining the integration of hedonic (gratitude) and eudaimonic (meaning) wellbeing in relation to the extent of yoga practice'. The study looked at 124 people with varying levels of yoga experience (from none to over six years), assessed in terms of the number of years for which these individuals had practised yoga at least twice a week. The participants completed the Meaning in Life Questionnaire (MLQ) and the Gratitude Questionnaire (GQ-6). The findings revealed a positive relationship between the extent of a person's yoga practice and their level of meaning in life and gratitude.

Patañjali's Yoga Sutras, also known as rāja yoga, comprise 196 *sutras* – meaning thread/line, written in Sanskrit – covering many aspects of life, beginning with a code of conduct and culminating in the goal of yoga, attaining one's 'true Self', i.e., mystical union with Brahman (Satchidananda, 2012). One of the most important sutras states is *Yoga citta vritti nirodhah* (Chapter 1, v. 2), which translates as 'yoga is the resolution of the agitations of the mind'. Thus, yoga aims towards the attainment of a state of mind that dissolves and resolves the ceaseless chatter and comment of discursive thoughts, leaving only the freedom of stillness. The conceptual overlap between yoga and meditation is evident here. The next sutra states *Tada drastuh svarupe vasthanam* (Chapter 1, v. 3): 'Then the seer [awareness, consciousness] abides in its own nature.' This state is what we are refering to here as 'awareness+'. The observer (conscious awareness) transcends the self (ceases to identify with narrow identity constructs) and experiences connection with the sacred. According to yogic tradition, this transcendence is a state of unconditional bliss, peace and love (Wilber, 2007). The level of discipline and training required to reach this state means few people are perhaps capable of attaining it in any stable or enduring way. However, many of us may have had glimpses of such bliss on rare occasions, the type of event Maslow (1972) described as 'peak experiences'. Wong (2009) refers to this as *chaironic* happiness, from the Greek root *chairo*, meaning blessing or joy. In contrast to hedonic and to some extent eudaimonic wellbeing, chaironic happiness is inherently spiritual: the self is transcended and one experiences a sense of unity with something greater than the self (whatever name we give to this something).

REFLECTION . . .

Have you ever experienced chaironic happiness? This could be the kind of happiness and joy you feel standing on a mountain top and watching the sun set. Suddenly everything falls into place, and one is flooded with an overwhelming surge of love. Or it could be the first time a person sets eyes on their newborn child, or the instant when you feel yourself falling in love with another person, or simply a quiet transcendent moment when everything seems just perfect with the world as it is. If you have felt this state, try to recall it, and dwell in the memory of it. How might it feel to inhabit this state more of the time? Perhaps through yoga or meditation you might find a path to help you make this a reality?

Patañjali's sutras are essentially a technical manual, describing a structured stage-wise developmental path – known as the 'eight limbs' of yoga – designed to help one attain self-transcendence. The first limb is *Yama*, the beginning of the yogic path: this step concerns ethical behaviour, including *ahimsa* (non-violence) and *satya* (truthfulness), both of which are vital for self-growth. (There are parallels here with the Buddhist precepts. Indeed, it is argued that Patañjali's work was influenced by Buddhist teachings, and vice versa. More specifically, it is suggested that Patañjali's work was a response by Hinduism to the growing popularity of Buddhism at that time (Johnson, 2012).) The second limb is *Niyama*, which concerns self-discipline and spiritual observation, and includes *santosha* (contentment) and *swadhayaya* (self-study). Here the path develops, moving from one's relationship with others and the environment to one's relationship with one's own self. The third limb is *Asana*, which mainly deals with the practice of physical postures. According to yogic tradition, the body is the temple of the spirit and therefore is key to our spiritual growth. Physical practice allows people to direct their awareness to their body, thus 'uniting' it with the mind. The fourth limb is *Pranayama*. This stage teaches breath control and awareness. As one gains mastery over the breathing process, one recognises the connection between mind, breath and body in a way that enhances self-awareness. These first four stages allow us to refine our self-development and self-knowledge; this is in preparation for the final four stages, which lead us deeper into meditation.

The fifth limb is *Pradyahara*. This stage teaches withdrawal or sensory transcendence; one is aware of the external world, yet learns how to detach from sensory input. Levenson et al. (2012) illustrated this stage by using functional magnetic resonance imaging (fMRI) to study the startle response of an experienced meditator: relative to control subjects, the meditator had significantly weaker physiological responses to noise – he was aware of stimuli, but was less reactive. The sixth limb is *Dharana* – focused attention (FA) on a mental object. (Recall in Chapter 2 that the first parameter for differentiating meditation practices was 'behaviours of mind', which distinguished between FA and 'open-monitoring' (OM) (Lutz et al., 2008).) Notice how each stage prepares us for the next one: it would be hard to maintain a single-pointed focus if one had not already developed non-reactivity. The seventh limb is *Meditation*. Here, this refers to OM, where awareness is relaxed and open, with no focal point; the mind is quiet and deep stillness is experienced. The eighth and final limb is *Samadhi*, in which the meditating yogi reaches self-transcendence. In Samadhi, one feels a profound connection to the sacred, together with deep feelings of bliss and interconnectedness with all living beings. This is the final stage of yogic transformation, a state that many spiritual teachings refer to as enlightenment (Wilber, 1995). Paradoxically, this omega point of personal development is the very point at which one ceases to experience oneself as a separate person, and enters into an experiential union with the sacred.

There are many different varieties of yoga on offer in the world today, with various styles to suit all kinds of tastes and temperament. A popular form is Iyengar yoga (www. bksiyengar.com), founded by B.K.S. Iyengar (born 1918), which is based on Patañjali's eight limbs. Another prominent type is Ashtanga Vinyāsa (www.ashtanga.com), popularised by Sri K. Pattabhi Jois (1915–2009), which has a progressive, dynamic series of postures. Perhaps you could find a class near you and give it a try?

Religion, spirituality and positive psychology

In this chapter, we have touched upon ideas and practices that would perhaps be considered esoteric by mainstream psychology. Nevertheless, in contemplating the journeys offered by yoga and meditation, it is clear that these have many meeting points with the journey offered by PP: yoga, meditation and PP all offer an invitation for a *psycho-spiritual* transformation, and share a deep interest in concepts like meaning, acceptance, awareness, development, compassion and love. However, our knowledge and understanding of the kind of personal transformation offered by practices such as meditation and yoga is only in its infancy. The task of PP is to help develop a systematic scientific understanding of these disciplines – without losing a sense of wonder and appreciation of their sacred dimensions – so that we can better help people achieve greater wellbeing. Moreover, our interest in the potential value of religion/spirituality to PP should not stop at Buddhism and Hinduism. We have focused on these two traditions, with their associated practices of meditation and yoga, as these practices have been widely studied and utilised in clinical settings. As such, these practices, particularly meditation, are already being brought into psychology and harnessed in APP as the basis for PPIs. However, the other great religious/spiritual traditions have likewise spent centuries developing ideas and practices to encourage wellbeing, personal development and ultimately salvation (however we interpret this).

Do you personally affiliate to and engage with a particular religious or spiritual tradition? Are there any aspects of this tradition – rituals, practices, beliefs, aesthetics, communal participation – that you find particularly rewarding or fulfilling? What kind of PPIs might we develop on the basis of these?

As such, all traditions may have valuable lessons to offer PP. Our task going forward is to explore and engage with these traditions, such that we might develop new PPIs and further our understanding of how to promote wellbeing. For example, most traditions have their own forms of meditation. We may be able to develop other meditation-based PPIs from these forms, including: contemplative prayer in Christianity (Ryan, 2001); visualisation prayers in Kabbalistic Judaism, e.g., imagining the name of God written in letters that are 'infinitely large' (Kaplan, 1989, p. 142); 'Islamic relaxation' techniques that incorporate prayer and recitation of the holy Qur'an (Mardiyono et al., 2011); and 'Sama' in Sufi Islam, which involves 'reverently listening to music and/or the singing of mystical poetry' (Lewisohn, 1997, p. 3). Or, we might develop interventions based on the ethical frameworks of these traditions. For instance, Hackney (2007) has examined the intersection of PP and Christianity under the rubric of Christian Positive Psychology. Similarly, Jafari (1993) has considered the relevance of incorporating Islamic values into counselling practice. One does not have to follow or adhere to these traditions to potentially benefit from their values, ideas and practices, as emphasised by Alain de Botton (2012) in his book *Religion for Atheists*. Moreover, these suggestions here are only scratching the surface of a great, deep ocean of wisdom, accumulated and developed over the centuries. In exploring this ocean further, PP has an exciting journey ahead of it.

SUMMARY – THIS CHAPTER HAS…

- Differentiated religion and spirituality, and considered the relevance of the sacred to PP
- Explored the impact of religion and spirituality on wellbeing using the LIFE model
- Re-contextualised meditation by exploring its Buddhist roots
- Outlined aspects of Buddhist philosophy, including wisdom, compassion and ethics
- Considered possible PPIs relating to Buddhism
- Re-contextualised yoga by exploring its Hindu roots
- Detailed the various branches of yoga, and introduced Patañjali's eight limbs
- Highlighted the potential contributions of other religious traditions to PP

QUIZ…

1 What percentage of people worldwide are thought to be involved in some kind of religious or spiritual practice?
2 In Ivtzan et al.'s (2011) study, participants were placed into four groups according to whether they had high or low religious involvement and high or low spirituality. Which group had the lowest levels of wellbeing?

3　What is the original historical name of the Buddha?

4　What possible date for the birth of the Buddha was cited in the text?

5　Name any two of the components of the Noble Eightfold Path.

6　In Buddhism, what are the four universal virtues?

7　How many adults in the US currently practise yoga – 1 million, 16 million or 32 million?

8　Which branch of yoga is the path of devotion/love?

9　In which century BCE is Patañjali thought to have composed his yoga sutras?

10　What is the eighth and final limb of Patañjali's system?

RESOURCES AND SUGGESTIONS…

- To deepen your spiritual journey, we recommend you read *No Boundary: Eastern and Western Approaches to Personal Growth*, by Ken Wilber (2001). For more challenging expositions of the spiritual quest, please try *Doing Nothing: Coming to the End of the Spiritual Search*, by Steven Harrison (2002), and *Zen and the Art of Motorcycle Maintenance*, by Robert Pirsig (1974).
- Meditation resources are provided in Chapter 2. For yoga, www.yogajournal.com offers excellent information on yogic philosophy, postures, teaching, lifestyle and health.
- An interesting new meditative approach in Christianity is the Taizé movement (www.taize.fr/en). This involves contemplative prayer services, usually focused around meditative music and held in candlelit settings. Taizé services can now be found in many churches. We recommend that you try attending one if you can.

8

ETHICAL AND REFLECTIVE PRACTICE

The only journey is the one within.

Rainer Maria Rilke

LEARNING OBJECTIVES: AT THE END OF THE CHAPTER YOU WILL BE ABLE TO...

- Understand the importance of an ethical framework for applied disciplines
- Contemplate the relevance of values, morals and ethics to PP
- Appreciate what PP can learn from fields such as counselling and psychotherapy
- Consider the question 'who is a positive psychologist'?
- Understand the importance of reflective practice
- Differentiate reflection-in-action, reflection-on-action, reflexivity, and rumination
- Consider your personal growth in the context of PP practice

LIST OF TOPICS...

- Values, morals and ethics
- Development of the VIA character strengths
- The professionalisation of PP
- Counselling and psychotherapy
- The British Association of Counselling and Psychotherapy (BACP)

- The BACP ethical framework
- Professional supervision
- Reflection and reflexivity
- Self-awareness and insight
- Schön's 'reflective practice'
- Stages and levels of reflection
- The Personal Growth Initiative
- The Johari Window

This book has taken us on quite a journey. As we suggested at the very beginning, we can look at this journey in two ways: the adventure that PP as a whole is undertaking as it emerges, takes shape, and starts to flourish as a discipline; and the path that you, the reader, are travelling along as you read this book and engage with PP. The bulk of the book has focused primarily on the former aspect, looking at the evolution and development of different aspects of PP, and how we can apply our understanding in diverse practical fields. Now, in this final chapter, we turn the focus more explicitly on you, the reader who has accompanied us this far. Throughout the book we have been highlighting the applied dimension of PP, and the use of PPIs to promote wellbeing. Here, the question is: *Who* is the person who will be applying PP and using these PPIs? In reading this book, one answer to this is perhaps *you the reader*. The question then becomes: What kind of qualities do we hope such practitioners would embody and cultivate, and what kind of developmental arc do we envisage them being on? On the whole, these are not the kinds of questions that PP is currently asking as a discipline. However, as the field develops and matures, it is increasingly important that such questions are asked. Indeed, just *asking* these questions itself takes the field forward, and helps it to flourish.

So, how can we answer these questions? One way is to turn to applied psychological disciplines that have already developed a degree of professional maturity, such as clinical or counselling psychology, and to learn from these, which is what we shall do here. In particular, we will focus on two elements that are central to professional training in these disciplines: ethical and reflective practice. In adopting these professional elements, this of course does not mean that PP becomes a professional discipline itself. However, it does help to *professionalise* PP: *not* necessarily in the sense of making it exclusive to a specific cadre of accredited people – although this is one possible option for the future, as we discuss below – but in the sense of making it more responsible and mature. The chapter is thus in two parts. First, we consider the notion of ethical practice. This relates to our responsibilities as practitioners, including the importance of safeguarding the people who are the subjects/participants of our PPIs. Second, we explore the idea of reflective practice. Here our focus is on the wellbeing and development of practitioners themselves. Together, these two elements will help us develop a more sensitive and thoughtful approach to APP.

PRACTICE ESSAY QUESTIONS . . .

- PP is potentially dangerous at present as it lacks a systematic approach to ethics. Discuss.
- Critically evaluate the importance of reflective practice within PP.

Ethical practice

In this first section we discuss the importance of developing an ethical framework to guide APP. First, however, we need to ask, what *are* ethics? In order to answer this, it is also helpful to conceptualise two other similar constructs: values and morals. Values are defined as 'desirable goals, varying in importance, that serve as guiding principles in people's lives' (Sagiv & Schwartz, 2000, p. 178). Thus, values are not necessarily about good/bad or right/wrong, but are 'conceptions of the desirable' that drive behaviour and motivate life choices (Schwartz, 1999, p. 24). In contrast, morals are explicitly about 'notions of right and wrong' (Hazard, 1994, p. 451). However, there is an intimate relationship between values and morals: the values that are held in common in a society often *become* the basis for a shared moral framework. The word 'morals' derives from the Latin *mores*, which signifies 'usage in a community' or, more specifically, 'customs or usages of social life sanctioned by the conscience of the community' (Muzzey, 1906, p. 29). So, how does ethics fit in here? Essentially, ethics refers to the explicit codification of a system of morals, in which these are communally defined and recognised. The term 'ethics' is derived from the Greek *ethikos*, meaning 'custom or usage', and refers to norms that are 'shared by a group on the basis of mutual and usually reciprocal recognition' (Hazard, 1994, p. 453). Moreover, as we will see, systems of ethics can often be domain-specific, pertaining to specific contexts. Indeed, this is the case in professional disciplines, like clinical psychology, where ethics refers to 'rules and standards of conduct recognized as binding in a professional body or an association' (Mathenge, 2013, p. 9).

Before we consider a potential ethical framework for APP, it is worth examining how PP currently approaches the question of values, morals and ethics. Here, we find a certain tension: on the one hand, PP emphasises the importance of people cultivating and living from a sense of values; yet on the other hand, in order to be taken seriously as a science, there is often an avowed commitment in PP to the scientific ideal of being 'value-neutral' (Sundararajan, 2005). A good example of this tension is found in the concept of signature strengths, as conceptualised using the VIA (values-in-action) framework (Peterson, 2006b). The 24 strengths of the VIA taxonomy were generated by consulting seminal texts of the world's religious and philosophical traditions, looking for 'ubiquitous values and virtues' (Dahlsgaard et al., 2005, p. 204). As such, VIA strengths which people are exhorted to enact, like justice or temperance, are explicitly drawn from moral frameworks like the Mosaic Ten Commandments. However, in PP, these strengths have become somewhat de-contextualised from their initial moral underpinnings. As Sundararajan (2005) points out, in his book *Authentic Happiness*, Seligman (2002) characterises the 'good life' as the gratification that arises from utilising one's signature strengths. Seligman then gives the striking case of 'a hit man who derives enormous gratification from stalking and slaying' (p. 303). He then asks rhetorically whether such a person could be said to have achieved 'the good life'. His response: 'The answer is yes. I condemn their actions, of course, but on grounds independent of the theory in this book.' That is, Seligman of course denounces such behaviour, but states that this condemnation cannot be made within the context of his theory as, since it is a scientific theory, it should aim for the scientific ideal of value neutrality.

REFLECTION . . .

What is your take on Seligman's hit man example above? In his book, Seligman of course states that this action would be 'morally despicable'. However, he then suggests that his theory is 'not a morality or a world-view', and that since science should be 'morally neutral', it is not with possible within the bounds of his theory to assert that a person *shouldn't* derive gratification from violence. Thus, Seligman refuses to align his theory with a moral position, to assert that some ways of pursuing wellbeing are *better* than others. What do you think? If a person finds pleasure, gratification or fulfilment through acts such as killing, can they be said to be living a pleasant, good or meaningful life? Or consider the case of flow: would it be problematic if a person found a state of flow through gambling? What role should morals play in PP?

As such, in terms of our distinction above, we might say that PP currently places a strong emphasis on values (desirable goals), but is somewhat reticent to weigh in on issues around morals and ethics. It could be argued that in not articulating a specific moral position, PP is pursuing the creditable goal of not seeking to *moralise*, i.e., telling people prescriptively to act in particular ways. However, critical theorists suggest that it is impossible *not* to act and think from a 'moral horizon' – i.e., no position is ever neutral – and that the only question is whether one acknowledges one's moral framework or not (Taylor, 1989). Indeed, paradoxically, the scientific commitment to value neutrality *is itself* a value choice, one which values 'objectivity' over making explicit moral commitments. In any case, it could be argued that PP *does* currently involve value-judgements and moral hierarchies, indeed inherently so. (This is not to say that the authors necessarily agree with these judgements and hierarchies.) Even the prefix 'positive' could be seen as a value-judgement, as could the elevation of concepts such as happiness and flourishing be seen as being ultimately *better* than outcomes like sadness, and as goals worth aiming for. Thus, as Taylor (1989) argues, we cannot be value-neutral in PP. This is *OK* – one cannot avoid being guided by values; we just need to identify and acknowledge these values. Moreover, doing so becomes especially important when we consider the *applied* aspects of PP. In a theoretical context, debates around the role and relevance of values, morals and ethics in academic disciplines are acceptable and even to be encouraged. However, in practical settings, working with real people and intervening in actual lives, it becomes imperative to develop an ethical framework to guide our actions.

So, what ethical framework should PP practitioners adopt? What guidelines should be followed? Is there a specific protocol one could adhere to? These are some of the questions we must ask ourselves when we engage in the practice of PP. Most professions have formal ethical codes, articulating how people in that profession should act. Such codes involve various 'ethical statements' that are used as a way of explaining how work in the field is 'best undertaken to achieve the greatest good and minimise any potential wrongs' (Mitchels & Bond, 2010, p. 5). For example, medicine, law and psychotherapy share in common two ethical precepts, namely, client–practitioner confidentiality and record keeping. Confidentiality is recognised as being a human right of those seeking the service of such professionals – from medical patients to legal clients – and must be respected to protect such people, and to facilitate a professional relationship based on trust and openness (Gallagher & Hodge, 2012). Record keeping is vital if the practitioner is to provide consistent service, taking into account all the relevant elements of the treatment (Jenkins, 2007). Record keeping may also be important for other reasons: for instance, in many professions, practitioners may be required to give evidence in a court of law (Soisson et al., 1987). These ethical protocols are not only recognised as standards for good practice, but are upheld through various mechanisms, including being embedded into the training and accreditation of these professions, and monitoring by special inspection staff within these professions.

So, where does APP presently stand in terms of having an ethical framework? Unfortunately, it does not currently have one. That is not to say that practitioners implementing PPIs in various fields are all necessarily unregulated or operating unethically. Indeed, many people will be affiliated to professions that have their *own* ethical standards, such as medical professionals using PPIs in clinical contexts, or educators deploying these in schools. Thus, many practitioners of PP will *already* be guided by ethics protocols within their own discipline, which means APP is already being practised ethically in many instances. However, what about the field of PP as a whole? It may be argued that there is no field 'as a whole' and that PP is more a collective term uniting people interested in constructs pertaining to wellbeing. Indeed, such was the vision of many of those who established PP (Linley & Joseph, 2004). The issue with this formulation is that people are nevertheless able to present themselves as 'positive psychologists' and offer their services to others, e.g., providing PPIs. Under such circumstances, there is no guarantee that such people will practise ethically or safely. A possible solution to this dilemma would be to develop PP into a professional discipline, complete with doctoral training, accreditation, and a fully-developed system of ethical practice. This may indeed be the way the field develops over the coming years, and we discuss the merits of this in the box below. However, in the meantime, we contend that it would be helpful for APP to begin to develop a set of non-binding ethical guidelines.

In some ways, PP is already moving towards a situation where a centralised body provides guidance and even regulation around ethical issues. The main professional body that oversees PP activity is the International Positive Psychology Association (IPPA). IPPA offers members information and support, including teaching programmes, PP resources, conferences and various research divisions. It also has an ethics committee that makes decisions relating to the conduct of the association and its members. However, as yet, so far neither IPPA nor any other PP body has issued an ethical framework to which its members must commit in order to be recognised by or affiliated to that body. The reason is simple: IPPA is very young, being established in 2007. Although it has made impressive progress in this short time, appointing committees, setting up divisions and forming a students' body, establishing a comprehensive ethical framework takes time; it would be unrealistic to expect IPPA to have achieved this already. Nevertheless, we can begin to work towards this goal. Thus, we contend that IPPA, and PP in general, can learn from other similar associations, and eventually create an ethical code suited to its aims and purposes. Specifically, we can be guided by the fields of counselling and psychotherapy, which similarly involve working with people to enhance their wellbeing. Indeed, there is already a close overlap between PP and these fields through the emergence of PPIs like positive psychotherapy (Seligman et al., 2006) and wellbeing therapy (Fava & Ruini, 2013).

Compared to PP, counselling and psychotherapy are relatively well-established fields. In the UK, there are two main associations encompassing these: the British Association for Counselling and Psychotherapy (BACP) and the United Kingdom Council for Psychotherapy (UKCP). The BACP was established in 1970, a completely different time scale from PP. Interestingly, in previous decades, counselling/psychotherapy have been (and still are) on comparable journeys to that being embarked upon by PP, asking similarly fundamental questions around the nature of their discipline, who has the 'right' to practise it, and how high standards in practice can be upheld. The regulation of counselling and psychotherapy is an ongoing debate within these fields. Indeed, some practitioners disagree with the very idea of regulation (Gabriel, 2009). Nevertheless, these bodies have established frameworks to protect both clients and practitioners. Given the strong overlap between APP and these fields, without formally adopting their ethical frameworks, PP can learn from them. Moreover, even though PP does not yet have its own framework that people are obliged to follow, *as practitioners* we can develop and evolve by voluntarily emulating the ethical ethos of counselling/psychotherapy.

So, what kind of ethical frameworks are there in counselling/psychotherapy? The BACP (2010, p. 1) system of ethical prescriptions is set out in a statement entitled *Ethical Framework for Good Practice in Counselling and Psychotherapy*. It touches on three dimensions: values, principles and personal moral qualities. We can consider these in turn. First, in terms of values, the framework holds that practitioners should be committed to:

- *Respecting* human rights and dignity
- *Protecting* the safety of clients
- *Ensuring* the integrity of practitioner–client relationships
- *Enhancing* the quality of professional knowledge and its application
- *Alleviating* personal distress and suffering
- *Fostering* a sense of self that is meaningful to the person(s) concerned
- *Increasing* personal effectiveness
- *Enhancing* the quality of relationships between people
- *Appreciating* the variety of human experience and culture
- *Striving* for the fair and adequate provision of counselling and psychotherapy services

Looking through this list, it is hard to imagine anybody interested in PP, and particularly anybody who is applying PP in practical contexts, objecting to any of these values. Indeed, these values relate closely to a number of constructs that are at the heart of PP, and reflect the kind of outcomes we endeavour to promote in APP. For example, the idea of fostering a meaningful sense of self is central to theories of wellbeing, such as Ryff's (1989) PWB model. Likewise, increasing personal effectiveness is aligned with constructs such as self-determination (Ryan & Deci, 2000). Or again, enhancing the quality of relationships between people is central to many of the PPIs discussed in this book, such as family-centred positive psychology (Sheridan et al., 2004). Thus already we can see that it would not be too much of a leap for PP to incorporate ethical principles such as these. Returning to the BACP (2010) ethical framework, the second dimension is 'principles'. Here, the values listed above are the foundation for various action-oriented principles which outline the main ethical responsibilities of the counselling/psychotherapy practitioner:

- **Trustworthiness**: Respect for the trust placed in the practitioner (also referred to as fidelity). Strict patient–practitioner confidentiality is an important aspect of this trust. Practitioners must also honour any agreement made with the client.
- **Autonomy**: Respect for the client's right to self-determination. The practitioner must provide accurate information, obtain the client's informed consent, and emphasise the voluntary nature of their participation. This principle is designed to minimise the potential for manipulation of clients.
- **Beneficence**: Commitment to promote the client's wellbeing. This principle prescribes acting in the client's best interest based on a professional assessment. One should work strictly within one's limits of competence, and only provide services based on adequate and relevant training and experience. One's practice should also be backed up by scientific research and systematic reflection.
- **Non-maleficence**: Commitment to not harming the client. The practitioner must avoid any sexual, financial, emotional or other abuse and mistreatment of the client, and also not offer services in a state of incapacitating illness or other adverse personal circumstances.
- **Justice**: Fair and impartial treatment of all clients, and provision of adequate services. This principle underscores the practitioner's legal obligations, and their commitment to not discriminating against any clients (or other individuals/ groups).
- **Self-respect**: Fostering the practitioner's self-knowledge and self-care. Practitioners should also apply the principles above to *themselves*, and seek therapy and other paths of personal development. Supervision, discussed later in this chapter, is part of this principle.

As with the values above, it is hard to imagine people studying or practising PP objecting to any of these principles. Some principles are *already* at the heart of PP, especially beneficence, which mirrors our definition of APP as 'the science and practice of improving wellbeing'. Likewise, other principles relate closely to constructs within PP, such as the principle of autonomy, which is coterminous with the concept of self-determination (Ryan & Deci, 2000). Other principles resonate with PP values, but in this context are somewhat legalistic, and so have hitherto not explicitly been formalised within the field. For example, although most PP practitioners would surely implicitly recognise and uphold the principle of non-maleficence, an explicit commitment to this is currently not required of practitioners. In putting PP on a more secure professional footing, this is the kind of principle one would want to see actively recognised. The final quality, self-respect, is also particularly intriguing. While many PP practitioners would arguably take a strong interest in their own wellbeing and development, this principle makes this an explicit part of professional development. The second part of this chapter, on reflective practice, discusses this aspect of PP practice in more detail.

Finally, to return to the BACP (2010) ethical framework, the third dimension of this is 'personal moral qualities'. This refers to the practitioner's way of being, their personal character that binds together all the other values and principles. It would be unrealistic to expect practitioners to fully embody all the qualities listed below. Nevertheless, practitioners are encouraged to recognise the value of these, and be guided by them. One may be struck by the overlap between these qualities and the strengths of the VIA taxonomy (Peterson & Seligman, 2004). This reinforces the point that all these ethical guidelines are *already* familiar territory for PP. The introduction of an explicit ethical framework in PP would simply formally recognise these valued qualities and processes. The BACP moral qualities are:

- *Empathy*: The ability to communicate understanding of another person's experience from that person's perspective.
- *Sincerity*: The commitment to stand behind one's words.
- *Integrity*: The commitment to be honest and straightforward in dealing with others.
- *Resilience*: The capacity to withstand being involved with the concerns of others without being personally affected by them.
- *Respect*: The ability to respect other people and the way they understand themselves.
- *Humility*: The ability to accept and acknowledge one's strengths and weaknesses.
- *Competence*: The effective deployment of the skills and knowledge required for the task at hand.
- *Fairness*: The consistent application of appropriate criteria in taking decisions and actions.
- *Wisdom*: Sound judgement and informed practice.
- *Courage*: The capacity to overcome fears, risks and uncertainty.

In the fields of counselling and psychotherapy, these ethical guidelines are not simply articulated, but structures are in place to help trainees and practitioners cultivate and uphold these. Principle among such structures is a process of *supervision*, where a practitioner's work is monitored and supported by an experienced colleague. Such supervision has a number of goals (Inskipp & Proctor, 1993). The first is formative: to enrich the practitioner's education, training and skills, with a view to enhancing the quality of their work. One method here involves role-playing based on client material. The second goal is normative. The supervisor directs the practitioner in following ethical guidelines, maintaining adequate standards and observing boundaries. The third and final goal is restorative. Not only does supervision maintain and empower the implementation of values, principles and personal qualities, but it also provides the practitioner with a support system. Thus, in a more pastoral sense, supervision is one answer to the important question of 'who will care for the carers?' (Juvenal & Richlin, 1986). People working in caring professions are themselves in need of care and support to help them cope with the demands of the work, and to attain a healthy and balanced life more generally. Without this, workers may struggle to care for others effectively, and can even experience burnout (Leiter & Maslach, 2005). Thus, a helpful and caring supervisor can offer invaluable support.

REFLECTION . . .

Do you feel supported in your current occupation (whether in work, studying, or otherwise using your time)? Might you benefit from developing and being nurtured by a pastoral supervision-type relationship in this occupation?

The BACP ethical framework suggests that all practitioners should participate in regular supervision. Currently, there is no such model of supervision for the field of PP as a whole. However, as with the values/principles above, the idea of supervision resonates with the ethos of PP. Indeed, not only could PP benefit from incorporating supervision principles and practices, but the practice of supervision itself can in turn learn from PP, as demonstrated by the fact that a new branch of supervision is explicitly based on PP, namely Strengths Based Supervision (Edwards, 2012; Wade & Jones, 2013). This model uses Peterson and Seligman's (2004) work on the VIA taxonomy to enhance supervision, reframing the process in a way that capitalises on the supervisee's strengths. Edwards (2012) proposes numerous ways to harness strengths in supervision, including enhancing optimism; empowering supervisees to realise that they are capable of healing others; helping develop supervisees' self-efficacy; supporting them in applying their strengths; and encouraging them to invite clients to engage in a similar way. In this way, bringing a PP ethos to clinical work offers a transformative approach to supervision. Currently, the only type of formal supervision in the field of PP occurs in the context of academic research, e.g., students taking psychology courses at university will have an academic supervisor to guide them through their dissertation. However, one can see the value of all PP practitioners being able to access supervision, particularly a deeper supervisory relationship that safeguards and promotes their wellbeing and personal development.

So, we have seen what PP might gain from formulating an ethical framework, perhaps influenced by guidelines in counselling and psychotherapy. However, as emphasised throughout, these ethical ideas are already at the heart of PP in many ways, imbued as they are with PP constructs like empathy and integrity. Moreover, people studying and practising PP may already be implicitly adopting the ethical values and principles of counselling/psychotherapy in their study or practice. However, as we have suggested, PP might benefit from a more systematic and explicit ethical framework to guide all those practising PP in whatever context. This is arguably the kind of step that PP as a whole needs to take to mature as a discipline. Until then, all those practising PP might benefit from trying to emulate the guidelines of counselling/psychotherapy, if only for their own development as practitioners. Relating to this last point – developing as practitioners – we now turn to an aspect of professional practice that we would also like to promote in PP: reflective practice. In some ways, this is part of ethical practice, as represented by principles such as self-respect. However, it is of such importance to our development, as practitioners but more generally as people, that it warrants its own section.

Reflective practice

At the beginning of this chapter we suggested that we would now be shining a light upon you, the reader and potential PP practitioner. So far we have discussed general ethical principles that can guide our behaviour and help ensure that PP is practised safely and well collectively. Now, we invite you to shine a light upon *yourselves* in a more personal and intimate way. That is, we are encouraging you to become a reflective practitioner. Reflecting on oneself, one's actions, and indeed on one's journey in a deeper sense through life, is essential for a PP practitioner. In whatever way one engages with PP – whether conducting PPIs in professional settings, as a student, a researcher, or an interested reader – self-awareness is a fundamental aspect of the experience. We can describe the process of trying to become self-aware using the general term *reflective practice.*[1] So, why is reflective practice important? Here we will consider its value in three respects, constituting three sequentially deeper forms of reflection: on specific actions/events; on our career and practice of PP generally; and finally, the deepest level, on our life journey as a whole. We will explore these in turn.

So, first, in an immediate sense we can reflect on specific actions and thoughts. A very influential model in this respect, especially in the context of professional practice, is Schön's (1983) notion of the 'reflective practitioner'. Schön identifies two key forms of reflective practice: reflection-in-action and reflection-on-action. The former involves trying to be aware *in the moment* of how we are impacting upon a situation or being impacted by it: 'on-the-spot surfacing, criticizing, restructuring, and testing of intuitive understandings of experienced phenomena' (p. 241). The latter means reflecting on one's actions in retrospect, *after the event*. These two processes reinforce each other, with both serving to develop one's professional practice. For example, take the case of a PP practitioner administering a PPI like LKM to a client. Reflection-in-action means paying attention to the dynamics of the interaction *as it is happening*; the practitioner might reflect on how they are guiding the meditation – too fast or too slow, speaking too loudly or too quietly? Then, afterwards, the practitioner can reflect on how well it went – what was positive, how they might improve next time. This model of reflective practice has been applied across disciplines, from clinical psychology (Cushway & Gatherer, 2003) to social work (Gardner, 2001) to teaching (Korthagen & Vasalos, 2005). A nice way to think about reflective practice is that it means combining applied science with *artistry* (Schön, 1983). Applied forms of science – in which we include PP – to an extent revolve around certain skills that can be used in a somewhat mechanical way. However, what *really* elevates a practitioner is being able to apply such skills with the creativity, self-awareness and care that we associate with people engaged in artistic pursuits.

---

[1] In speaking about reflective practice, we are referring more to self-awareness than self-reflection. In PP, the latter – with its connotations of pre-occupation and rumination – is more often seen as detrimental to wellbeing. Influential researchers such as Lyubomirsky (2001, p. 244) suggest that 'happy individuals are less inclined than unhappy ones to self-reflect and dwell about themselves, their outcomes and their moods'. Conversely, the type of reflective practice we are referring to here is more aligned with the gentle and non-judgemental openness of mindfulness, which, as shown in Chapter 2, is positively linked to wellbeing. In addition, it is worth clarifying the relationship between our notion of reflective practice and a similar term in the literature, namely *reflexivity*. There are subtle differences between these terms: reflection is a self-aware state of mind, whereas reflexivity refers more to critical thinking about one's particular cognitive biases (Hardy et al., 2001). We prefer the general term reflective practice, since this is closer to the type of mindful self-awareness we would hope to encourage. However, we urge the reader to also imbue this awareness with the kind of critical thinking implied in the concept of reflexivity, yet without losing the kindly, accepting, compassionate and non-judgemental spirit of mindfulness.

RESEARCH AND PRACTICE CASE STUDIES . . .

Readers undertaking research projects, perhaps as part of a university course, are encouraged to bring reflective practice to bear on these. In this context, the term 'reflexivity' is more appropriate, as we are concerned with critically interrogating the way we influence our data throughout the research process (Cutcliffe, 2003). This commitment to reflexivity is based on a postpositivist constructivist epistemology. Positivism is the belief that there is an external world, which we can observe in a neutral, objective way. However, constructivist theorists have criticised this stance, which is common in many branches of science, arguing that the research process inextricably influences the observed data. As Charmaz (2000, p. 524) says, data do not provide a window onto reality, but rather are generated by the 'temporal, cultural and structural contexts' of the research. In qualitative research, say, the way interviews are conducted – which questions are asked, who is asking them – determines the answers that are received (Enosh & Buchbinder, 2005). That we affect our data does not invalidate the research; it is an inherent facet of it. Nevertheless, reflexivity means we try to acknowledge our impact, so that other scholars can at least appreciate the way our particular biases have influenced the research process and its results.

So, we recognise that reflective practice is important. However, how can we develop this skill? Training courses for therapists or clinical psychologists often endeavour to teach reflective practice to their trainees (Guiffrida, 2005). As with ethics, PP can learn from such fields and apply practices they have developed, many of which are *already* at the heart of PP. For example, in counselling/psychotherapy, a key activity for helping practitioners become more reflective is mindfulness (Shapiro et al., 2007). Indeed, mindfulness is almost conceptually identical to reflection, and to aspects of reflexivity (Finlay and Gough's (2003, p. ix) definition of reflexivity as an 'immediate, dynamic and continuing self-awareness' would serve well as a definition of mindfulness). We have already discussed the impact of mindfulness on wellbeing in Chapter 2. Here we see its value extending to practitioners themselves, which is why mindfulness practice is being incorporated into training in many professions, including counselling (Shapiro et al., 2007), medicine (Irving et al., 2012), nursing (Mackenzie et al., 2006), teaching (Napoli, 2004) and even law (Riskin, 2004). Mindfulness enhances in-action reflectivity, and provides the practitioner with rich real-time information on how they are acting in a professional context. As such, we would encourage PP practitioners to practise mindfulness, even if only for their professional development (though it is likely to improve their wellbeing too!).

REFLECTION . . .

It is vital to differentiate between reflection and rumination (Silvia et al., 2005). Both involve a focus on one's self. However, the motivation is fundamentally different in each case. Trapnell and Campbell (1999, p. 297) define rumination as 'self-attentiveness motivated by perceived threats, losses, or injustices to the self'. Conversely, reflection is 'self-attentiveness motivated by curiosity or epistemic interest in the self'. Rumination overlaps with constructs such as worry and anxiety. In contrast, reflection is akin to mindfulness, involving open-minded curiosity towards one's present-moment experience (Kabat-Zinn, 2003). Thus, reflection and rumination delineate circumstances in which investigation of the self is either productive and beneficial (reflection) or generative of dysphoria (rumination). To differentiate between them, all one needs to do is ask: *'Why am I attending to myself right now?'* If one is mired in anger or dissatisfaction, then one may well be ruminating. However, if the answer is about curiosity, noticing and understanding new aspects of yourself, then you are reflecting.

Beyond reflecting on particular actions/experiences, one can also reflect in a longer-term way about how one's practice is developing generally. This is more an overarching assessment of how one is changing and hopefully evolving in one's career over time. Ideally, most people would naturally engage in this type of reflection, whatever occupation they were in. However, as with ethics, professions like counselling/psychotherapy have also built up structures to encourage this kind of reflection, such as supervision (Edwards, 2012). Moreover, there are specific models of reflection that practitioners can engage in to promote long-term development. One such model is Korthagen and Vasalos's (2005) five-stage ALACT framework. We can illustrate this with the example of a person implementing a PPI. The first stage is *Action*, i.e., actually running the intervention. Next is *Looking back* on the action, i.e., reflecting on the way it was conducted. The process continues with *Awareness* of essential aspects, where the practitioner analyses the impact of the techniques chosen. In the fourth stage, *Creating* alternative methods of action, the practitioner considers other possible strategies that could enhance the intervention in future. Finally, in the fifth stage, *Trial*, the practitioner tries out the amended intervention and examines the consequences. These stages, ALACT in short, generate an ongoing cycle of reflection that can facilitate continual professional development.

Moreover, the kind of reflection prompted by the ALACT framework is not just about one's professional performance, but can lead to deeper, more personal reflections on one's self, empowering self-growth. In Korthagen and Vasalos's model, there are not only stages, but six progressively deep and personal *levels* of reflection. This progression is known as the 'onion model', i.e., peeling away layers to get to the core. The most superficial level is reflection on the **environment**: the practitioner reflects on everything that they encounter 'outside' themselves, such as the client's actions. At a slightly deeper level, they consider the ongoing **behaviours** in the practitioner–client dyad (the nature of the interaction). Deeper still, the practitioner focuses on their own **competence**, the knowledge/experience they possess to handle the situation. Going further 'in', the practitioner can contemplate the underlying **beliefs** which influence his or her actions (with parallels to Seligman's (1990) notion of 'icebergs', discussed in Chapter 6). Underneath this, the practitioner can consider their professional **identity**, i.e., what kind of person are they *becoming* in the context of their work. Finally, at an even deeper existential level, the practitioner can reflect on their **mission**. Also known as the 'level of spirituality' (Dilts, 1990), this last level is a reflection on the very nature of our being, on what gives meaning and significance to our lives, and how we have chosen to spend our time on earth.

TRY ME! . . .

Consider your own occupation, i.e., the way you productively occupy your time, whether as a practitioner, a student, or in any other capacity. Use Korthagen and Vasalos's (2005) levels of reflection to contemplate this endeavour. Proceed through the levels, getting progressively deeper until you engage with the question of *why* you do what you do. What kinds of self-awareness and insight does this process generate for you?

As we explore the deeper reflective levels of Korthagen and Vasalos's (2005) model, we move beyond simply considering our professional development and initiate a more fundamental enquiry into the nature of our lives and the journeys we are on. We would invite you, the reader, to consider such an enquiry in the context of your own lives. In whatever capacity you are engaging with this book – and PP more generally – all of you are on a personal journey, and may well have been changed in some way by reading this. You may have been persuaded that the **LIFE model in Chapter 1** offers a useful way of appraising existence, energised by trying the **mental practices in Chapter 2**, intrigued by **body/ brain-based discussions in Chapter 3**, motivated by **socio-cultural reflections in Chapter 4**, struck by notions of **positive development in Chapter 5**, inspired by **work-related PPIs in Chapter 6**, tantalised by the transformative power of **religion and spirituality in Chapter 7**, or convinced of the importance of **ethical and reflective practice** in this last chapter. As such, as we near the end of the book, we would encourage you to reflect on the journey you have undertaken in reading this book, and on where this journey fits into your broader life path. At its deepest level, reflection involves 'a personal journey of reflective sense-making' (Waddock, 2011, p. 177). This can be a process that touches the core of who we are as people, and can engender transformative change. In APP, self-awareness reveals itself as a powerful force driving psychological development, a practical path for change and transformation. A wonderful construct for appreciating this transformational process is the Personal Growth Initiative (PGI) (Robitschek, 1998), described in the box below.

PSYCHOMETRIC SCALES . . .

The PGI is defined by Robitschek (1998) as 'active, intentional engagement in the process of personal growth' (p. 184). This process has two dimensions. First, a cognitive dimension that is rooted in reflection and self-awareness, where one knows *how* to intentionally grow/change. This is equivalent to the awareness component of the ALACT model. Second, there is a behavioural dimension, where actual action is initiated, which is akin to the trial component of ALACT. Individuals with high PGI consciously seek opportunities to capitalise on the change process and are aware of their development over time. PGI is strongly linked to many aspects of wellbeing (Robitschek & Keyes, 2004). It is measured using the Personal Growth Initiative Scale (Robitschek, 1998), which assesses whether people consider personal growth to be important, and actively seek opportunities to facilitate this. Perhaps you might like to try it. Using the scale below, choose the number that best describes the extent to which you agree or disagree with each statement: 1 = *definitely disagree*, 2 = *mostly disagree*, 3 = *somewhat disagree*, 4 = *somewhat agree*, 5 = *mostly agree*, 6 = *definitely agree*.

Answer

1   I know how to change specific things that I want to
    change in my life.   _____
2   I have a good sense of where I am headed in my life.   _____
3   If I want to change something in my life, I initiate the
    transition process.   _____
4   I can choose the role that I want to have in a group.   _____
5   I know what I need to do to get started toward
    reaching my goals.   _____
6   I have a specific action plan to help me reach my goals.   _____
7   I take charge of my life.   _____
8   I know what my unique contribution to the world might be.   _____
9   I have a plan for making my life more balanced.   _____

Total = _____

To determine your PGI score, sum the scores on all nine items. Higher scores indicate a greater personal growth initiative.

In reflecting in a deeper sense on our life journey, we can contemplate the path we have taken so far, and consider where we stand now. However, the future lies over the horizon – the great unknown. As such, our potential for transformation may be hidden to ourselves at present. Almost by definition, the person we may become in future is unknown to our present self; if it were known, it would simply be *part* of our present self. Thus, change derives from inner potentials of which we may at best be only dimly aware. An intriguing way to consider this process of change is the 'Johari Window' (Luft, 1969), which illustrates aspects of ourselves that are known or unknown to us and to others. Aspects that are **known to us and to others** are our persona, our clear and visible 'character'. Aspects that are **known to us but unknown to others** are our masked features, secret dimensions of the self that we conceal from others. Aspects of us that are **known to others but unknown to ourselves** are our blind spots. Finally, there are aspects of the self that are **unknown to others and to ourselves**, dimensions of the self that have not yet been brought to light. This last dimension is the origin of growth, which arises from unveiling the unknown. Although this dimension is elusive, we can help bring it into the light through transformative practices of reflection, such as meditation. These practices can be vehicles for self-discovery, shining a light of self-awareness on our hidden potentials and encouraging these to grow and flourish. The Delphic injunction to 'know thyself' is a most difficult challenge, and yet is at the heart of personal development. We hope this final chapter, and the book as a whole, helps you on your own journey of discovery. This book is a personal invitation for you to search for and find that which *makes life better*, both for yourself and others. Accepting the invitation will hopefully change your life deeply, as we know it has changed ours.

SUMMARY – THIS CHAPTER HAS...

- Conceptualised values, morals and ethics, and considered the relevance of these to PP
- Discussed the desirability of APP developing an ethical framework
- Highlighted the use of ethical frameworks in other professional disciplines
- Raised the issue of who has the 'right' to call themselves a 'positive psychologist'
- Explored what PP can learn from the fields of counselling and psychotherapy
- Outlined the dimensions of the BACP ethical framework
- Highlighted the value of a supervisory relationship in a professional context
- Distinguished between reflection, reflexivity and rumination
- Introduced strategies to promote reflection-in-action and reflection-on-action
- Discussed personal development and transformation

QUIZ...

1 Which religious code is mentioned in the text as one of the sources for the VIA taxonomy?
2 When was IPPA founded?

3   When was the BACP founded?
4   What are the three dimensions of the BACP ethical framework?
5   How many values are specified in the BACP ethical framework?
6   Which BACP principle upholds a commitment to not harming the client?
7   In research, reflexivity pertains to which type of epistemology?
8   What are the five stages of Korthagen and Vasalos's (2005) ALACT framework?
9   What are the six levels of reflection in the ALACT framework?
10 Who is cited as creating the PGI?

RESOURCES AND SUGGESTIONS...

- To learn more about the BACP ethical framework, please visit their website at www. bacp.co.uk/ethical_framework/.
- IPPA is the main body that oversees PP. You can follow their work at www. ippanetwork.org/.

GLOSSARY OF TERMS

ACC	Anterior Cingulate Cortex
AI	Appreciative Inquiry
ALACT	Action, Looking back, Awareness, Creating, Trial
APA	American Psychological Association
APP	Applied Positive Psychology
ATP	Awareness Training Program
BA	Body Awareness
BACP	British Association for Counselling and Psychotherapy
BAT	Body Awareness Therapy
BBAT	Basic Body Awareness Therapy
BCE	Before Common Era
BDI	Buddhist-Derived Intervention
BMI	Body Mass Index
CE	Common Era
DMT	Dance/Movement Therapy
DNA	Deoxyribonucleic Acid
EEG	Electroencephalography
EHRC	Equality and Human Rights Commission
EI	Emotional Intelligence
FA	Focused Attention
FCPP	Family-Centred Positive Psychology
fMRI	Functional Magnetic Resonance Imaging
FWP	Family Wellbeing Programme
GDP	Gross Domestic Product
GNH	Gross National Happiness
HPA	Hypothalmic-Pituitary-Adrenal
HRV	Heart Rate Variability
IPP	Integrated Positive Practice
IPPA	International Positive Psychology Association
J D-R	Job Demands-Resources
LIFE	Layered Integrated Framework Example
LKM	Loving-Kindness Meditation

MAPP	MSc in Applied Positive Psychology
MBCT	Mindfulness-Based Cognitive Therapy
MBSR	Mindfulness-Based Stress Reduction
MBWB	Mindfulness Based Well-Being
MMP	Mindfulness Meditation Practices
MRT	Master Resilience Training
MSCEIT	Mayer Salovey Caruso Emotional Intelligence Test
MSLSS	Multidimensional Students' Life Satisfaction Scale
MT	Music Therapy
NA	Negative Affect
NCC	Neural Correlates of Consciousness
NEF	New Economics Foundation
NHS	National Health Service
NT	Neurotransmitter
OM	Open Monitoring
ONS	Office for National Statistics
PA	Positive Affect
PERMA	Positive emotions, Engagement, Relationships, Meaning, and Achievement
PFC	Prefrontal Cortex
PGI	Personal Growth Initiative
PHWP	Psychologically Healthy Workplace Program
POB	Positive Organizational Behaviour
POS	Positive Organizational Scholarship
PP	Positive Psychology
PPI	Positive Psychology Intervention
PRP	Penn Resilience Program
PsyCap	Psychological Capital
PTSD	Posttraumatic Stress Disorder
PWB	Psychological Wellbeing
PYD	Positive Youth Development
SEL	Social and Emotional Learning
SES	Socio-Economic Status
SSRI	Selective Serotonin Reuptake Inhibitor
SWB	Subjective Wellbeing
WHO	World Health Organisation
UEL	University of East London
UK	United Kingdom
UKCP	United Kingdom Council for Psychotherapy
UN	United Nations
US	United States
VIA	Values-in-Action
VIA-IS	VIA Inventory of Strengths

QUIZ ANSWERS

Chapter 1

1. 1948
2. Neural Correlates of Consciousness (NCC)
3. David Bakan
4. Intersubjective
5. Arthur Koestler
6. The ecosystem
7. Karl Marx
8. Participatory research, collaborative inquiry, or emancipatory research
9. Mesosystem
10. Phineas Quimby

Chapter 2

1. Sustained, executive, selective, and switching
2. Focused Attention and Open Monitoring
3. Molecular biology
4. Massachusetts Medical Center
5. MMPs, ATPs, and BDIs
6. Emotions as embodied and transient
7. Emotional management
8. Coherence and purpose
9. Vienna
10. Personal projects and possible selves

Chapter 3

1. 23
2. Short
3. 100
4. Prefrontal cortex
5. Theta
6. The sympathetic

7. The hypothalmic-pituitary-adrenal axis
8. Edmund Husserl
9. Aesthetics
10. Pythagoras

Chapter 4

1. Close relationships
2. Wil Gesler
3. Home and school
4. 120
5. New York
6. Australia
7. 1972
8. Nudge
9. Mary Wollstonecraft
10. Rachel Carson

Chapter 5

1. Five months pre-birth to one month post-birth
2. The sensorimotor stage
3. John Bowlby, and Mary Ainsworth
4. Secure, anxious-avoidant, anxious-resistant, and disorganised
5. Warmth versus hostility, and restrictiveness versus permissiveness
6. Australia
7. Penn Resilience Program
8. Competence, confidence, connection, character and caring
9. Beck and Cowan
10. Choose from: not smoking, adaptive coping styles, absence of alcohol abuse, healthy weight, stable marriage, exercise, and years of education

Chapter 6

1. Vigour, dedication and absorption
2. 24
3. Self-efficacy, optimism, hope, resilience
4. 'Space Oddity', by David Bowie
5. Activating event, beliefs, consequences, disputation, energisation
6. 48 hours

7. Google
8. Discovery, dream, design, delivery/destiny
9. 40
10. 6.5 million

Chapter 7

1. 90
2. High religious involvement and low spirituality
3. Siddhartha Gautama
4. 480 BCE
5. Correct answers include: right vision, conception, speech, conduct, livelihood, effort, mindfulness, and concentration
6. Benevolence, compassion, joy and equanimity
7. 16 million
8. Bhakti yoga
9. Second century BCE
10. Samadhi

Chapter 8

1. The Ten Commandments
2. 2007
3. 1970
4. Values, principles, and personal moral qualities
5. Ten
6. Non-maleficence
7. Positivist and/or constructivist
8. Action, looking back, awareness, creating, and trial
9. Environment, behaviours, competence, beliefs, identity, and mission
10. Robitschek (1998)

REFERENCES

Abramson, L. Y., Seligman, M. E., & Teasdale, J. D. (1978). Learned helplessness in humans: Critique and reformulation. *Journal of Abnormal Psychology, 87*(1), 49–74.

Acevedo, E. (2012). Exercise psychology: Understanding the mental health benefits of physical activity and the public health challenges of inactivity. In E. Acevedo (Ed.), *The Oxford Handbook of Exercise Psychology* (pp. 3–8). New York: Oxford University Press.

Adamson, S., & Metzner, R. (1988). The nature of the MDMA experience and its role in healing, psychotherapy and spiritual practice. *ReVision, 10*, 59–72.

Advertising and Commercial Archives (2012). XXXX: Advertising and Commercial Archives. Retrieved 6 February, 2013, from http://www.advertolog.com/xxxx-6335855/print-outdoor/meditation-camp-16031855/

Ainsworth, M. D. S., Blehar, M. C., Waters, E., & Wall, S. (1979). *Patterns of Attachment: A Psychological Study of the Strange Situation*. Hillsdale, NJ: Lawrence Erlbaum Associates.

Alexander, B., Warner-Schmidt, J., Eriksson, T. M., Tamminga, C., Arango-Lievano, M., Ghose, S., . . . Flajolet, M. (2010). Reversal of depressed behaviors by p11 gene therapy in the nucleus accumbens. *Science Translational Medicine, 2*(54), 54–76.

Alicea, S., Pardo, G., Conover, K., Gopalan, G., & McKay, M. (2012). Step-up: Promoting youth mental health and development in inner-city high schools. *Clinical Social Work Journal, 40*(2), 175–186.

American Psychiatric Association (APA) (1994). *Diagnostic and Statistical Manual of Mental Disorders* (4th edition). Washington, DC: American Psychiatric Association.

American Psychological Association (APA) (1999). What is a Psychologically Healthy Workplace? From http://www.apahelpcenter.org/articles/article.php?id=34

Ando, M., Morita, T., Miyashita, M., Sanjo, M., Kira, H., & Shima, Y. (2010). Effects of bereavement life review on spiritual well-being and depression. *Journal of Pain and Symptom Management, 40*(3), 435–459.

Aquinas, St Thomas (1981 (1273)). *Summa Theologia*. London: Christian Classics.

Arendt, H. (1958). *The Human Condition*. Chicago, IL: University of Chicago Press.

Arendt, M., Munk-Jørgensen, P., Sher, L., & Jensen, S. O. W. (2011). Mortality among individuals with cannabis, cocaine, amphetamine, MDMA, and opioid use disorders: A nationwide follow-up study of Danish substance users in treatment. *Drug and Alcohol Dependence, 114*(2–3), 134–139.

Argyle, M., & Beit-Hallahmi, B. (1975). *The Social Psychology of Religion*. London and Boston, MA: Routledge and Kegan Paul.

Aristotle. (2000 (350 BCE)). *Nicomachean Ethics* (R. Crisp Ed.). Cambridge: Cambridge University Press.

Arnold, K. A., Turner, N., Barling, J., Kelloway, E. K., & McKee, M. C. (2007). Transformational leadership and psychological well-being: The mediating role of meaningful work. *Journal of Occupational Health Psychology*, *12*(3), 193–203.

Arnold, M. (1867). *New Poems*. London: Macmillan and Co.

Arrindell, W. A., & Luteijn, F. (2000). Similarity between intimate partners for personality traits as related to individual levels of satisfaction with life. *Personality and Individual Differences*, *28*(4), 629–637.

Aspinwall, L., & Tedeschi, R. (2010). Of babies and bathwater: A reply to Coyne and Tennen's views on positive psychology and health. *Annals of Behavioral Medicine*, *39*(1), 27–34.

Austin, J. H. (1998). *Zen and the Brain: Toward an Understanding of Meditation and Consciousness*. Cambridge, MA: MIT Press.

Avey, J. B., Luthans, F., Smith, R. M., & Palmer, N. F. (2010a). Impact of positive psychological capital on employee well-being over time. *Journal of Occupational Health Psychology*, *15*(1), 17–28.

Avey, J. B., Luthans, F., & Youssef, C. M. (2010b). The additive value of positive psychological capital in predicting work attitudes and behaviors. *Journal of Management*, *36*(2), 430–452.

Avolio, B. J., Bass, B. M., & Jung, D. I. (1999). Re-examining the components of transformational and transactional leadership using the Multifactor Leadership. *Journal of Occupational and Organizational Psychology*, *72*(4), 441–462.

Bache, I., & Reardon, L. (2013). An idea whose time has come? Explaining the rise of well-being in British politics. *Political Studies*, *61*(4), 898–914.

Bailey, C., Murphy, R., & Porock, D. (2011). Professional tears: Developing emotional intelligence around death and dying in emergency work. *Journal of Clinical Nursing*, *20*(23–24), 3364–3372.

Bakan, D. (1966). *The Duality of Human Existence*. Chicago, IL: Rand McNally.

Bakker, A. B. (2005). Flow among music teachers and their students: The crossover of peak experiences. *Journal of Vocational Behavior*, *66*(1), 26–44.

Bakker, A. B., Demerouti, E., & Euwema, M. C. (2005). Job resources buffer the impact of job demands on burnout. *Journal of Occupational Health Psychology*, *10*, 170–180.

Bakker, A. B., & Schaufeli, W. B. (2008). Positive organizational behavior: Engaged employees in flourishing organizations. *Journal of Organizational Behavior*, *29*(2), 147–154.

Baltes, M. M., & Carstensen, L. L. (2003). The process of successful aging: Selection, optimization, and compensation. *Understanding Human Development* (pp. 81–104). London: Springer.

Bandura, A. (1977). Self efficacy: Toward a unifying theory of behavioral change. *Psychological Review*, *84*, 191–215.

Barad, J. (2007). The understanding and experience of compassion: Aquinas and the Dalai Lama. *Buddhist-Christian Studies*, *27*, 11–29.

Baron-Cohen, S., Wheelwright, S., Hill, J., Raste, Y., & Plumb, I. (2001). The 'reading the mind in the eyes' test revised version: A study with normal adults, and adults with Asperger syndrome or high-functioning autism. *Journal of Child Psychology and Psychiatry*, *42*(2), 241–251.

Basar, E., Basar-Eroglu, C., Karakas, S., & Schürmann, M. (2001). Gamma, alpha, delta, and theta oscillations govern cognitive processes. *International Journal of Psychophysiology, 39*(2–3), 241–248.

Basner, M., Babisch, W., Davis, A., Brink, M., Clark, C., Janssen, S., & Stansfeld, S. (2014). Auditory and non-auditory effects of noise on health. *The Lancet, 383*(9925), 1325–1332.

Bass, B. M. (1991). From transactional to transformational leadership: Learning to share the vision. *Organizational Dynamics, 18*(3), 19–31.

Bauman, Z. (2005). Education in liquid modernity. *Review of Education, Pedagogy, and Cultural Studies, 27*(4), 303–317.

Baumeister, R. F. (1991). *Meanings of Life*. New York: Guilford Press.

Baumrind, D. (1967). Child care practices anteceding three patterns of preschool behavior. *Genetic Psychology Monographs, 75*(1), 43–88.

Bayat, M. (2007). Evidence of resilience in families of children with autism. *Journal of Intellectual Disability Research, 51*(9), 702–714.

Beck, A. T., Rush, A. J., Shaw, B. F., & Emery, G. (1979). *Cognitive Therapy of Depression*. New York: Guilford Press.

Beck, D. E., & Cowan, C. (1996). *Spiral Dynamics: Mastering Values, Leadership and Change*. Cambridge, MA: Blackwell.

Becker, D., & Marecek, J. (2008). Dreaming the American dream: Individualism and positive psychology. *Social and Personality Psychology Compass, 2*(5), 1767–1780.

Becker, L. C. (1992). Good lives: Prolegomena. *Social Philosophy and Policy, 9*(2), 15–37.

Belfiore, E. (2002). Art as a means of alleviating social exclusion: Does it really work? A critique of instrumental cultural policies and social impact studies in the UK. *International Journal of Cultural Policy, 8*(1), 91–106.

Bellah, R. N., Madsen, R., Sullivan, W. M., Swidler, A., & Tipton, S. M. (1996). *Habits of the Heart: Individualism and Commitment in American Life*. Berkeley, CA: University of California Press.

Belsky, J., Bakermans-Kranenburg, M. J., & Van IJzendoorn, M. H. (2007). For better and for worse: Differential susceptibility to environmental influences. *Current Directions in Psychological Science, 16*(6), 300–304.

Benería, L. (2001). Shifting the risk: New employment patterns, informalization, and women's work. *International Journal of Politics, Culture, and Society, 15*(1), 27–53.

Bergs, J. (2002). Effect of healthy workplaces on well-being and productivity of office workers. Paper presented at the Proceedings of International Plants for People Symposium, Amsterdam, NL.

Berridge, K. C., & Kringelbach, M. L. (2011). Building a neuroscience of pleasure and well-being. *Psychology of Well-being, 1*(1), 1–26.

Berson, I. R., & Berson, M. J. (2002). Emerging risks of violence in the digital age. *Journal of School Violence, 1*(2), 51–71.

Bertollo, M., Saltarelli, B., & Robazza, C. (2009). Mental preparation strategies of elite modern pentathletes. *Psychology of Sport and Exercise, 10*(2), 244–254.

Biddle, S. J. H., & Mutrie, N. (2008). *Psychology of Physical Activity: Determinants, Well-Being, and Interventions*. London: Routledge.

Biswas-Diener, R. (2009). Personal coaching as a positive intervention. *Journal of Clinical Psychology*, *65*(5), 544–553.

Biswas-Diener, R., Kashdan, T. B., & Minhas, G. (2011a). A dynamic approach to psychological strength development and intervention. *The Journal of Positive Psychology*, *6*(2), 106–118.

Biswas-Diener, R., Linley, P. A., Givindji, R., & Woolston, L. (2011b). Positive psychology as a force for social change. In K. Sheldon, T. Kashdan & M. Steger (Eds.), *Designing Positive Psychology: Taking Stock and Moving Forward* (pp. 410–419). New York: Oxford University Press.

Blanchflower, D. G., & Oswald, A. J. (2004). Well-being over time in Britain and the USA. *Journal of Public Economics*, *88*(7–8), 1359–1386.

Blanchflower, D. G., & Oswald, A. J. (2008). Is well-being U-shaped over the life cycle? *Social Science & Medicine*, *66*(8), 1733–1749.

Blanchflower, D. G., Oswald, A., & Stewart-Brown, S. (2013). Is psychological well-being linked to the consumption of fruit and vegetables? *Social Indicators Research*, *114*(3), 785–801.

Block, N. (1995). On a confusion about a function of consciousness. *Behavioral and Brain Sciences*, *18*(2), 227–287.

Boecker, H., Sprenger, T., Spilker, M. E., Henriksen, G., Koppenhoefer, M., Wagner, K. J., . . . Tolle, T. R. (2008). The runner's high: Opioidergic mechanisms in the human brain. *Cerebral Cortex*, *18*(11), 2523–2531.

Bögels, S., Lehtonen, A., & Restifo, K. (2010). Mindful parenting in mental health care. *Mindfulness*, *1*(2), 107–120.

Bolino, M. C., Turnley, W. H., & Bloodgood, J. M. (2002). Citizenship behavior and the creation of social capital in organizations. *Academy of Management Review*, *27*(4), 505–522.

Bongi, S. M., & Del Rosso, A. (2012). Mind body therapies in the rehabilitation program of fibromyalgia syndrome. In W. S. Wilke (Ed.), *New Insights into Fibromyalgia* (pp. 169–186). Rijeka, Croatia: InTech.

Bourdieu, P. (1986). The forms of capital. In J. G. Richardson (Ed.), *Handbook of Theory and Research for the Sociology of Education* (pp. 241–258). New York: Greenwood.

Bowen, S., & Marlatt, A. (2009). Surfing the urge: Brief mindfulness-based intervention for college student smokers. *Psychology of Addictive Behaviors*, *23*(4), 666–671.

Bowen, S., Witkiewitz, K., Dillworth, T. M., Chawla, N., Simpson, T. L., Ostafin, B. D., . . . Marlatt, G. A. (2006). Mindfulness meditation and substance use in an incarcerated population. *Psychology of Addictive Behaviors*, *20*(3), 343–347.

Bowlby, J. (1969). *Attachment and Loss: Attachment* (Vol. 1). New York: Basic Books.

Boyd, J., & Banzhaf, S. (2007). What are ecosystem services? The need for standardized environmental accounting units. *Ecological Economics*, *63*(2), 616–626.

Bradt, J., Goodill, S. W., & Dileo, C. (2011). Dance/movement therapy for improving psychological and physical outcomes in cancer patients. *Cochrane Database of Systematic Reviews*, *10*.

Brani, O., Hefferon, K., Lomas, T., Ivtzan, I., & Painter, J. (2014). The impact of body awareness on subjective wellbeing: The role of mindfulness. *International Journal of Body Psychotherapy*, *13*(1), 94–107.

Braun, A. A. (2009). Gross National Happiness in Bhutan: A living example of an alternative approach to progress. *Social Impact Research Experience Journal (Sire)* (pp. 1–142). Wharton, PA: University of Pennsylvania.

Bressan, R. A., & Crippa, J. A. (2005). The role of dopamine in reward and pleasure behaviour – review of data from preclinical research. *Acta Psychiatrica Scandinavica*, *111*, 14–21.

Brewer, S., Van Eerd, D., Amick III, B. C., Irvin, E., Daum, K. M., Gerr, F., . . . Rempel, D. (2006). Workplace interventions to prevent musculoskeletal and visual symptoms and disorders among computer users: A systematic review. *Journal of Occupational Rehabilitation*, *16*(3), 317–350.

British Association for Counselling and Psychotherapy (BACP) (2010). *Ethical Framework for Good Practice in Counselling and Psychotherapy*. Lutterworth: British Association for Counselling and Psychotherapy.

Bronfenbrenner, U. (1977). Toward an experimental ecology of human development. *American Psychologist*, *32*(7), 513–531.

Bronfenbrenner, U. (1986). Ecology of the family as a context for human development: Research perspectives. *Developmental Psychology*, *22*(6), 723–742.

Bronfenbrenner, U. (1993). Ecological models of human development. In M. Gauvain & M. Cole (Eds.), *Readings on the Development of Children* (pp. 37–43). New York: Freeman.

Brown, K. W., & Ryan, R. M. (2003). The benefits of being present: Mindfulness and its role in psychological well-being. *Journal of Personality and Social Psychology*, *84*(4), 822–848.

Brown, K. W., Ryan, R. M., & Creswell, J. D. (2007). Mindfulness: Theoretical foundations and evidence for its salutary effects. *Psychological Inquiry*, *18*(4), 211–237.

Brown, R. P., & Gerbarg, P. L. (2009). Yoga breathing, meditation, and longevity. *Annals of the New York Academy of Sciences*, *1172*(1), 54–62.

Brown, S., Martinez, M. J., & Parsons, L. M. (2006). The neural basis of human dance. *Cerebral Cortex*, *16*(8), 1157–1167.

Bruce, A., & Davies, B. (2005). Mindfulness in hospice care: Practising meditation-in-action. *Qualitative Health Research*, *15*(10), 1329–1344.

Brunwasser, S. M., Gillham, J. E., & Kim, E. S. (2009). A meta-analytic review of the Penn Resiliency Program's effect on depressive symptoms. *Journal of Consulting and Clinical Psychology*, *77*(6), 1042–1054.

Bulygo, Z. (2013). Inside Google's Culture of Success and Employee Happiness. Retrieved 11 February, 2013, from http://blog.kissmetrics.com/googles-culture-of-success/.

Burke, J., O'Campo, P., Salmon, C., & Walker, R. (2009). Pathways connecting neighborhood influences and mental well-being: Socioeconomic position and gender differences. *Social Science & Medicine*, *68*(7), 1294–1304.

Burkhardt, J., & Brennan, C. (2012). The effects of recreational dance interventions on the health and well-being of children and young people: A systematic review. *Arts & Health*, *4*(2), 148–161.

Burkhardt, J., & Rhodes, J. (2012). *Commissioning Dance for Health and Well-Being: Guidance and Resources for Commissioners*. Birmingham: DanceXchange.

Burns, J. W. (2006). The role of attentional strategies in moderating links between acute pain induction and subsequent psychological stress: Evidence for symptom specific reactivity among patients with chronic pain versus healthy non patients. *Emotions, 6*, 180–192.

Burris, J. L., Sauer, S. E., & Carlson, C. R. (2011). A test of religious commitment and spiritual transcendence as independent predictors of underage alcohol use and alcohol-related problems. *Psychology of Religion and Spirituality, 3*(3), 231–240.

Burton, C. M., & King, L. A. (2004). The health benefits of writing about intensely positive experiences. *Journal of Research in Personality, 38*(2), 150–163.

Bushe, G. R. (2011). Appreciative inquiry: Theory and critique. In D. Boje, B. Burnes & J. Hassard (Eds.), *The Routledge Companion to Organizational Change* (pp. 87–103). Oxford: Routledge.

Cacioppe, R., & Edwards, M. (2005). Seeking the Holy Grail of organisational development: A synthesis of integral theory, spiral dynamics, corporate transformation and action inquiry. *Leadership & Organization Development Journal, 26*(2), 86–105.

Cacioppo, J. T., Tassinary, L. G., & Berntson, G. G. (2007). *Handbook of Psychophysiology* (3rd edition). Cambridge: Cambridge University Press.

Cahn, B. R., & Polich, J. (2006). Meditation states and traits: EEG, ERP, and neuroimaging studies. *Psychological Bulletin, 132*(2), 180–211.

Cameron, K. S., & Caza, A. (2004). Contributions to the discipline of positive organizational scholarship. *American Behavioral Scientist, 47*(6), 731–739.

Cameron, K. S., Dutton, J. E., & Quinn, R. E. (2003). Foundations of positive organizational scholarship. In K. S. Cameron, J. E. Dutton & R. E. Quinn (Eds.), *Positive Organizational Scholarship: Foundations of a New Discipline* (pp. 3–13). San Francisco, CA: Berrett-Koehler.

Cameron, S., & Maginn, C. (2011). Living psychology: The 'emotional warmth' dimension of professional childcare. *Educational and Child Psychology, 28*(3), 44–62.

Camus, A. (1942). *L'etranger* (S. Gilbert, Trans.). New York: Vintage Books.

Carman, T. (2000). The body in Husserl and Merleau-Ponty. *Philosophical Topics, 27*(2), 205–226.

Carr, W., & Kemmis, S. (1986). *Becoming Critical: Education, Knowledge and Action Research*. London: The Falmer Press.

Carson, R. (2002 (1962)). *Silent Spring*. New York: First Mariner Books.

Carver, C. S., & Scheier, M. F. (2003). Optimism. In C. R. Snyder & S. J. Lopez (Eds.), *Handbook of Positive Psychology* (pp. 231–243). Oxford: Oxford University Press.

Carver, C. S., Scheier, M. F., & Weintraub, J. K. (1989). Assessing coping strategies: A theoretically based approach. *Journal of Personality and Social Psychology, 56*(2), 267–283.

Casey, B., Jones, R. M., & Hare, T. A. (2008). The adolescent brain. *Annals of the New York Academy of Sciences, 1124*(1), 111–126.

Caspersen, C. J., Powell, K. E., & Christenson, G. M. (1985). Physical activity, exercise, and physical fitness: Definitions and distinctions for health-related research. *Public Health Reports, 100*(2), 126–130.

Caspi, A., Sugden, K., Moffitt, T. E., Taylor, A., Craig, I. W., Harrington, H., . . . Poulton, R. (2003). Influence of life stress on depression: Moderation by a polymorphism in the 5-HTT gene. *Science, 301*(5631), 386–389.

Castronova, E. (2003). Theory of the Avatar. *CESifo Working Papers*.

Catalano, R. F., & Toumbourou, J. W. (2012). Positive youth development. In S. Lopez (Ed.), *The Encyclopedia of Positive Psychology* (pp. 759–765). Oxford: Wiley-Blackwell.

Chakrabortty, A. (2013, 16 December). For a real-life Hunger Games, look no further than your local bank, *The Guardian*.

Chalmers, D. J. (1995). Facing up to the problem of consciousness. *Journal of Consciousness Studies, 2*, 200–219.

Chalmers, D. J. (2004). How can we construct a science of consciousness? In M. Gazzaniga (Ed.), *The Cognitive Neurosciences*. Cambridge, MA: MIT Press.

Chan, D. W. (2010). Gratitude, gratitude intervention and subjective well-being among Chinese school teachers in Hong Kong. *Educational Psychology, 30*(2), 139–153.

Charmaz, K. (2000). Grounded theory: Objectivist and constructivist methods. In N. Denzin & Y. Lincoln (Eds.), *Handbook of Qualitative Research* (pp. 509–535). Thousand Oaks, CA: SAGE.

Chauhan, S. (1992). Role of yogic exercises in the withdrawal symptoms of drug-addicts. *Yoga Mimamsa, 30*, 21–23.

Chiesura, A. (2004). The role of urban parks for the sustainable city. *Landscape and Urban Planning, 68*(1), 129–138.

Cioffi, D. (1991). Beyond attentional strategies: Cognitive perceptual model of somatic interpretation. *Psychological Bulletin, 109*, 25–41.

Clifton, D. O., & Harter, J. K. (2003). Investing in strengths. In K. S. Cameron, J. E. Dutton & R. E. Quinn (Eds.), *Positive Organizational Scholarship: Foundations of a New Discipline* (pp. 111–121). San Francisco, CA: Berrett-Koehler.

Clow, A., & Fredhoi, C. (2006). Normalisation of salivary cortisol levels and self-report stress by a brief lunchtime visit to an art gallery by London City workers. *Journal of Holistic Healthcare, 3*(2), 29–32.

CNN (2013, 25 August 2012). Fighting loneliness and disease with meditation. Retrieved 16 February, 2013, from http://edition.cnn.com/2012/08/25/health/meditation-loneliness-inflammation-enayati

Coffey, L. (2012). *What's Your Dharma? Discover the Vedic Way to Your Life's Purpose*. Westlake Village, CA: Bamboo Entertainment.

Cohen, A. B., Pierce Jr, J. D., Chambers, J., Meade, R., Gorvine, B. J., & Koenig, H. G. (2005). Intrinsic and extrinsic religiosity, belief in the afterlife, death anxiety, and life satisfaction in young Catholics and Protestants. *Journal of Research in Personality, 39*(3), 307–324.

Cohen, S., Alper, C. M., Doyle, W. J., Treanor, J. J., & Turner, R. B. (2006). Positive emotional style predicts resistance to illness after experimental exposure to rhinovirus or influenza A virus. *Psychosomatic Medicine, 68*(6), 809–815.

Colberg, S. R., Sigal, R. J., Fernhall, B., Regensteiner, J. G., Blissmer, B. J., Rubin, R. R., ... Braun, B. (2010). Exercise and type 2 diabetes. The American College of Sports Medicine and the American Diabetes Association: Joint position statement. *Diabetes Care, 33*(12), e147–e167.

Coningham, R., Acharya, K., Strickland, K., Davis, C., Manuel, M., Simpson, I., . . . Sanderson, D. (2013). The earliest Buddhist shrine: Excavating the birthplace of the Buddha, Lumbini (Nepal). *Antiquity, 87*(338), 1104–1123.

Connell, R. W. (1995). *Masculinities*. Berkeley, CA: University of California Press.

Cook, E. A. (1998). Effects of reminiscence on life satisfaction of elderly female nursing home residents. *Health Care for Women International, 19*(2), 109–118.

The Cooperative (2012). *Ethical Consumer Markets Report 2012*. Manchester: The Cooperative Group.

Cooperrider, D. L., & Srivastva, S. (1987). Appreciative inquiry in organizational life. *Research in Organizational Change and Development, 1*(1), 129–169.

Costa, P. T., & McCrae, R. R. (1992). Normal personality assessment in clinical practice: The NEO Personality Inventory. *Psychological Assessment, 4*(1), 5–13.

Courtenay, W. H. (2000). Constructions of masculinity and their influence on men's well-being: A theory of gender and health. *Social Science & Medicine, 50*(10), 1385–1401.

Cousins, L. S. (1996). The dating of the historical Buddha: A review article. *Journal of the Royal Asiatic Society (Third Series), 6*(1), 57–63.

Cox, H. (1999). The market as God. *The Atlantic Monthly, 283*(3), 18–23.

Coyne, J., & Tennen, H. (2010). Positive psychology in cancer care: Bad science, exaggerated claims, and unproven medicine. *Annals of Behavioral Medicine, 39*(1), 16–26.

Crabb, S. (2011). The use of coaching principles to foster employee engagement. *The Coaching Psychologist, 7*(1), 27–34.

Crabtree, S., & Pelham, B. (2009). What Alabamians and Iranians Have in Common. Retrieved 14 March, 2013, from http://www.gallup.com/poll/114211/Alabamians-Iranians-Common.aspx

Crombie, D., Lombard, C., & Noakes, T. (2011). Increasing emotional intelligence in cricketers: An intervention study. *International Journal of Sports Science and Coaching, 6*(1), 69–86.

Croom, A. M. (2012). Music, neuroscience, and the psychology of wellbeing: A précis. *Frontiers in Psychology, 2*, 1–15.

Cruz-Ferreira, A., Fernandes, J., Gomes, D., Bernardo, L. M., Kirkcaldy, B. D., Barbosa, T. M., & Silva, A. (2011). Effects of Pilates-based exercise on life satisfaction, physical self-concept and health status in adult women. *Women & Health, 51*(3), 240–255.

Csikszentmihalyi, M. (1990). *Flow: The Psychology of Optimal Experience*. New York: Harper Perennial.

Curtis, B. M., & O'Keefe Jr, J. H. (2002). Autonomic tone as a cardiovascular risk factor: The dangers of chronic fight or flight. *Mayo Clinic Proceedings, 77*(1), 45–54.

Cushway, D., & Gatherer, A. (2003). Reflecting on reflection. *Clinical Psychology, 27*, 6–10.

Cutcliffe, J. R. (2003). Reconsidering reflexivity: Introducing the case for intellectual entrepreneurship. *Qualitative Health Research, 13*(1), 136–148.

da Costa, B. R., & Vieira, E. R. (2008). Stretching to reduce work-related musculoskeletal disorders: A systematic review. *Journal of Rehabilitation Medicine, 40*(5), 321–328.

Dahl, R. E. (2004). Adolescent brain development: A period of vulnerabilities and opportunities. Keynote address. *Annals of the New York Academy of Sciences, 1021*(1), 1–22.

Dahlsgaard, K., Peterson, C., & Seligman, M. E. (2005). Shared virtue: The convergence of valued human strengths across culture and history. *Review of General Psychology, 9*(3), 203–213.

Dalen, J., Smith, B. W., Shelley, B. M., Sloan, A. L., Leahigh, L., & Begay, D. (2010). Pilot study: Mindful Eating and Living (MEAL): Weight, eating behavior, and psychological outcomes associated with a mindfulness-based intervention for people with obesity. *Complementary Therapies in Medicine, 18*(6), 260–264.

Dalke, H., Little, J., Niemann, E., Camgoz, N., Steadman, G., Hill, S., & Stott, L. (2006). Colour and lighting in hospital design. *Optics & Laser Technology, 38*(4), 343–365.

Daltroy, L. H., Iversen, M. D., Larson, M. G., Lew, R., Wright, E., Ryan, J., . . . Liang, M. H. (1997). A controlled trial of an educational program to prevent low back injuries. *New England Journal of Medicine, 337*(5), 322–328.

Damasio, A. R., Everitt, B. J., & Bishop, D. (1996). The somatic marker hypothesis and the possible functions of the prefrontal cortex. *Philosophical Transactions of the Royal Society of London. Series B: Biological Sciences, 351*(1346), 1413–1420.

Darmstadt, G. L., Donnay, F., & Starrs, A. (2013). Healthy mother, healthy newborn: An interconnected continuum. *The Journal of Maternal-Fetal & Neonatal Medicine, 26*(S1), 1–2.

Dasen, P. (2000). Rapid social change and the turmoil of adolescence: A cross-cultural perspective. *International Journal of Group Tensions, 29*(1–2), 17–49.

Davidson, R. J. (2000). Affective style, psychopathology, and resilience: Brain mechanisms and plasticity. *American Psychologist, 55*(11), 1196–1214.

Davidson, R. J. (2003). Affective neuroscience and psychophysiology: Toward a synthesis. *Psychophysiology, 40*(5), 655–665.

Davis, M. C. (2004). Life review therapy as an intervention to manage depression and enhance life satisfaction in individuals with right hemisphere cerebral vascular accidents. *Issues in Mental Health Nursing, 25*(5), 503–515.

Davis-Kean, P. E. (2005). The influence of parent education and family income on child achievement: The indirect role of parental expectations and the home environment. *Journal of Family Psychology, 19*(2), 294–304.

Day, A. L., & Carroll, S. A. (2004). Using an ability-based measure of emotional intelligence to predict individual performance, group performance, and group citizenship behaviours. *Personality and Individual Differences, 36*(6), 1443–1458.

de Botton, A. (2012). *Religion for Atheists: A Non-Believer's Guide to the Uses of Religion.* New York: Pantheon Books.

de Chavez, A. C., Backett-Milburn, K., Parry, O., & Platt, S. (2005). Understanding and researching wellbeing: Its usage in different disciplines and potential for health research and health promotion. *Health Education Journal, 64*(1), 70–87.

de Neve, J.-E., Christakis, N. A., Fowler, J. H., & Frey, B. S. (2012). Genes, economics, and happiness. *Journal of Neuroscience, Psychology, and Economics, 5*(4), 193–211.

Deci, E. L., & Ryan, R. M. (1985). *Intrinsic Motivation and Self-Determination in Human Behavior.* New York: Plenum.

Deci, E. L., & Ryan, R. M. (2000). The "what" and "why" of goal pursuits: Human needs and the self-determination of behavior. *Psychological Inquiry, 11*, 319–338.

DeLuca, K. M., Lawson, S., & Sun, Y. (2012). Occupy Wall Street on the public screens of social media: The many framings of the birth of a protest movement. *Communication, Culture & Critique, 5*(4), 483–509.

Demerouti, E., Bakker, A. B., Nachreiner, F., & Schaufeli, W. B. (2001). The job demands–resources model of burnout. *Journal of Applied Psychology*, *86*(3), 499–512.

Dennett, D. (1990). *Consciousness Explained*. London: Allen Lane.

Department for Business, Innovation and Skills (2013). *Cut EU Red Tape: Report from the Business Taskforce*. London: Department for Business, Innovation and Skills.

Descartes, R. (2008 (1641)). *Meditations on First Philosophy: With Selections from the Objections and Replies* (M. Moriarty, Trans.). Oxford: Oxford University Press.

Diaz, F. M. (2010). A preliminary investigation into the effects of a brief mindfulness induction on perceptions of attention, aesthetic response, and flow during music listening. PhD thesis, Florida State University.

Diener, E., & Chan, M. Y. (2011). Happy people live longer: Subjective well-being contributes to health and longevity. *Applied Psychology: Health and Well-Being*, *3*(1), 1–43.

Dik, B. J., Duffy, R. D., & Eldridge, B. M. (2009). Calling and vocation in career counseling: Recommendations for promoting meaningful work. *Professional Psychology: Research and Practice*, *40*(6), 91–127.

Dik, B. J., Steger, M. F., Gibson, A., & Peisner, W. (2011). Make your work matter: Development and pilot evaluation of a purpose-centered career education intervention. *New Directions for Youth Development*, *132*, 59–73.

Dilts, R. (1990). *Changing Belief Systems with NLP*. Cupertino, CA: Meta Publications.

Ditto, B., Eclache, M., & Goldman, N. (2006). Short-term autonomic and cardiovascular effects of mindfulness body scan meditation. *Annals of Behavioral Medicine*, *32*(3), 227–234.

Donaldson, S. I., Csikszentmihalyi, M., & Nakamura, J. (Eds.). (2011). *Applied Positive Psychology: Improving Everyday Life, Health, Schools, Work, and Society*. London: Taylor & Francis.

Dowling, M., & Aribi, Z. A. (2013). Female directors and UK company acquisitiveness. *International Review of Financial Analysis*, *29*, 79–86.

Dubow, E. F., & Ippolito, M. F. (1994). Effects of poverty and quality of the home environment on changes in the academic and behavioral adjustment of elementary school-age children. *Journal of Clinical Child Psychology*, *23*(4), 401–412.

Duncan, G. (2010). Should happiness-maximization be the goal of government? *Journal of Happiness Studies*, *11*(2), 163–178.

Duncan, L. G., & Bardacke, N. (2010). Mindfulness-based childbirth and parenting education: Promoting family mindfulness during the perinatal period. *Journal of Child and Family Studies*, *19*(2), 190–202.

Duncan, L. G., Coatsworth, J. D., & Greenberg, M. T. (2009). A model of mindful parenting: Implications for parent–child relationships and prevention research. *Clinical Child and Family Psychology Review*, *12*(3), 255–270.

Dunphy, K. F. (2009). *Developing and Revitializing Rural Communities through Arts and Creativity: Australia*. Vancouver, BC: Creative City Network of Canada.

Dupuy, J. (2013). *Integral Recovery: A Revolutionary Approach to the Treatment of Alcoholism and Addiction*. New York: SUNY Press.

Durkheim, E. (2001 (1912)). *The Elementary Forms of Religious Life* (C. Cosman, Trans.). Oxford: Oxford University Press.

Durlak, J. A., Weissberg, R. P., & Pachan, M. (2010). A meta-analysis of after-school programs that seek to promote personal and social skills in children and adolescents. *American Journal of Community Psychology, 45*(3–4), 294–309.

Dutton, J. E., Roberts, L. M., & Bednar, J. (2010). Pathways for positive identity construction at work: Four types of positive identity and the building of social resources. *Academy of Management Review, 35*(2), 265–293.

Dweck, C. S. (2006). *Mindset: The New Psychology of Success.* New York: Random House.

Dweck, C. S., Chiu, C. & Hong, Y. (1995). Implicit theories: Elaboration and extension of the model. *Psychological Inquiry, 6*(4), 322–333.

Easterlin, R. A. (1995). Will raising the incomes of all increase the happiness of all? *Journal of Economic Behavior & Organization, 27*(1), 35–47.

Edwards, J. K. (2012). *Strengths-Based Supervision in Clinical Practice.* New York: SAGE.

Ehrenreich, B. (2009). *Smile or Die: How Positive Thinking Fooled America and the World.* London: Granta.

Ellens, J. H. (2008). *Understanding Religious Experiences: What the Bible Says about Spirituality.* Westport, CT: Praeger.

Elliott, M., & Hayward, R. D. (2007). Religion and the search for meaning in life. *Journal of Counselling Psychology, 53*, 80–93.

Ellis, A. (1987). *The Practice of Rational-Emotive Therapy.* New York: Springer.

Ellison, C. G., & Levin, J. S. (1998). The religion–health connection: Evidence, theory, and future directions. *Health Education & Behavior, 25*(6), 700–720.

Emmons, R. A., & McCullough, M. E. (2003). Counting blessings versus burdens: An experimental investigation of gratitude and subjective well-being in daily life. *Journal of Personality and Social Psychology, 84*(2), 377–389.

Emmons, R. A., & Paloutzian, R. F. (2003). The psychology of religion. *Annual Review of Psychology, 54*(1), 377–402.

Engel, G. L. (1977). The need for a new medical model: A challenge for biomedicine. *Science, 196*(4286), 129–136.

Enns, C. Z., & Kasai, M. (2003). Hakoniwa: Japanese sandplay therapy. *The Counseling Psychologist, 31*(1), 93–112.

Enosh, G., & Buchbinder, E. (2005). The interactive construction of narrative styles in sensitive interviews: The case of domestic violence research. *Qualitative Enquiry, 11*(4), 588–617.

Equality and Human Rights Commission (2010). *Equality, Human Rights and Good Relations in 2010.* London: Equality and Human Rights Commission.

Erikson, E. H. (1963 (1950)). *Childhood and Society* (2nd edition). New York: W. W. Norton.

Erricker, C., & Erricker, J. (2001). *Meditation in Schools: A Practical Guide to Calmer Classrooms.* New York: Continuum.

Esbjörn-Hargens, S. (2006). Integral research: A multi-method approach to investigating phenomena. *Constructivism and the Human Sciences, 11*(1–2), 79–107.

Ettner, S. L., & Grzywacz, J. G. (2001). Workers' perceptions of how jobs affect health: A social ecological perspective. *Journal of Occupational Health Psychology*, 6(2), 101–113.

Evans, J. H. (2002). *Playing God?: Human Genetic Engineering and the Rationalization of Public Bioethical Debate*. Chicago, IL: University of Chicago Press.

Evans, S., Ferrando, S., Findler, M., Stowell, C., Smart, C., & Haglin, D. (2008). Mindfulness-based cognitive therapy for generalized anxiety disorder. *Journal of Anxiety Disorders*, 22(4), 716–721.

Faiver, C. M., O'Brien, E. M., & Ingersoll, R. E. (2000). Religion, guilt, and mental health. *Journal of Counseling & Development*, 78(2), 155–161.

Farrell, M., Howes, S., Bebbington, P., Brugha, T., Jenkins, R., Lewis, G., . . . Meltzer, H. (2001). Nicotine, alcohol and drug dependence and psychiatric comorbidity: Results of a national household survey. *British Journal of Psychiatry*, 179, 432–437.

Fava, G. A., & Ruini, C. (2013). Well-being therapy: Theoretical background, clinical implications, and future directions. In S. A. David, I. Boniwell & A. C. Ayers (Eds.), *The Oxford Handbook of Happiness*. Oxford: Oxford University Press.

Feldenkrais, M. (1977). *Awareness through Movement*. London: Penguin.

Feldman, R., Keren, M., Gross-Rozval, O., & Tyano, S. (2004). Mother–child touch patterns in infant feeding disorders: Relation to maternal, child, and environmental factors. *Journal of the American Academy of Child & Adolescent Psychiatry*, 43(9), 1089–1097.

Fell, J. (2004). Identifying neural correlates of consciousness: The state space approach. *Consciousness and Cognition*, 13(4), 709–729.

Fell, J., Axmacher, N., & Haupt, S. (2010). From alpha to gamma: Electrophysiological correlates of meditation-related states of consciousness. *Medical Hypotheses*, 75(2), 218–224.

Ferguson, J. M. (2001). SSRI antidepressant medications: Adverse effects and tolerability. *Journal of Clinical Psychiatry*, 3(1), 22–27.

Fetzer Institute. (1999). *National Institute on Aging Working Group: Multidimensional Measurement of Religiousness/Spirituality for Use in Health Research*. Kalamazoo, MI: Fetzer Institute.

Feuerstein, G. (2002). *The Yoga Tradition: Its History, Literature, Philosophy, and Practice*. New Delhi: Bhavana Books.

Field, T., Diego, M., & Hernandez-Reif, M. (2010). Preterm infant massage therapy research: A review. *Infant Behavior and Development*, 33(2), 115–124.

Fincham, F. D., & Beach, S. R. (2010). Of memes and marriage: Toward a positive relationship science. *Journal of Family Theory & Review*, 2(1), 4–24.

Fine, S., Horowitz, I., Weigler, H., & Basis, L. (2010). Is good character good enough? The effects of situational variables on the relationship between integrity and counterproductive work behaviors. *Human Resource Management Review*, 20(1), 73–84.

Finlay, B., & Walther, C. S. (2003). The relation of religious affiliation, service attendance, and other factors to homophobic attitudes among university students. *Review of Religious Research*, 44(4), 370–393.

Finlay, F., & Gough, B. (2003). *Reflexivity: A Practical Guide for Researchers in Health and Social Sciences*. Oxford: Blackwell Science.

Firth, S. (2005). End-of-life: A Hindu view. *The Lancet*, *366*(9486), 682–686.

Fischer, C. (2008). Feedback on household electricity consumption: A tool for saving energy? *Energy Efficiency*, *1*(1), 79–104.

Flett, G. L., Vredenburg, K., & Krames, L. (1997). The continuity of depression in clinical and nonclinical samples. *Psychological Bulletin*, *121*(3), 395–416.

Ford, P. A., Jaceldo-Siegl, K., Lee, J. W., Youngberg, W., & Tonstad, S. (2013). Intake of Mediterranean foods associated with positive affect and low negative affect. *Journal of Psychosomatic Research*, *74*(2), 142–148.

Foster, W. (1986). A critical perspective on administration and organization in education. *Critical Perspectives on the Organization and Improvement of Schooling* (Vol. 13, pp. 95–129). Amsterdam: Springer.

Foucault, M. (1973). *Madness and Civilization*. New York: Vintage Books.

Foucault, M. (1979). *Discipline and Punish*. New York: Vintage Books.

Fowler, R. D., Seligman, M. E. P., & Koocher, G. P. (1999). The APA 1998 Annual Report. *American Psychologist*, *54*(8), 537–568.

Fox, K. R., Biddle, S., & Boutcher, S. (2001). The effects of exercise on self-perceptions and self-esteem. In S. J. H. Biddle, K. R. Fox & S. H. Boutcher (Eds.), *Physical Activity and Psychological Well-being* (pp. 88–117). London: Routledge.

Frank, A. W. (1990). Bringing bodies back in: A decade review. *Theory, Culture & Society*, *7*(1), 131–162.

Frank, A. W. (1997). *The Wounded Storyteller: Body, Illness and Ethics*. Chicago, IL: University of Chicago Press.

Frankl, V. E. (1963). *Man's Search for Meaning: An Introduction to Logotherapy*. New York: Washington Square Press.

Fredrickson, B. L. (2005). The broaden-and-build theory of positive emotions. In F. A. Huppert, N. Baylis & B. Keverne (Eds.), *The Science of Well-Being* (pp. 217–240). Oxford: Oxford University Press.

Fredrickson, B. L., Cohn, M. A., Coffey, K. A., Pek, J., & Finkel, S. M. (2008). Open hearts build lives: Positive emotions, induced through loving-kindness meditation, build consequential personal resources. *Journal of Personality and Social Psychology*, *95*(5), 1045–1062.

Fredrickson, B. L., & Roberts, T. A. (1997). Objectification theory. *Psychology of Women Quarterly*, *21*(2), 173–206.

Fresco, D. M., Moore, M. T., van Dulmen, M. H. M., Segal, Z. V., Ma, S. H., Teasdale, J. D., & Williams, J. M. G. (2007). Initial psychometric properties of the experiences questionnaire: Validation of a self-report measure of decentering. *Behavior Therapy*, *38*(3), 234–246.

Friedman, M. (1951). Neo-liberalism and its prospects. Unpublished paper available in the archives of the Hoover Institution. Stanford, CA: Stanford University.

Fry, L. W. (2003). Toward a theory of spiritual leadership. *The Leadership Quarterly*, *14*(6), 693–727.

Fuster, J. M. (2008). *The Prefrontal Cortex* (4th edition). London: Academic Press.

Gable, S. L., Reis, H. T., Impett, E. A., & Asher, E. R. (2004). What do you do when things go right? The intrapersonal and interpersonal benefits of sharing positive events. *Journal of Personality and Social Psychology*, *87*(2), 228–245.

Gabriel, L. (2009). Regulation: Refusing to participate – BACP response. *Therapy Today*, *20*(6). doi: http://www.therapytoday.net/article/show/547/

Gallace, A. (2012). Living with touch. *The Psychologist*, *25*(12), 896–899.

Gallagher, A., & Hodge, S. (2012). *Ethics, Law and Professional Issues: A Practice Based Approach for Health Professionals*. Basingstoke: Palgrave Macmillan.

Gallup, G., & Johnson, B. R. (2003). New Index Tracks 'Spiritual State of the Union'. *Gallup Poll News Service*. Retrieved from http://www.gallup.com/poll/7657/New-Index-Tracks-Spiritual-State-Union.aspx.

Ganpat, T. S., & Nagendra, H. (2011). Yoga therapy for developing emotional intelligence in mid-life managers. *Journal of Mid-Life Health*, *2*(1), 28–30.

Garber, C. E., Blissmer, B., Deschenes, M. R., Franklin, B., Lamonte, M. J., Lee, I.-M., . . . Swain, D. P. (2011). American College of Sports Medicine position stand. Quantity and quality of exercise for developing and maintaining cardiorespiratory, musculoskeletal, and neuromotor fitness in apparently healthy adults: Guidance for prescribing exercise. *Medicine and Science in Sports and Exercise*, *43*(7), 1334–1359.

Gard, G. (2005). Body awareness therapy for patients with fibromyalgia and chronic pain. *Disability & Rehabilitation*, *27*(12), 725–728.

Gardner, F. (2001). Social work students and self-awareness: How does it happen? *Reflective Practice*, *2*(1), 27–40.

Gardner, H. (1985). *Frames of Mind: The Theory of Multiple Intelligences*. New York: Basic Books.

Garland, S. N., Carlson, L. E., Cook, S., Lansdell, L., & Speca, M. (2007). A non-randomized comparison of mindfulness-based stress reduction and healing arts programs for facilitating post-traumatic growth and spirituality in cancer outpatients. *Supportive Care in Cancer*, *15*(8), 949–961.

Gebser, J. (1985). *The Ever-Present Origin* (N. Barstad & A. Mickunas, Trans.). Athens, OH: Ohio University Press

Germer, C. K., Siegel, R. D., & Fulton, P. R. (2005). *Mindfulness and Psychotherapy*. New York: Guilford Press.

Gesler, W. M. (1992). Therapeutic landscapes: Medical issues in light of the new cultural geography. *Social Science & Medicine*, *34*(7), 735–746.

Giacalone, R., & Promislo, M. (2010). Unethical and unwell: Decrements in well-being and unethical activity at work. *Journal of Business Ethics*, *91*(2), 275–297.

Giddens, A., & Dallmayr, F. R. (1982). *Profiles and Critiques in Social Theory*. Berkeley, CA: University of California Press.

Gillham, J. E., Jaycox, L. H., Reivich, K. J., Seligman, M. E. P., & Silver, T. (1990). The Penn Resiliency Program. Unpublished Manual, University of Pennsylvania, Philadelphia, PA.

Gillham, J. E., Reivich, K. J., Freres, D. R., Lascher, M., Litzinger, S., Shatté, A., & Seligman, M. E. P. (2006). School-based prevention of depression and anxiety symptoms in early adolescence: A pilot of a parent intervention component. *School Psychology Quarterly*, *21*(3), 323–348.

Gokcen, N., Hefferon, K., & Attree, E. (2012). University students' constructions of 'flourishing' in British higher education: An inductive content analysis. *International Journal of Wellbeing*, *2*(1), 1–21.

Gold, C., Wigram, T., & Elefant, C. (2006). Music therapy for autistic spectrum disorder. *Cochrane Database of Systematic Reviews, 2*.

Gold, E., Smith, A., Hopper, I., Herne, D., Tansey, G., & Hulland, C. (2010). Mindfulness-based stress reduction (MBSR) for primary school teachers. *Journal of Child and Family Studies, 19*(2), 184–189.

Goldstein, E. D. (2007). Sacred moments: Implications on well-being and stress. *Journal of Clinical Psychology, 63*(10), 1001–1019.

Goswami, A. (1990). Consciousness in quantum physics and the mind–body problem. *Journal of Mind and Behavior, 11*(1), 75–96.

Graeser, S. (2011). Salutogenic factors for mental health promotion in work settings and organizations. *International Review of Psychiatry, 23*(6), 508–515.

Grant, A. M. (2006). A personal perspective on professional coaching and the development of coaching psychology. *International Coaching Psychology Review, 1*(1), 12–22.

Grant, A. M., Curtayne, L., & Burton, G. (2009). Executive coaching enhances goal attainment, resilience and workplace well-being: A randomised controlled study. *The Journal of Positive Psychology, 4*(5), 396–407.

Grau, A., & Jordan, S. (2002). *Europe Dancing: Perspectives on Theatre, Dance, and Cultural Identity*. London: Routledge.

Graves, C. W. (1970). Levels of existence: An open system theory of values. *Journal of Humanistic Psychology, 10*(2), 131–155.

Griffin, C. (1997). Troubled teens: Managing disorders of transition and consumption. *Feminist Review, 55*, 4–21.

Griffiths, R. R., Richards, W. A., McCann, U., & Jesse, R. (2006). Psilocybin can occasion mystical-type experiences having substantial and sustained personal meaning and spiritual significance. *Psychopharmacology, 187*(3), 268–283.

Grimshaw, D., & Rubery, J. (2012). Reinforcing neoliberalism: Crisis and austerity in the UK. In S. Lehndorff (Ed.), *A Triumph of Failed Ideas: European Models of Capitalism in the Crisis* (pp. 41–58). Brussels: European Trade Union Initiative.

Griswold, E. (2012, 23 September). How 'Silent Spring' ignited the environmental movement, *New York Times*.

Gross, J. J. (1999). Emotion regulation: Past, present, future. *Cognition & Emotion, 13*(5), 551–573.

Grossman, P., Niemann, L., Schmidt, S., & Walach, H. (2004). Mindfulness-based stress reduction and health benefits: A meta-analysis. *Journal of Psychosomatic Research, 57*(1), 35–43.

Gruzelier, J. H., Foks, M., Steffert, T., Chen, M. J. L., & Ros, T. (2013). Beneficial outcome from EEG-neurofeedback on creative music performance, attention and well-being in school children. *Biological Psychology, 95*(0), 86–95.

Guest, D. E. (2002). Perspectives on the study of work–life balance. *Social Science Information, 41*(2), 255–279.

Guiffrida, D. A. (2005). The emergence model: An alternative pedagogy for facilitating self-reflection and theoretical fit in counseling students. *Counselor Education and Supervision, 44*(3), 201–213.

Gyatso, T. (2006). Science at the crossroads. *Explore: The Journal of Science and Healing*, *2*(2), 97–99.

Gyllensten, A. L. (2001). *Basic Body Awareness Therapy: Assessment, Treatment and Interaction*. Lund, Sweden: University of Lund.

Hackney, C. H. (2007). Possibilities for a Christian positive psychology. *Journal of Psychology and Theology*, *35*(3), 211–221.

Hadfield, C. (2013). *An Astronaut's Guide to Life on Earth*. London: Macmillan.

Halliday, J. L. (1948). *Psychosocial Medicine: A Study of the Sick Society*. London: W. W. Norton.

Halstead, M. T., & Mickley, J. R. (1997). Attempting to fathom the unfathomable: Descriptive views of spirituality. *Seminars in Oncology Nursing*, *13*(4), 225–230.

Hamilton, N. A., Kitzman, H., & Guyotte, S. (2006). Enhancing health and emotion: Mindfulness as a missing link between cognitive therapy and positive psychology. *Journal of Cognitive Psychotherapy*, *20*(2), 123–134.

Hamilton-Baillie, B. (2008). Shared space: Reconciling people, places and traffic. *Built Environment*, *34*(2), 161–181.

Hammond, D. C. (2005). Neurofeedback treatment of depression and anxiety. *Journal of Adult Development*, *12*(2–3), 131–137.

Hanh, T. N. (1993). *The Blooming of a Lotus: Guided Meditation Exercises for Healing and Transformation* (A. Laity, Trans.). Boston, MA: Beacon Press.

Hanlon, P., Carlisle, S., Reilly, D., Lyon, A., & Hannah, M. (2010). Enabling well-being in a time of radical change: Integrative public health for the 21st century. *Public Health*, *124*(6), 305–312.

Haque, U. (2011). *Betterness: Economics for Humans*. Cambridge, MA: Harvard Business Press.

Harcourt, B. E. (1998). Reflecting on the subject: A critique of the social influence conception of deterrence, the broken windows theory, and order-maintenance policing New York style. *Michigan Law Review*, *97*(2), 291–389.

Hardy, C., Phillips, N., & Clegg, S. (2001). Reflexivity in organization and management theory: A study of the production of the research subject. *Human Relations*, *54*(5), 531–560.

Harrison, S. (2002). *Doing Nothing: Coming to the End of the Spiritual Search*. New York: Jeremy P. Tarcher.

Harter, J. K., Schmidt, F. L., & Keyes, C. L. M. (2003). Wellbeing in the workplace and its relationship to business outcomes. In C. L. Keyes & J. Haidt (Eds.), *Flourishing: The Positive Person and the Good Life* (pp. 205–224). Washington, DC: Americal Psychological Association.

Harvey, P. (2012). *An Introduction to Buddhism: Teachings, History and Practices*. Cambridge: Cambridge University Press.

Hayes, S. C. (2002). Buddhism and acceptance and commitment therapy. *Cognitive and Behavioral Practice*, *9*(1), 58–66.

Hays, T. (2005). Well-being in later life through music. *Australasian Journal on Ageing*, *24*(1), 28–32.

Hays, T., & Minichiello, V. (2005). The meaning of music in the lives of older people: A qualitative study. *Psychology of Music, 33*(4), 437–451.

Hazard Jr, G. C. (1994). Law, morals, and ethics. *Southern Illinois University Law Journal, 19*, 447–458.

Health and Safety Executive (1998). *The Working Time Regulations 1998*. Retrieved from http://www.hse.gov.uk/contact/faqs/workingtimedirective.htm

Heaphy, E. D., & Dutton, J. E. (2008). Positive social interactions and the human body at work: Linking organizations and physiology. *Academy of Management Review, 33*(1), 137–162.

Hefferon, K. (2013). *Positive Psychology and the Body: The Somatopsychic Side to Flourishing*. Maidenhead: Open University Press.

Hefferon, K., & Boniwell, I. (2011). *Positive Psychology: Theory, Research and Applications*. Maidenhead: Open University Press.

Hefferon, K., & Mutrie, N. (2012). Physical activity as a 'stellar' positive psychology intervention. In E. O. Acevedo (Ed.), *The Oxford Handbook of Exercise Psychology* (pp. 117–130). Oxford and New York: Oxford University Press.

Hefferon, K., & Pluess, M. (2013). Genetics and their role in wellbeing. In *The Body and Positive Psychology: The Somatopsychic Side to Flourishing* (pp. 59–76). Maidenhead: Open University Press/McGraw Hill.

Hefferon, K. M., & Ollis, S. (2006). 'Just clicks': An interpretive phenomenological analysis of professional dancers' experience of flow. *Research in Dance Education, 7*(2), 141–159.

Heidegger, M. (1927). *Being and Time* (J. MacQuarrie & E. Robinson, Trans.). London: Blackwell.

Held, B. S. (2002). The tyranny of the positive attitude in America: Observation and speculation. *Journal of Clinical Psychology, 58*(9), 965–991.

Held, B. S. (2004). The negative side of positive psychology. *Journal of Humanistic Psychology, 44*(1), 9–46.

Helliwell, J. F., & Huang, H. (2010). How's the job? Well-being and social capital in the workplace. *ILR Review, 63*, 205–227.

Helliwell, J. F., Layard, R., & Sachs, J. (Eds.). (2013). *World Happiness Report 2013*. Geneva: United Nations.

Helliwell, J. F., & Putnam, R. D. (2004). The social context of well-being. *Philosophical Transactions of the Royal Society of London. Series B: Biological Sciences, 359*(1449), 1435–1446.

Herring, M. P., O'Connor, P. J., & Dishman, R. K. (2010). The effect of exercise training on anxiety symptoms among patients: A systematic review. *Archives of Internal Medicine, 170*(4), 321–331.

Hertenstein, M. J. (2010). Tactile stimulation. In S. Goldstein & J. Naglieri (Eds.), *Encyclopedia of Child Behavior and Development*. New York: Springer.

Highwater, J. (1992). *Dance: Rituals of Experience*. Oxford: Oxford University Press.

Hill, P. C., Pargament, K. I., Hood, R. W., McCullough Jr, M. E., Swyers, J. P., Larson, D. B., & Zinnbauer, B. J. (2000). Conceptualizing religion and spirituality: Points of commonality, points of departure. *Journal for the Theory of Social Behaviour, 30*(1), 51–77.

Hillman, C. H., Erickson, K. I., & Kramer, A. F. (2008). Be smart, exercise your heart: Exercise effects on brain and cognition. *Nature Reviews Neuroscience, 9*(1), 58–65.

His Holiness the Dalai Lama (1997). *The Heart of Compassion.* Twin Lakes, WI: Lotus Press.

HM Treasury (2011). *The Plan for Growth.* London: HM Treasury.

Hobel, C., & Culhane, J. (2003). Role of psychosocial and nutritional stress on poor pregnancy outcome. *The Journal of Nutrition, 133*(5), 1709S–1717S.

Hochschild, A. R. (1979). Emotion work, feeling rules, and social structure. *The American Journal of Sociology, 85*(3), 551–575.

Hoffman, B. M., Babyak, M. A., Craighead, W. E., Sherwood, A., Doraiswamy, P. M., Coons, M. J., & Blumenthal, J. A. (2011). Exercise and pharmacotherapy in patients with major depression: One-year follow-up of the SMILE study. *Psychosomatic Medicine, 73*(2), 127–133.

Hollingsworth, A. (2008). Implications of interpersonal neurobiology for a spirituality of compassion. *Zygon, 43*(4), 837–860.

Holt, N., Bremner, A., Sutherland, E., Vliek, M., Passer, M., & Smith, R. (2012). *Psychology: The Science of Mind and Behaviour.* Maidenhead: McGraw Hill.

Hölzel, B. K., Ott, U., Hempel, H., Hackl, A., Wolf, K., Stark, R., & Viatl, D. (2007). Differential engagement of anterior cingulate and adjacent medial frontal cortex in adept meditators and non-meditators. *Neuroscience Letters, 421*(1), 16–21.

Hoover, T. (2010). *Zen Culture.* New York: Random House.

Hopper, J. R., & Nielsen, J. M. (1991). Recycling as altruistic behavior: Normative and behavioral strategies to expand participation in a community recycling program. *Environment and Behavior, 23*(2), 195–220.

House, R. J. (1977). A 1976 theory of charismatic leadership. In J. G. Hunt & L. L. Larson (Eds.), *Leadership: The Cutting Edge* (pp. 189–207). Carbondale, IL: Southern Illinois University Press.

Hsu, M. C., Schubiner, H., Stracks, J. S., & Clauw, D. J. (2010). Sustained pain reduction through affective self-awareness in fibromyalgia: A randomized controlled trial. *Journal of General Internal Medicine, 25*(10), 1064–1070.

Hudson, A. (2011, 10 March). Are call centres the factories of the 21st Century? *BBC.*

Huebner, E. S. (1994). Preliminary development and validation of a multidimensional life satisfaction scale for children. *Psychological Assessment, 6*(2), 149–158.

Huebner, E. S. (2001). *Manual for the Multidimensional Students' Life Satisfaction Scale.* Columbia, SC: University of South Carolina Press.

Husserl, E. (1952). *Ideas Pertaining to a Pure Phenomenology and to a Phenomenological Philosophy.* The Hague: Martinus Nijhoff.

Inskipp, F., & Proctor, B. (1993). *The Art, Craft and Tasks of Counselling Supervision.* New York: Cascade Publications.

Irving, J. A., Park-Saltzman, J., Fitzpatrick, M., Dobkin, P. L., Chen, A., & Hutchinson, T. (2012). Experiences of health care professionals enrolled in mindfulness-based medical practice: A grounded theory model. *Mindfulness, 5*(1), 60–71.

Ivtzan, I., Chan, C. P., Gardner, H. E., & Prashar, K. (2011). Linking religion and spirituality with psychological well-being: Examining self-actualisation, meaning in life, and personal growth initiative. *Journal of Religion and Health, 51,* 13–30.

Ivtzan, I., & Papantoniou, A. (2014). Yoga meets positive psychology: Examining the integration of hedonic (gratitude) and eudaimonic (meaning) wellbeing in relation to the extent of yoga practice. *Journal of Bodywork & Movement Therapies, 18*(2), 183–189.

Jacobs, A. B. (1985). *Looking at Cities.* Cambridge, MA: Harvard University Press.

Jacobson, K. (2012, 4 April). The shareholder fallacy. *Salon.*

Jafari, M. F. (1993). Counseling values and objectives: A comparison of Western and Islamic perspectives. *The American Journal of Islamic Social Sciences, 10*(3), 326–339.

Jahoda, M. (1958). *Current Concepts of Positive Mental Health.* New York: Basic Books.

Janoff-Bulman, R., & Yopyk, D. J. (2004). Random outcomes and valued commitments. In J. Greenberg, S. L. Koole & T. Pyszczynski (Eds.), *Handbook of Experimental Existential Psychology* (pp. 122–140). New York: Guilford Press.

Jenkinson, C. E., Dickens, A. P., Jones, K., Thompson-Coon, J., Taylor, R. S., Rogers, M., . . . Richards, S. H. (2013). Is volunteering a public health intervention? A systematic review and meta-analysis of the health and survival of volunteers. *BMC Public Health, 13*(1), 1–10.

Jeong, Y.-J., Hong, S.-C., Lee, M. S., Park, M.-C., Kim, Y.-K., & Suh, C.-M. (2005). Dance movement therapy improves emotional responses and modulates neurohormones in adolescents with mild depression. *International Journal of Neuroscience, 115*(12), 1711–1720.

Johnson, D. P., Penn, D. L., Fredrickson, B. L., Meyer, P. S., Kring, A. M., & Brantley, M. (2009). Loving-kindness meditation to enhance recovery from negative symptoms of schizophrenia. *Journal of Clinical Psychology, 65*(5), 499–509.

Johnson, E., & Goldstein, D. (2003). Do defaults save lives? *Science, 302,* 1338–1339.

Johnson, M. E. (2012). The Buddha and Patañjali: The impact of Buddhism on the yoga sūtras of Patañjali. *Sri Lanka International Journal of Buddhist Studies, 2,* 225–251.

Johnston, S. J., Boehm, S. G., Healy, D., Goebel, R., & Linden, D. E. J. (2010). Neurofeedback: A promising tool for the self-regulation of emotion networks. *Neuroimage, 49*(1), 1066–1072.

Josipovic, Z. (2010). Duality and nonduality in meditation research. *Consciousness and Cognition, 19*(4), 1119–1121.

Juvenal, & Richlin, A. (1986). *Juvenal Satire VI.* London: Bryn Mawr Commentaries.

Kabat-Zinn, J. (1982). An outpatient program in behavioral medicine for chronic pain patients based on the practice of mindfulness meditation: Theoretical considerations and preliminary results. *General Hospital Psychiatry, 4*(1), 33–47.

Kabat-Zinn, J. (2003). Mindfulness-based interventions in context: Past, present, and future. *Clinical Psychology: Science and Practice, 10*(2), 144–156.

Kabat-Zinn, J., Lipworth, L., Burncy, R., & Sellers, W. (1987). Four-year follow-up of a meditation-based program for the self-regulation of chronic pain: Treatment outcomes and compliance. *The Clinical Journal of Pain, 2*(3), 159–173.

Kahn, R. L., Wolfe, D. M., Quinn, R., Snoek, J. D., & Rosenthal, R. A. (1964). *Organizational Stress.* New York: Wiley.

Kahneman, D., Krueger, A. B., Schkade, D. A., Schwarz, N., & Stone, A. A. (2004). A survey method for characterizing daily life experience: The Day Reconstruction Method. *Science, 306*(5702), 1776–1780.

Kaplan, A. (1989). *Meditation and Kabbalah*. Boston, MA: Weiser Books.

Kauffman, C., & Silberman, J. (2009). Finding and fostering the positive in relationships: Positive interventions in couples therapy. *Journal of Clinical Psychology*, *65*(5), 520–531.

Kaufman, J. C. (2001). The Sylvia Plath effect: Mental illness in eminent creative writers. *The Journal of Creative Behavior*, *35*(1), 37–50.

Kaufmann, D., Kraay, A., & Mastruzzi, M. (2009). *Governance Matters VIII: Aggregate and Individual Governance Indicators, 1996–2008*. World Bank Policy Research Working Paper No. 4978. Washington, DC: World Bank.

Kaufmann, D., Kraay, A., & Zoido-Lobatón, P. (1999). *Aggregating Governance Indicators*. World Bank Policy Research Working Paper No. 2195. Washington, DC: World Bank.

Kawachi, I., & Berkman, L. (2001). Social ties and mental health. *Journal of Urban Health*, *78*(3), 458–467.

Kearney, A. R., & De Young, R. (1995). A knowledge-based intervention for promoting carpooling. *Environment and Behavior*, *27*(5), 650–678.

Keenan, J. P., Rubio, J., Racioppi, C., Johnson, A., & Barnacz, A. (2005). The right hemisphere and the dark side of consciousness. *Cortex*, *41*(5), 695–704.

Kelling, G. L., & Bratton, W. J. (1998). Declining crime rates: Insiders' views of the New York City story. *The Journal of Criminal Law and Criminology*, *88*(4), 1217–1232.

Kelloway, E. K., & Day, A. L. (2005). Building healthy workplaces: What we know so far. *Canadian Journal of Behavioural Science/Revue canadienne des sciences du comportement*, *37*(4), 223–235.

Keltner, D., & Haidt, J. (2003). Approaching awe, a moral, spiritual, and aesthetic emotion. *Cognition & Emotion*, *17*(2), 297–314.

Kemeny, M. E. (2003). The psychobiology of stress. *Current Directions in Psychological Science*, *12*(4), 124–129.

Kemmis, S., & McTaggart, R. (1982). *The Action Research Planner*. Geelong, Victoria, Australia: Deakin University Press.

Kennedy, C. A., Amick III, B. C., Dennerlein, J. T., Brewer, S., Catli, S., Williams, R., . . . Mahood, Q. (2010). Systematic review of the role of occupational health and safety interventions in the prevention of upper extremity musculoskeletal symptoms, signs, disorders, injuries, claims and lost time. *Journal of Occupational Rehabilitation*, *20*(2), 127–162.

Kenway, J., & Fitzclarence, L. (1997). Masculinity, violence and schooling: Challenging 'poisonous pedagogies'. *Gender and Education*, *9*(1), 117–134.

Kets de Vries, M. F. R. (2001). Creating authentizotic organizations: Well-functioning individuals in vibrant companies. *Human Relations*, *54*(1), 101–111.

Keyes, C. L. M. (2002). The mental health continuum: From languishing to flourishing in life. *Journal of Health and Social Behavior*, *43*(2), 207–222.

Khalsa, S. (2007). Yoga as a therapeutic intervention. *Principles and Practice of Stress Management*, *48*, 449–462.

Killeen, P. R., & Glenberg, A. M. (2010). Resituating cognition. *Comparative Cognition & Behavior Reviews*, *5*, 66–85.

King, L. A. (2001). The health benefits of writing about life goals. *Personality and Social Psychology Bulletin*, *27*(7), 798–807.

King, N. (2013). Local authority sport services under the UK coalition government: Retention, revision or curtailment? *International Journal of Sport Policy and Politics*. doi: 10.1080/19406940.2013.825873

King, R. (1999). *Orientalism and Religion: Post-Colonial Theory, India and 'The Mystic East'*. London: Routledge.

Kish, S., Furukawa, Y., Ang, L., Vorce, S., & Kalasinsky, K. (2000). Striatal serotonin is depleted in brain of a human MDMA (Ecstasy) user. *Neurology, 55*(2), 294–296.

Kivy, P. (2009). *The Blackwell Guide to Aesthetics*. London: John Wiley & Sons.

Kiyota, M. (1978). *Mahayana Buddhist Meditation: Theory and Practice*. Hawaii: University Press.

Kleen, M., & Reitsma, B. (2011). Appliance of heart rate variability biofeedback in acceptance and commitment therapy: A pilot study. *Journal of Neurotherapy, 15*(2), 170–181.

Klein, N. (2007). *The Shock Doctrine: The Rise of Disaster Capitalism*. New York: Macmillan.

Klein Velderman, M., Bakermans-Kranenburg, M. J., Juffer, F., & van Ijzendoorn, M. H. (2006). Effects of attachment-based interventions on maternal sensitivity and infant attachment: Differential susceptibility of highly reactive infants. *Journal of Family Psychology, 20*(2), 266–274.

Koch, C., & Tsuchiya, N. (2007). Attention and consciousness: Two distinct brain processes. *Trends in Cognitive Sciences, 11*(1), 16–22.

Koenig, H. G. (2009). Research on religion, spirituality, and mental health: A review. *Canadian Journal of Psychiatry, 54*(5), 283–291.

Koestler, A. (1964). *The Act of Creation*. London: Hutchinson & Co.

Koestler, A. (1978). *Janus: A Summing Up*. London: Hutchinson & Co.

Kohlberg, L. (1981). *The Philosophy of Moral Development: Moral Stages and the Idea of Justice*. London: Harper & Row.

Kohn, D. B., & Candotti, F. (2009). Gene therapy fulfilling its promise. *New England Journal of Medicine, 360*(5), 518–521.

Koltko-Rivera, M. E. (2006). Rediscovering the later version of Maslow's hierarchy of needs: Self-transcendence and opportunities for theory, research, and unification. *Review of General Psychology, 10*(4), 302–317.

Koplan, J. P., Siscovick, D. S., & Goldbaum, G. M. (1985). The risks of exercise: A public health view of injuries and hazards. *Public Health Reports, 100*(2), 189–195.

Korthagen, F., & Vasalos, A. (2005). Levels in reflection: Core reflection as a means to enhance professional growth. *Teachers and Teaching, 11*(1), 47–71.

Kosmin, B. A., & Keysar, A. (2013). *American Religious Identification Survey (ARIS 2012)*. Hartford, CT: ISSSC, Trinity College.

Kouzes, J. M., & Pozner, B. Z. (1987). *The Leadership Challenge*. San Francisco, CA: Jossey-Bass.

Kramer, K. (1986). *World Scriptures: An Introduction to Comparative Religions*. Mahwah, NJ: Paulist Press.

Kramer, K. (1988). *The Sacred Art of Dying: How World Religions Understand Death*. Mahwah, NJ: Paulist Press.

Krause, N. (2009). Religious involvement, gratitude, and change in depressive symptoms over time. *International Journal for the Psychology of Religion, 19*(3), 155–172.

Kringelbach, M. L., & Berridge, K. C. (2010). The functional neuroanatomy of pleasure and happiness. *Discovery Medicine*, *9*(49), 579–587.

Kumar, A., Tims, F., Cruess, D., Mintzer, M., Ironson, G., Loewenstein, D., . . . Kumar, M. (1999). Music therapy increases serum melatonin levels in patients with Alzheimer's disease. *Alternative Therapies in Health and Medicine*, *5*(6), 49–57.

Kumar, S. M. (2002). An introduction to Buddhism for the cognitive-behavioral therapist. *Cognitive and Behavioral Practice*, *9*(1), 40–43.

Larson, J. S. (1999). The conceptualization of health. *Medical Care Research and Review*, *56*(2), 123–136.

Larson, R., Jarrett, R., Hansen, D., Pearce, N., Sullivan, P., Walker, K., . . . Wood, D. (2004). Organized youth activities as contexts for positive development. In P. A. Linley & S. Joseph (Eds.), *Positive Psychology in Practice* (pp. 540–560). Hoboken, NJ: John Wiley & Sons.

Larson, R. W. (2000). Toward a psychology of positive youth development. *American Psychologist*, *55*(1), 170–183.

Latey, P. (2001). The Pilates method: History and philosophy. *Journal of Bodywork and Movement Therapies*, *5*(4), 275–282.

Latham, G. I. (1994). *The Power of Positive Parenting*. North Logan, UT: P&T Ink.

Lawler-Row, K. A., & Piferi, R. L. (2006). The forgiving personality: Describing a life well lived? *Personality and Individual Differences*, *41*(6), 1009–1020.

Layard, R. (2005). *Happiness: Lessons from a New Science*. London: Penguin.

Laybourn, K. (1997). *A History of British Trade Unionism*. London: Sutton Publishing.

Layder, D. (1993). *New Strategies in Social Research*. Cambridge: Polity Press.

Lazar, S. W., Kerr, C. E., Wasserman, R. H., Gray, J. R., Greve, D. N., Treadway, M. T., . . . Benson, H. (2005). Meditation experience is associated with increased cortical thickness. *Neuroreport*, *16*(17), 1893–1897.

Lazarus, R. S. (2003). Does the positive psychology movement have legs? *Psychological Inquiry*, *14*(2), 93–109.

Leiter, M. P., & Maslach, C. (2005). A mediation model of job burnout. In A. S. G. Antoniou & C. L. Cooper (Eds.), *Research Companion to Organizational Health Psychology* (pp. 544–564). Cheltenham: Edward Elgar.

Lerner, R. (2009). The positive youth development perspective: Theoretical and empirical bases of a strengths based approach to adolescent development. In S. Lopez & C. R. Snyder (Eds.), *Handbook of Positive Psychology* (2nd edition, pp. 149–164). New York: Oxford University Press.

Lesch, K.-P., Balling, U., Gross, J., Strauss, K., Wolozin, B., Murphy, D., & Riederer, P. (1994). Organization of the human serotonin transporter gene. *Journal of Neural Transmission*, *95*(2), 157–162.

Levenson, R. W., Ekman, P., & Ricard, M. (2012). Meditation and the startle response: A case study. *Emotion*, *12*(3), 650–658.

Levering, R. (1988). *A Great Place to Work*. New York: Avon Books.

Levine, D. N. (1984). The liberal arts and the martial arts. *Liberal Education*, *70*(3), 235–251.

Lomas, T., Hefferon, K., & Ivtzan, I. (forthcoming). The LIFE model: A conceptual map for applied positive psychology.

Lomas, T., Cartwright, T., Edginton, T., & Ridge, D. (2014a). A religion of wellbeing?: The appeal of Buddhism to men in London, UK. *Psychology of Religion and Spirituality*. doi: 10.1037/a0036420.

Lomas, T., Edginton, T., Cartwright, T., & Ridge, D. (2014b). Engagement with meditation as a positive health trajectory: Divergent narratives of progress in male mediators. *Psychology and Health*, 29(2), 218–236.

Lopez, S. J., Snyder, C. R., Magyar-Moe, J. L., Edwards, L. M., Pedrotti, J. T., Janowksi, K., . . . Pressgrove, C. (2004). Strategies for accentuating hope. In P. A. Linley & S. Joseph (Eds.), *Positive Psychology in Practice* (pp. 388–403). Hoboken, NJ: John Wiley & Sons.

Louis, M. C. (2011). Strengths interventions in higher education: The effect of identification versus development approaches on implicit self-theory. *The Journal of Positive Psychology*, 6(3), 204–215.

Lucas, R. E., Clark, A. E., Georgellis, Y., & Diener, E. (2004). Unemployment alters the set point for life satisfaction. *Psychological Science*, 15(1), 8–13.

Lucas, R. E., & Schimmack, U. (2009). Income and well-being: How big is the gap between the rich and the poor? *Journal of Research in Personality*, 43(1), 75–78.

Luft, J. (1969). *Of Human Interactions: The Johari Model*. Palo Alto, CA: Mayfield.

Lumley, J., Chamberlain, C., Dowswell, T., Oliver, S., Oakley, L., & Watson, L. (2009). Interventions for promoting smoking cessation during pregnancy. *Cochrane Database of Systematic Reviews*, 3.

Lund, C., Breen, A., Flisher, A. J., Kakuma, R., Corrigall, J., Joska, J. A., . . . Patel, V. (2010). Poverty and common mental disorders in low and middle income countries: A systematic review. *Social Science & Medicine*, 71(3), 517–528.

Luthans, F. (2002). The need for and meaning of positive organizational behavior. *Journal of Organizational Behavior*, 23(6), 695–706.

Luthans, F., Avey, J. B., Avolio, B. J., & Peterson, S. J. (2010). The development and resulting performance impact of positive psychological capital. *Human Resource Development Quarterly*, 21(1), 41–67.

Luthans, F., Youssef, C. M., & Avolio, B. J. (2007). *Psychological Capital*. Oxford: Oxford University Press.

Lutz, A., Greischar, L. L., Perlman, D. M., & Davidson, R. J. (2009). BOLD signal in insula is differentially related to cardiac function during compassion meditation in experts vs. novices. *NeuroImage*, 47(3), 1038–1046.

Lutz, A., Slagter, H. A., Dunne, J. D., & Davidson, R. J. (2008). Attention regulation and monitoring in meditation. *Trends in Cognitive Sciences*, 12(4), 163–169.

Lykken, D., & Tellegen, A. (1996). Happiness is a stochastic phenomenon. *Psychological Science*, 7(3), 186–189.

Lynch, J. W., Kaplan, G. A., & Shema, S. J. (1997). Cumulative impact of sustained economic hardship on physical, cognitive, psychological, and social functioning. *New England Journal of Medicine*, 337(26), 1889–1895.

Lyubomirsky, S. (2001). Why are some people happier than others? The role of cognitive and motivational processes in well-being. *American Psychologist*, 56(3), 239–249.

Lyubomirsky, S., Sheldon, K. M., & Schkade, D. (2005). Pursuing happiness: The architecture of sustainable change. *Review of General Psychology, 9*(2), 111–131.

Ma, S. H., & Teasdale, J. D. (2004). Mindfulness-based cognitive therapy for depression: Replication and exploration of differential relapse prevention effects. *Journal of Consulting and Clinical Psychology, 72*(1), 31–40.

Mabbett, D. (2013). The second time as tragedy? Welfare reform under Thatcher and the coalition. *The Political Quarterly, 84*(1), 43–52.

Maccoby, E. E., & Jacklin, C. N. (1974). *The Psychology of Sex Differences* (Vol. 1). Stanford, CA: Stanford University Press.

Mackenzie, C. S., Poulin, P. A., & Seidman-Carlson, R. (2006). A brief mindfulness-based stress reduction intervention for nurses and nurse aides. *Applied Nursing Research, 19*(2), 105–109.

MacLean, P. D. (1990). *The Triune Brain in Evolution: Role in Paleocerebral Functions*. New York: Springer.

Macy, D. (2008). 'Yoga in America' market study: Practitioner spending grows to nearly $6 billion a year. Retrieved 6 May, 2011, from http://www.yogajournal.com/advertise/press_releases/10.

Magill, L. (2000). The use of music therapy to address the suffering in advanced cancer pain. *Journal of Palliative Care, 17*(3), 167–172.

Maratos, A., Gold, C., Wang, X., & Crawford, M. (2008). Music therapy for depression. *Cochrane Database of Systematic Reviews, 1*.

Marcus, C. C., & Barnes, M. (1999). *Healing Gardens: Therapeutic Benefits and Design Recommendations*. New York: John Wiley & Sons.

Mardiyono, M., Songwathana, P., & Petpichetchian, W. (2011). Spirituality intervention and outcomes: Cornerstone of holistic nursing practice. *Nurse Media Journal of Nursing, 1*(1), 117–127.

Markus, H., & Nurius, P. (1986). Possible selves. *American Psychologist, 41*(9), 954–969.

Martikainen, P., Bartley, M., & Lahelma, E. (2002). Psychosocial determinants of health in social epidemiology. *International Journal of Epidemiology, 31*(6), 1091–1093.

Marx, K. (1977 (1845)). Theses on Feuerbach: Thesis 11. *Karl Marx: Selected Writings*. New York: Oxford University Press.

Mascaro, N., & Rosen, D. H. (2006). The role of existential meaning as a buffer against stress. *Journal of Humanistic Psychology, 46*(2), 168–190.

Maslow, A. H. (1972). *The Farther Reaches of Human Nature*. London: Maurice Bassett.

Maslow, A. H. (1987 (1954)). *Motivation and Personality. With New Material by Ruth Cox and Robert Frager* (R. Frager, Ed., 3rd edition). New York: Harper & Row.

Masten, A. S. (2001). Ordinary magic: Resilience processes in development. *American Psychologist, 56*, 227–239.

Mathenge, G. D. (2013). Ethical issues in advertising and marketing: An empirical analysis of the hindrances to efficient marketing and product communication management in Kenya. *European Journal of Business and Innovation Research, 1*(4), 9–19.

Mayer, J. D., Roberts, R. D., & Barsade, S. G. (2008). Human abilities: Emotional intelligence. *Annual Review of Psychology, 59*, 507–536.

Mayer, J. D., & Salovey, P. (1997). What is emotional intelligence? In P. Salovey & D. J. Sluyter (Eds.), *Emotional Development and Emotional Intelligence* (pp. 3–31). New York: Basic Books.

Mayer, J. D., Salovey, P., & Caruso, D. R. (2002). *Mayer-Salovey-Caruso Emotional Intelligence Test (MSCEIT) User's Manual.* Toronto: MHS Publications.

McCalman, J., McEwan, A., Tsey, K., Blackmore, E., & Bainbridge, R. (2010). Towards social sustainability: The case of the family wellbeing community empowerment education program. *Journal of Economic and Social Policy, 13*(2, article 8).

McCright, A., Dunlap, R., & Xiao, C. (2013). Perceived scientific agreement and support for government action on climate change in the USA. *Climatic Change, 119*(2), 511–518.

McCullough, M. E., & Worthington, J. E. L. (1999). Religion and the forgiving personality. *Journal of Personality, 67*(6), 1141–1164.

McGrath, H., & Noble, T. (2003). *Bounce Back! Teacher's Handbook.* Sydney, Australia: Pearson Education.

Mclaughlin, K. (2005). From ridicule to institutionalization: Anti-oppression, the state and social work. *Critical Social Policy, 25*(3), 283–305.

McMillan, L., Owen, L., Kras, M., & Scholey, A. (2011). Behavioural effects of a 10-day Mediterranean diet: Results from a pilot study evaluating mood and cognitive performance. *Appetite, 56*(1), 143–147.

McNulty, J. K. (2011). The dark side of forgiveness: The tendency to forgive predicts continued psychological and physical aggression in marriage. *Personality and Social Psychology Bulletin, 37*(6), 770–783.

Mehling, W. E., Gopisetty, V., Daubenmier, J., Price, C. J., Hecht, F. M., & Stewart, A. (2009). Body awareness: Construct and self report measures. *PLoS One, 4*(5), e5614.

Mendelson, T., Greenberg, M. T., Dariotis, J. K., Gould, L. F., Rhoades, B. L., & Leaf, P. J. (2010). Feasibility and preliminary outcomes of a school-based mindfulness intervention for urban youth. *Journal of Abnormal Child Psychology, 38*(7), 985–994.

Mensendieck, B. M. (1937). *The Mensendieck System of Functional Exercises.* Portland, ME: Southworth-Anthoensen Press.

Merleau-Ponty, M. (1962). *Phenomenology of Perception* (C. Smith, Trans.). London: Routledge & Kegan Paul.

Mikulas, W. I. (1990). Mindfulness, self-control, and personal growth. In M. G. T. Kwee (Ed.), *Psychotherapy, Meditation, and Health* (pp. 151–164). London: East-West Publications.

Mikulincer, M., & Shaver, P. R. (2013). Adult attachment and happiness: Individual differences in the experience and consequences of positive emotions. In S. A. David, I. Boniwell & A. C. Ayers (Eds.), *The Oxford Handbook of Happiness* (pp. 834–846). Oxford: Oxford University Press.

Milevsky, A., Schlechter, M., Netter, S., & Keehn, D. (2007). Maternal and paternal parenting styles in adolescents: Associations with self-esteem, depression and life-satisfaction. *Journal of Child and Family Studies, 16*(1), 39–47.

Miller, J. B. (1986). *What Do We Mean by Relationships?* Wellesley, MA: Stone Center Working Paper Series.

Miller, W. R., & Thoresen, C. E. (2003). Spirituality, religion, and health: An emerging research field. *American Psychologist, 58*(1), 24–35.

Milligan, C., Gatrell, A., & Bingley, A. (2004). 'Cultivating health': Therapeutic landscapes and older people in northern England. *Social Science & Medicine, 58*, 1781–1793.

Mills, N., & Allen, J. (2000). Mindfulness of movement as a coping strategy in multiple sclerosis: A pilot study. *General Hospital Psychiatry, 22*(6), 425–431.

Mirsky, A., Anthony, B., Duncan, C., Ahearn, M., & Kellam, S. (1991). Analysis of the elements of attention: A neuropsychological approach. *Neuropsychology Review, 2*(2), 109–145.

Mischel, W. (1975). A social-learning view of sex differences in behavior. In E. E. Maccoby (Ed.), *The Development of Sex Differences* (pp. 56–81). Stanford, CA: Stanford University Press.

Mitchels, B., & Bond, T. (2010). *Essential Law for Counsellors and Psychotherapists.* Lutterworth: British Association for Counselling and Psychotherapy.

Moadel, A., Morgan, C., Fatone, A., Grennan, J., Carter, J., Laruffa, G., . . . Dutcher, J. (1999). Seeking meaning and hope: Self-reported spiritual and existential needs among an ethnically-diverse cancer patient population. *Psycho-Oncology, 8*(5), 378–385.

Mongkolnchaiarunya, J. (2005). Promoting a community-based solid-waste management initiative in local government: Yala municipality, Thailand. *Habitat International, 29*(1), 27–40.

Monroe, S. M., & Simons, A. D. (1991). Diathesis-stress theories in the context of life stress research: Implications for the depressive disorders. *Psychological Bulletin, 110*(3), 406–425.

Moravia, S. (1995). *The Enigma of the Mind: The Mind–Body Problem in Contemporary Thought.* Cambridge: Cambridge University Press.

Morgan, A. (2000). *What is Narrative Therapy?* Adelaide: Dulwich Centre Publications.

Moskowitz, M., Levering, R., Akhtar, O., Fry, E., Leahey, C., & Vandermey, A. (2013). The 100 best companies to work for. *Fortune, 167*(2), 85–93.

Moss, D. (2009). Neurofeedback. In S. Lopez (Ed.), *The Encyclopedia of Positive Psychology* (pp. 646–647). Chichester: Blackwell Publishing.

Mueller, C. M., & Dweck, C. S. (1998). Intelligence praise can undermine motivation and performance. *Journal of Personality and Social Psychology, 75*, 33–52.

Mulla, Z. R., & Krishnan, V. R. (2006). Karma Yoga: A conceptualization and validation of the Indian philosophy of work. *Journal of Indian Psychology, 24*(1), 26–43.

Munson, S., Lauterbach, D., Newman, M., & Resnick, P. (2010). Happier together: Integrating a wellness application into a social network site. In T. Ploug, P. Hasle & H. Oinas-Kukkonen (Eds.), *Persuasive Technology* (pp. 27–39). Berlin: Springer.

Musafer, S. (2012, 25 January). Trade unions: Not dead yet, *BBC*. Retrieved from http://www.bbc.co.uk/news/business-16609527

Muzik, M., Hamilton, S. E., Lisa Rosenblum, K., Waxler, E., & Hadi, Z. (2012). Mindfulness yoga during pregnancy for psychiatrically at-risk women: Preliminary results from a pilot feasibility study. *Complementary Therapies in Clinical Practice, 18*(4), 235–240.

Muzzey, D. S. (1906). Medieval morals. *International Journal of Ethics, 17*(1), 29–47.

Nahrgang, J. D., Morgeson, F. P., & Hofmann, D. A. (2011). Safety at work: A meta-analytic investigation of the link between job demands, job resources, burnout, engagement, and safety outcomes. *Journal of Applied Psychology, 96*(1), 71–94.

Nakamura, Y., Lipschitz, D. L., Landward, R., Kuhn, R., & West, G. (2011). Two sessions of sleep-focused mind–body bridging improve self-reported symptoms of sleep and PTSD in veterans: A pilot randomized controlled trial. *Journal of Psychosomatic Research, 70*(4), 335–345.

Nakhaie, R., & Arnold, R. (2010). A four year (1996–2000) analysis of social capital and health status of Canadians: The difference that love makes. *Social Science & Medicine, 71*(5), 1037–1044.

Napoli, M. (2004). Mindfulness training for teachers: A pilot program. *Complementary Health Practice Review, 9*(1), 31–42.

National Endowment for the Arts (2013). *2012 Survey of Public Participation in the Arts.* Washington, DC: National Endowment for the Arts.

National Institue for Health and Care Excellence [National Institute for Clinical Excellence] (2004). *Depression: Management of Depression in Primary and Secondary Care.* Clinical Guideline 23. London: National Institute for Clinical Excellence.

Nayak, S., Wheeler, B. L., Shiflett, S. C., & Agostinelli, S. (2000). Effect of music therapy on mood and social interaction among individuals with acute traumatic brain injury and stroke. *Rehabilitation Psychology, 45*(3), 274–283.

Neff, K. D. (2003). Self-compassion: An alternative conceptualization of a healthy attitude toward oneself. *Self and Identity, 2*(2), 85–101.

Neff, K. D., & Germer, C. K. (2013). A pilot study and randomized controlled trial of the mindful self-compassion program. *Journal of Clinical Psychology, 69*(1), 28–44.

Nelis, D., Quoidbach, J., Mikolajczak, M., & Hansenne, M. (2009). Increasing emotional intelligence: (How) is it possible? *Personality and Individual Differences, 47*(1), 36–41.

Nelson, S. K., Kushlev, K., English, T., Dunn, E. W., & Lyubomirsky, S. (2013). In defense of parenthood: Children are associated with more joy than misery. *Psychological Science, 24*(1), 3–10.

Nelson, S. K., Kushlev, K., & Lyubomirsky, S. (2014). The pains and pleasures of parenting: When, why, and how is parenthood associated with more or less well-being? *Psychological Bulletin, 140* (3), 846–895.

Nes, R. B., Røysamb, E., Reichborn-Kjennerud, T., Tambs, K., & Harris, J. R. (2005). Subjective well-being: Genetic and environmental contributions to sustainablity and change. *Behavior Genetics, 35*, 815–816.

New Economics Foundation (2013). *Happy Planet Index.* Retrieved 23 January 2014 from www.happyplanetindex.org.

Newberg, A. B., & Iversen, J. (2003). The neural basis of the complex mental task of meditation: Neurotransmitter and neurochemical considerations. *Medical Hypotheses, 61*(2), 282–291.

NHS (2011). Statistics on Drug Use: England, 2011. Leeds: The Health and Social Care Information Centre.

NHS (2014a). 5 a day. Retrieved 14 February, 2014, from http://www.nhs.uk/livewell/5aday

NHS (2014b, 22 May 2013). NHS choices: Alcohol during pregnancy. Retrieved 22 January, 2014, from http://www.nhs.uk/conditions/pregnancy-and-baby/pages/alcohol-medi cines-drugs-pregnant.aspx#close.

NHS (2014c, 31 January 2013). NHS choices: Vitamins and nutrition in pregnancy. Retrieved 22 January, 2014, from http://www.nhs.uk/conditions/pregnancy-and-baby/ pages/vitamins-minerals-supplements-pregnant.aspx#close.

Nietzsche, F. (1976 (1888)). *Twilight of the Idols*. In W. Kaufmann (Ed.), *The Portable Nietzsche*. New York: Penguin.

Norrish, J. M., Williams, P., O'Connor, M., & Robinson, J. (2013). An applied framework for Positive Education. *International Journal of Wellbeing*, *3*(2), 147–161.

Nowak, C., & Heinrichs, N. (2008). A comprehensive meta-analysis of Triple P-Positive Parenting Program using hierarchical linear modeling: Effectiveness and moderating variables. *Clinical Child and Family Psychology Review*, *11*(3), 114–144.

O'Connor, M. J., & Whaley, S. E. (2007). Brief intervention for alcohol use by pregnant women. *American Journal of Public Health*, *97*(2), 252–258.

Office for National Statistics (ONS) (2011a). *Hours Worked in the Labour Market, 2011*. London: Office for National Statistics.

Office for National Statistics (ONS) (2011b). *Initial Investigation into Subjective Well-being from the Opinions Survey*. London: Office for National Statistics.

Office for National Statistics (ONS) (2012). *Religion in England and Wales 2011*. London: Office for National Statistics.

Ong, L. (2007). The kinesthetic Buddha, human form and function – Part 1: Breathing Torso. *Journal of Bodywork and Movement Therapies*, *11*(3), 214–222.

Ormandy, D., & Ezratty, V. (2012). Health and thermal comfort: From WHO guidance to housing strategies. *Energy Policy*, *49*, 116–121.

Ospina, M. B., Bond, K., Karkhaneh, M., Tjosvold, L., Vandermeer, B., Liang, Y., . . . Klassen, T. P. (2007). Meditation practices for health: State of the research. *Evidence Reports/Technology Assessments* (Full Report), 155, 1–263.

Oyserman, D., Terry, K., & Bybee, D. (2002). A possible selves intervention to enhance school involvement. *Journal of Adolescence*, *25*(3), 313–326.

Padilla, A., Hogan, R., & Kaiser, R. B. (2007). The toxic triangle: Destructive leaders, susceptible followers, and conducive environments. *The Leadership Quarterly*, *18*(3), 176–194.

Panksepp, J., & Bernatzky, G. (2002). Emotional sounds and the brain: The neuro-affective foundations of musical appreciation. *Behavioural Processes*, *60*(2), 133–155.

Pargament, K. I., & Mahoney, A. (2005). Sacred matters: Sanctification as a vital topic for the psychology of religion. *International Journal for the Psychology of Religion*, *15*(3), 179–198.

Parker, C. P., Baltes, B. B., Young, S. A., Huff, J., Altmann, R., LaCost, H., & Roberts, J. E. (2003). Relationships between psychological climate perceptions and work outcomes: A meta-analytic review. *Journal of Organizational Behavior*, *24*, 389–416.

Peifer, J. L. (2012). Review of Philippe Steiner's *Durkheim and the Birth of Economic Sociology* (Trans. Keith Tribe). Princeton, NJ: Princeton University Press. *Erasmus*, *5*(1), 121–127.

Penn, G., & Owen, L. (2002). Factors associated with continued smoking during pregnancy: Analysis of socio-demographic, pregnancy and smoking-related factors. *Drug and Alcohol Review, 21*(1), 17–25.

Pennebaker, J. W., & Seagal, J. D. (1999). Forming a story: The health benefits of narrative. *Journal of Clinial Psychology, 55*(10), 1243–1254.

Persson, D., Erlandsson, L.-K., Eklund, M., & Iwarsson, S. (2001). Value dimensions, meaning, and complexity in human occupation: A tentative structure for analysis. *Scandinavian Journal of Occupational Therapy, 8*(1), 7–18.

Peterson, C. (2006a). *A Primer in Positive Psychology.* New York: Oxford University Press.

Peterson, C. (2006b). The Values in Action (VIA) classification of strengths. In M. Csikszentmihalyi & I. S. Csikszentmihalyi (Eds.), *A Life Worth Living: Contributions to Positive Psychology* (pp. 29–48). Oxford: Oxford University Press.

Peterson, C., & Park, N. (2006). Character strengths in organizations. *Journal of Organizational Behavior, 27*(8), 1149–1154.

Peterson, C., & Seligman, M. E. P. (2004). *Character Strengths and Virtues: A Handbook and Classification.* Washington, DC: American Psychological Association.

Peterson, C., & Vaidya, R. S. (2003). Optimism as virtue and vice. In E. C. Chang & L. J. Sanna (Eds.), *Virtue, Vice, and Personality: The Complexity of Behaviour* (pp. 23–27). Washington, DC: American Psychological Association.

Phillips, D. R., Siu, O. L., Yeh, A. G., & Cheng, K. H. (2008). Informal social support and older persons' psychological well-being in Hong Kong. *Journal of Cross-cultural Gerontology, 23*(1), 39–55.

Phillips, G., Hayes, R., Bottomley, C., Petticrew, M., Watts, P., Lock, K., . . . Renton, A. (2012). OP06 Well London: Results of a cluster-randomised trial of a community development approach to improving health behaviours and mental wellbeing in deprived inner-city neighbourhoods. *Journal of Epidemiology and Community Health, 66*(Suppl 1), A3.

Phillips, K. (1993). *Boiling Point.* New York: Random House.

Piaget, J. (1971). *The Theory of Stages in Cognitive Development.* New York: McGraw-Hill.

Pickett, K. E., & Wilkinson, R. G. (2007). Child wellbeing and income inequality in rich societies: Ecological cross sectional study. *British Medical Journal, 335*(7629), 1080–1086.

Piedmont, R. L. (1999). Does spirituality represent the sixth factor of personality? Spiritual transcendence and the Five-Factor Model. *Journal of Personality, 67*(6), 985–1013.

Piedmont, R. L. (2004). *ASPIRES. Assessment of Spirituality and Religious Sentiments: Technical Manual.* Columbia, MD: Self-published.

Pirsig, R. M. (1974). *Zen and the Art of Motorcycle Maintenance.* New York: Vintage Books.

Plehwe, D., Walpen, B. J., & Neunhöffer, G. (Eds.). (2005). *Neoliberal Hegemony: A Global Critique.* New York: Routledge.

Pollard, E. L., & Davidson, L. (2001). Foundations of child wellbeing. *Action Research in Family and Early Childhood.* Paris: UNESCO.

Posner, M. I., & Dehaene, S. (1994). Attentional networks. *Trends in Neurosciences, 17*(2), 75–79.

Posner, M. I., & Petersen, S. E. (1990). The attention system of the human brain. *Annual Review of Neuroscience, 13*(1), 25–42.

Pratt, R. R. (2004). Art, dance, and music therapy. *Physical Medicine and Rehabilitation Clinics of North America, 15*, 827–842.

Price, J. (2010). *Sacred Scriptures of the World Religions: An Introduction.* New York: Continuum Books.

Prilleltensky, I. (2008). The role of power in wellness, oppression, and liberation: The promise of psychopolitical validity. *Journal of Community Psychology, 36*(2), 116–136.

Prilleltensky, I., Nelson, G., & Peirson, L. (2001). The role of power and control in children's lives: An ecological analysis of pathways toward wellness, resilience and problems. *Journal of Community & Applied Social Psychology, 11*(2), 143–158.

Prilleltensky, I., & Prilleltensky, O. (2005). Beyond resilience: Blending wellness and liberation in the helping professions. In M. Ungar (Ed.), *Handbook for Working with Children and Youth* (pp. 89–103). Thousand Oaks, CA: SAGE.

Proctor, C., Linley, P. A. & Maltby, J. (2009). Youth life satisfaction measures: A review. *The Journal of Positive Psychology, 4*(2), 128–144.

Proctor, C., & Fox-Eades, J. (2009). *Strengths Gym: Year 8.* St Peter Port, Guernsey: Positive Psychology Research Centre.

Puig, A., Lee, S. M., Goodwin, L., & Sherrard, P. A. (2006). The efficacy of creative arts therapies to enhance emotional expression, spirituality, and psychological well-being of newly diagnosed Stage I and Stage II breast cancer patients: A preliminary study. *The Arts in Psychotherapy, 33*(3), 218–228.

Quilty, M. T., Saper, R. B., Goldstein, R., & Khalsa, S. B. S. (2013). Yoga in the real world: Perceptions, motivators, barriers, and patterns of use. *Global Advances in Health and Medicine, 2*(1), 44–49.

Quimby, P. P. (2007 (1846–1865)). *The Quimby Manuscripts.* Digireads.com.

Raffone, A., & Srinivasan, N. (2010). The exploration of meditation in the neuroscience of attention and consciousness. *Cognitive Processing, 11*(1), 1–7.

Ragins, B. R., & Cotton, J. L. (1999). Mentor functions and outcomes: A comparison of men and women in formal and informal mentoring relationships. *Journal of Applied Psychology, 84*(4), 529–550.

Read, A. D. (1999). 'A weekly doorstep recycling collection, I had no idea we could!': Overcoming the local barriers to participation. *Resources, Conservation and Recycling, 26*(3–4), 217–249.

Reed, J., & Ones, D. S. (2006). The effect of acute aerobic exercise on positive activated affect: A meta-analysis. *Psychology of Sport and Exercise, 7*(5), 477–514.

Rego, A., & Cunha, M. Pina e (2008). Authentizotic climates and employee happiness: Pathways to individual performance? *Journal of Business Research, 61*(7), 739–752.

Reid, D. (2009). Capturing presence moments: The art of mindful practice in occupational therapy. *Canadian Journal of Occupational Therapy, 76*(3), 180–188.

Reis, H. T., & Gable, S. L. (2003). Toward a positive psychology of relationships. In C. L. M. Keyes & J. Haidt (Eds.), *Flourishing: Positive Psychology and the Life Well-Lived* (pp. 129–159). Washington, DC: American Psychological Association.

Reivich, K. J., Seligman, M. E. P. & McBride, S. (2011). Master resilience training in the US Army. *American Psychologist, 66*(1), 25–34.

Renton, A., Phillips, G., Daykin, N., Yu, G., Taylor, K., & Petticrew, M. (2012). Think of your art-eries: Arts participation, behavioural cardiovascular risk factors and mental well-being in deprived communities in London. *Public Health, 126, Supplement 1*(0), S57–S64.

Resnick, S., Warmoth, A., & Serlin, I. A. (2001). The humanistic psychology and positive psychology connection: Implications for psychotherapy. *Journal of Humanistic Psychology, 41*(1), 73–101.

Reynolds, F., & Lim, K. H. (2007). Turning to art as a positive way of living with cancer: A qualitative study of personal motives and contextual influences. *The Journal of Positive Psychology, 2*(1), 66–75.

Reznitskaya, A., & Sternberg, R. (2004). Teaching students to make wise judgements: The 'Teaching for wisdom' curriculum. In P. A. Linley & S. Joseph (Eds.), *Positive Psychology in Practice* (pp. 388–403). Hoboken, NJ: John Wiley & Sons.

Rhee, K. E., Lumeng, J. C., Appugliese, D. P., Kaciroti, N., & Bradley, R. H. (2006). Parenting styles and overweight status in first grade. *Pediatrics, 117*(6), 2047–2054.

Rickard, N., & Vella-Brodrick, D. (2013). Changes in well-being: Complementing a psychosocial approach with neurobiological insights. *Social Indicators Research, June*, 1–21.

Ridge, D., & Ziebland, S. (2006). 'The old me could never have done that': How people give meaning to recovery following depression. *Qualitative Health Research, 16*(8), 1038–1053.

Ridley-Duff, R., & Bennett, A. (2011). Towards mediation: Developing a theoretical framework to understand alternative dispute resolution. *Industrial Relations Journal, 42*(2), 106–123.

Riskin, L. L. (2004). Mindfulness: Foundational training for dispute resolution. *Journal of Legal Education, 54*, 79–90.

Robinson, D. A., & Harvey, M. (2008). Global leadership in a culturally diverse world. *Management Decision, 46*(3), 466–480.

Robitschek, C. (1998). Personal growth initiative: The construct and its measure. *Measurement and Evaluation in Counseling and Development, 30*, 183–198.

Robitschek, C., & Keyes, C. L. M. (2004). Personal Growth Initiative and Multidimensional Well-Being. Paper presented at the Annual Convention of the American Psychological Association, Honolulu, Hawaii.

Roche, B., & Hefferon, K. (2013). The assessment needs to go hand-in-hand with the debriefing: The importance of a structured coaching debriefing in understanding and applying a positive psychology strengths assessment. *International Coaching Psychology Review, 8*(1), 20–34.

Rodin, J., & Langer, E. J. (1977). Long-term effects of a control-relevant intervention with the institutionalized aged. *Journal of Personality and Social Psychology, 35*(12), 897–902.

Ross, C. E. (2000). Neighborhood disadvantage and adult depression. *Journal of Health and Social Behavior, 41*(2), 177–187.

Rosso, B. D., Dekas, K. H., & Wrzesniewski, A. (2010). On the meaning of work: A theoretical integration and review. *Research in Organizational Behavior, 30*, 91–127.

Roxendale, G. (1985). Body Awareness Therapy and the Body Awareness Scale. PhD thesis, University of Gothenburg.

Rudy, D., & Grusec, J. E. (2006). Authoritarian parenting in individualist and collectivist groups: Associations with maternal emotion and cognition and children's self-esteem. *Journal of Family Psychology*, *20*(1), 68–78.

Rusk, R. D., & Waters, L. E. (2013). Tracing the size, reach, impact, and breadth of positive psychology. *The Journal of Positive Psychology*, *8*(3), 207–221.

Ruud, E. (2008). Music in therapy: Increasing possibilities for action. *Music and Arts in Action*, *1*(1), 46–60.

Ruud, E. (2013). Can music serve as a 'cultural immunogen'? An explorative study. *International Journal of Qualitative Studies on Health and Well-Being*, *8*. doi: 10.3402/qhw.v8i0.20597

Ryan, L. (2013). Strengths-based coaching. Lecture on 14 December at the University of East London.

Ryan, M. T. (1995). Karl Marx: The human person as a worker. Introduction and commentary. In H. Brown, D. L. Hudecki, L. A. Kennedy & J. J. Snyder (Eds.), *Images of the Human: The Philosophy of the Human Person in a Religious Context* (pp. 253–256). Chicago, IL: Loyola Press.

Ryan, R. M., & Deci, E. L. (2000). Self-determination theory and the facilitation of intrinsic motivation, social development, and well-being. *American Psychologist*, *55*(1), 68–78.

Ryan, T. (2001). *Prayer of Heart and Body: Meditation and Yoga as Christian Spiritual Practice*. Mahwah, NJ: Paulist Press.

Ryff, C. D. (1989). Happiness is everything, or is it? Explorations on the meaning of psychological well-being. *Journal of Personality and Social Psychology*, *57*(6), 1069–1081.

Ryff, C. D., Dienberg Love, G., Urry, H. L., Muller, D., Rosenkranz, M. A., Friedman, E. M., . . . Singer, B. (2006). Psychological well-being and ill-being: Do they have distinct or mirrored biological correlates? *Psychotherapy and Psychosomatics*, *75*(2), 85–95.

Ryff, C. D., & Singer, B. (2003). Ironies of the human condition. Well-being and health on the way to mortality. In L. G. Aspinwall & U. M. Staudinger (Eds.), *A Psychology of Human Strengths* (pp. 271–287). Washington, DC: American Psychological Association.

Sagiv, L., & Schwartz, S. H. (2000). Value priorities and subjective well-being: Direct relations and congruity effects. *European Journal of Social Psychology*, *30*(2), 177–198.

Sale, R. (2008). Mindful yoga as a vehicle for childbirth education. *International Journal of Childbirth Education*, *23*(4), 7–8.

Salonen, H., Lahtinen, M., Lappalainen, S., Nevala, N., Knibbs, L. D., Morawska, L., & Reijula, K. (2013). Physical characteristics of the indoor environment that affect health and wellbeing in healthcare facilities: A review. *Intelligent Buildings International*, *5*(1), 3–25.

Salovey, P., & Mayer, J. D. (1989). Emotional intelligence. *Imagination, Cognition and Personality*, *9*(3), 185–211.

Salzberg, S. (1995). *Loving-Kindness: The Revolutionary Art of Happiness*. Boston, MA: Shambala Publications.

Sanders, M. R. (1999). Triple P-Positive Parenting Program: Towards an empirically validated multilevel parenting and family support strategy for the prevention of behavior and emotional problems in children. *Clinical Child and Family Psychology Review*, *2*(2), 71–90.

Sandgren, M. (2009). Evidence for strong immediate well-being effects of choral singing – with more enjoyment for women than for men. Paper presented at the 7th Triennial Conference of the European Society for the Cognitive Sciences of Music (ESCOM 2009), Jyväskylä, Finland.

Sangsue, J., & Vorpe, G. (2004). Professional and personal influences on school climate in teachers and pupils. *Psychologie du Travail et des Organisations, 10*(4), 341–354.

Sartre, J.-P. (1964 (1938)). *La nausée* (L. Alexander, Trans.). New York: New Directions.

Satchidananda, S. (2012). *Yoga Sutras of Patañjali*. Buckingham, VA: Integral Yoga Publications.

Satish, U., Mendell, M. J., Shekhar, K., Hotchi, T., Sullivan, D., Streufert, S., & Fisk, W. J. (2012). Is CO2 an indoor pollutant? Direct effects of low-to-moderate CO2 concentrations on human decision-making performance. *Environmental Health Perspectives, 120*(12), 1671–1677.

Sauter, S. L., Murphy, L. R., & Hurrell, J. J. (1990). Prevention of work-related psychological disorders: A national strategy proposed by the National Institute for Occupational Safety and Health (NIOSH). *American Psychologist, 45*, 1146–1158.

Sawni, A., & Breuner, C. C. (2012). Complementary, holistic, and integrative medicine: Depression, sleep disorders, and substance abuse. *Pediatrics in Review, 33*(9), 422–425.

Schaufeli, W. B., & Bakker, A. B. (2004). Job demands, job resources, and their relationship with burnout and engagement: A multi-sample study. *Journal of Organizational Behavior, 25*(3), 293–315.

Schaufeli, W. B., Bakker, A. B., & Salanova, M. (2006). The measurement of work engagement with a short questionnaire: A cross-national study. *Educational and Psychological Measurement, 66*(4), 701–716.

Schaufeli, W. B., Bakker, A. B., & Van Rhenen, W. (2009). How changes in job demands and resources predict burnout, work engagement, and sickness absenteeism. *Journal of Organizational Behavior, 30*(7), 893–917.

Schildkraut, J. J. (1965). The catecholamine hypothesis of affective disorders: A review of supporting evidence. *American Journal of Psychiatry, 122*, 509–522.

Schmidt-Wilk, J., Alexander, C., & Swanson, G. (1996). Developing consciousness in organizations: The transcendental meditation program in business. *Journal of Business and Psychology, 10*(4), 429–444.

Schnall, S., Haidt, J., Clore, G. L., & Jordan, A. H. (2008). Disgust as embodied moral judgment. *Personality and Social Psychology Bulletin, 34*(8), 1096–1109.

Schön, D. A. (1983). *The Reflective Practitioner: How Professionals Think in Action*. New York: Basic Books.

Schopenhauer, A. (1969 (1819)). *The World as Will and Representation*. New York: Dover Publications.

Schumacher, E. F. (2010 (1973)). *Small is Beautiful: Economics as if People Mattered*. London: Harper Collins.

Schwartz, S. H. (1999). A theory of cultural values and some implications for work. *Applied Psychology, 48*(1), 23–47.

Scruggs, L., & Benegal, S. (2012). Declining public concern about climate change: Can we blame the great recession? *Global Environmental Change, 22*(2), 505–515.

Seligman, M. E. P. (1990). *Learned Optimism*. New York: Pocket Books.

Seligman, M. E. P. (1999). Positive social science. *Journal of Positive Behavior Interventions, 1*(3), 181–182.

Seligman, M. E. P. (2002). *Authentic Happiness*. New York: Free Press.

Seligman, M. E. P. (2008). Positive health. *Applied Psychology, 57,* 3–18.

Seligman, M. E. P. (2012). *Flourish: A Visionary New Understanding of Happiness and Well-Being.* New York: Simon & Schuster.

Seligman, M. E. P., & Csikszentmihalyi, M. (2000). Positive psychology: An introduction. *American Psychologist, 55*(1), 5–14.

Seligman, M. E. P., Ernst, R. M., Gillham, J., Reivich, K., & Linkins, M. (2009). Positive education: Positive psychology and classroom interventions. *Oxford Review of Education, 35*(3), 293–311.

Seligman, M. E. P., Rashid, T., & Parks, A. C. (2006). Positive psychotherapy. *American Psychologist, 61*(8), 774–788.

Seligman, M. E. P., Steen, T. A., Park, N., & Peterson, C. (2005). Positive psychology progress: Empirical validation of interventions. *American Psychologist, 60*(5), 410–421.

Seligson, J. L., Huebner, E. S., & Valois, R. F. (2003). Preliminary validation of the brief multidimensional students' life satisfaction scale (BMSLSS). *Social Indicators Research, 61*(2), 121–145.

Sessa, B. (2007). Is there a case for MDMA-assisted psychotherapy in the UK? *Journal of Psychopharmacology, 21*(2), 220–224.

Shapiro, D. H. (1992). A preliminary study of long term meditators: Goals, effects, religious orientation, cognitions. *Journal of Transpersonal Psychology, 24*(1), 23–39.

Shapiro, D. H. (1994). Examining the content and context of meditation: A challenge for psychology in the areas of stress management, psychotherapy, and religion/values. *Journal of Humanistic Psychology, 34*(4), 101–135.

Shapiro, S. L., Brown, K. W., & Biegel, G. M. (2007). Teaching self-care to caregivers: Effects of mindfulness-based stress reduction on the mental health of therapists in training. *Training and Education in Professional Psychology, 1*(2), 105–115.

Shapiro, S. L., Carlson, L. E., Astin, J. A., & Freedman, B. (2006). Mechanisms of mindfulness. *Journal of Clinical Psychology, 62*(3), 373–386.

Sharif, F., Rezaie, S., Keshavarzi, S., Mansoori, P., & Ghadakpoor, S. (2013). Teaching emotional intelligence to intensive care unit nurses and their general health: A randomized clinical trial. *International Journal of Occupational & Environmental Medicine, 4*(3), 141–148.

Shaw, J. C. (1996). Intention as a component of the alpha-rhythm response to mental activity. *International Journal of Psychophysiology, 24*(1–2), 7–23.

Shear, J. (1998). Introduction. In J. Shear (Ed.), *Explaining Consciousness: The Hard Problem* (pp. 1–8). Cambridge, MA: MIT Press.

Sheldon, K. M. (2011). What's positive about positive psychology? Reducing value-bias and enhancing integration within the field. In K. M. Sheldon, T. Kashdan & M. F. Steger (Eds.), *Designing Positive Psychology: Taking Stock and Moving Forward* (pp. 421–429). Oxford: Oxford University Press.

Sheldon, K. M., Kasser, T., Smith, K., & Share, T. (2002). Personal goals and psychological growth: Testing an intervention to enhance goal attainment and personality integration. *Journal of Personality, 70*(1), 5–31.

Sheldrake, P. (2007). *A Brief History of Spirituality.* Boston, MA: Blackwell Publishing.

Sheridan, S. M., Warnes, E. D., Cowan, R. J., Schemm, A. V., & Clarke, B. L. (2004). Family-centered positive psychology: Focusing on strengths to build student success. *Psychology in the Schools, 41*(1), 7–17.

Sherkat, D. E., & Ellison, C. G. (1999). Recent developments and current controversies in the sociology of religion. *Annual Review of Sociology, 25*, 363–394.

Shin, J. (2008). Morality and internet behavior: A study of the internet troll and its relation with morality on the internet. Paper presented at the Proceedings of Society for Information Technology & Teacher Education International Conference, Chesapeake, VA: AACE.

Shonin, E., Van Gordon, W., & Griffiths, M. D. (2013a). Mindfulness-based interventions: Towards mindful clinical integration. *Frontiers in Psychology, 4*(194), doi: 10,3389/fpsyg.2013.00194.

Shonin, E., Van Gordon, W., Slade, K., & Griffiths, M. D. (2013b). Mindfulness and other Buddhist-derived interventions in correctional settings: A systematic review. *Aggression and Violent Behavior, 18*(3), 365–372.

Shorey, H. (2009). Attachment theory. In S. Lopez (Ed.), *Encyclopaedia of Positive Psychology*. Oxford: Wiley-Blackwell.

Silvia, P. J., Eichstaedt, J., & Phillips, A. G. (2005). Are rumination and reflection types of self-focused attention? *Personality and Individual Differences, 38*(4), 871–881.

Simon, L. S., Judge, T. A., & Halvorsen-Ganepola, M. D. K. (2010). In good company? A multi-study, multi-level investigation of the effects of coworker relationships on employee well-being. *Journal of Vocational Behavior, 76*(3), 534–546.

Sin, N. L., & Lyubomirsky, S. (2009). Enhancing well-being and alleviating depressive symptoms with positive psychology interventions: A practice-friendly meta-analysis. *Journal of Clinical Psychology, 65*(5), 467–487.

Singh, N. N., Wahler, R. G., Adkins, A. D., & Myers, R. E. (2003). Soles of the feet: A mindfulness-based self-control intervention for aggression by an individual with mild mental retardation and mental illness. *Research in Developmental Disabilities, 24*(3), 158–169.

Skatteboe, U.-B., Friis, S., Hope, M. K., & Vaglum, P. (1989). Body awareness group therapy for patients with personality disorders. *Psychotherapy and Psychosomatics, 51*(1), 11–17.

Smith, J. (2013, 6 March). The world's most ethical companies. *Forbes*.

Smith, L. M., Case, J. L., Smith, H. M., Harwell, L. C., & Summers, J. K. (2013). Relating ecoystem services to domains of human well-being: Foundation for a US index. *Ecological Indicators, 28*(0), 79–90.

Smith, M. B. (2003). Positive psychology: Documentation of a burgeoning movement [Review of the book *Handbook of Positive Psychology*]. *American Journal of Psychology, 116*, 159–163.

Smith, W. P., Compton, W. C., & West, B. W. (1995). Meditation as an adjunct to a happiness enhancement program. *Journal of Clinical Psychology, 51*(2), 269–273.

Snyder, C. R. (2000). *Handbook of Hope: Theory, Measures and Applications*. San Diego, CA: Academic Press.

Soisson, E. L., Van de Creek, L., & Knapp, S. (1987). Thorough record keeping: A good defense in a litigious era. *Professional Psychology: Research and Practice, 18*(5), 498–502.

Southwick, S. M., Gilmartin, R., Mcdonough, P., & Morrissey, P. (2006). Logotherapy as an adjunctive treatment for chronic combat-related PTSD: A meaning-based intervention. *American Journal of Psychotherapy, 60*(2), 161–174.

Sparks, K., Cooper, C. L., Fried, Y., & Shirom, A. (2013). The effects of working hours on health: A meta-analytic review. In C. L. Cooper (Ed.), *From Stress to Wellbeing Volume 1: The Theory and Research on Occupational Stress and Wellbeing* (pp. 292–314). Basingstoke: Palgrave Macmillan.

Spash, C. L. (2010). The brave new world of carbon trading. *New Political Economy, 15*(2), 169–195.

Spinelli, E. (1997). *Tales of Un-Knowing: Eight Stories of Existential Therapy*. New York: New York University Press.

Stambolovic, V. (2002). The case of Serbia/Yugoslavia: An analysis through spiral dynamics. *Medicine, Conflict and Survival, 18*(1), 59–70.

Stebbins, R. A. (2009). *Personal Decisions in the Public Square: Beyond Problem Solving into a Positive Sociology*. New Brunswick, NJ: Transaction.

Steffen, P., & Masters, K. (2005). Does compassion mediate the intrinsic religion–health relationship? *Annals of Behavioral Medicine, 30*(3), 217–224.

Steger, M. F., & Frazier, P. (2005). Meaning in life: One link in the chain from religiousness to well-being. *Journal of Counselling Psychology, 52*(4), 574–582.

Steptoe, A., Evans, O., & Fieldman, G. (1997). Perceptions of control over work: Psychophysiological responses to self-paced and externally-paced tasks in an adult population sample. *International Journal of Psychophysiology, 25*(3), 211–220.

Stern, J. (2006). *Terror in the Name of God*. New York: Harper Collins.

Steskens, P., & Loomans, M. (2010). Performance indicators for health, comfort and safety of the indoor environment. Paper presented at the Clima 2010-10th REHVA World Congress.

Stewart, J. B. (2013, 15 March). Looking for a lesson in Google's perks, *The New York Times*.

Strassel, J. K., Cherkin, D. C., Steuten, L., Sherman, K. J., & Vrijhoef, H. (2011). A systematic review of the evidence for the effectiveness of dance therapy. *Alternative Therapies in Health and Medicine, 17*(3), 50–59.

Stratakis, C. A., & Chrousos, G. P. (1995). Neuroendocrinology and pathophysiology of the stress system. *Annals of the New York Academy of Sciences, 771*(1), 1–18.

Ströhle, A. (2009). Physical activity, exercise, depression and anxiety disorders. *Journal of Neural Transmission, 116*(6), 777–784.

Suler, J. (2004). The online disinhibition effect. *Cyberpsychology & Behavior, 7*(3), 321–326.

Sullivan, M. J., Wood, L., Terry, J., Brantley, J., Charles, A., McGee, V., . . . Bosworth, H. B. (2009). The support, education, and research in chronic heart failure study (SEARCH): A mindfulness-based psychoeducational intervention improves depression and clinical symptoms in patients with chronic heart failure. *American Heart Journal, 157*(1), 84–90.

Sundararajan, L. (2005). Happiness donut: A Confucian critique of positive psychology. *Journal of Theoretical and Philosophical Psychology, 25*(1), 35–60.

Swahn, M. H., & Bossarte, R. M. (2009). Assessing and quantifying high risk: Comparing risky behaviors by youth in an urban, disadvantaged community with nationally representative youth. *Public Health Reports, 124*(2), 224–233.

Swindells, R., Lawthom, R., Rowley, K., Siddiquee, A., Kilroy, A., & Kagan, C. (2013). Eudaimonic well-being and community arts participation. *Perspectives in Public Health*, *133*(1), 60–65.

Symister, P., & Friend, R. (2003). The influence of social support and problematic support on optimism and depression in chronic illness: A prospective study evaluating self-esteem as a mediator. *Health Psychology*, *22*(2), 123–129.

Szasz, T. S. (1960). The myth of mental illness. *American Psychologist*, *15*(2), 113–118.

Taylor, B. R. (Ed.). (2005). *The Encyclopedia of Religion and Nature*. New York: Continuum.

Taylor, C. (1989). *Sources of the Self: The Making of the Modern Identity*. Cambridge, MA: Harvard University Press.

Taylor, S. (2003). Primal spirituality and the onto/philo fallacy: A critique of the claim that primal peoples were/are less spiritually and socially developed than modern humans. *International Journal of Transpersonal Studies*, *22*, 61–76.

Teasdale, J. D., Segal, Z. V., Williams, J. M. G., Ridgeway, V. A., Soulsby, J. M., & Lau, M. A. (2000). Prevention of relapse/recurrence in major depression by mindfulness-based cognitive therapy. *Journal of Consulting and Clinical Psychology*, *68*(4), 615–623.

Tedeschi, R. G., & Calhoun, L. G. (2004). Posttraumatic growth: Conceptual foundations and empirical evidence. *Psychological Inquiry*, *15*(1), 1–18.

Thaler, R. H., & Sunstein, C. R. (2003). Libertarian paternalism. *The American Economic Review*, *93*(2), 175–179.

Thaler, R. H., & Sunstein, C. R. (2008). *Nudge: Improving Decisions about Health, Wealth, and Happiness*. Boston. MA: Yale University Press.

Than, K. (2012, 14 June). World's oldest cave art found – made by Neanderthals? *National Geographic*.

Tharenou, P. (2013). The work of feminists is not yet done: The gender pay gap – a stubborn anachronism. *Sex Roles*, *68*(3–4), 198–206.

Thompson, S., Marks, N., & Jackson, T. (2013). Well-being and sustainable development. In S. A. David, I. Boniwell & A. C. Ayers (Eds.), *The Oxford Handbook of Happiness* (pp. 498–516). Oxford: Oxford University Press.

Thrangu, K. (1993). *The Practice of Tranquility and Insight: A Guide to Tibetan Buddhist Meditation* (R. Roberts, Trans.). Boston, MA: Shambhala Publications.

Thune, I., Brenn, T., Lund, E., & Gaard, M. (1997). Physical activity and the risk of breast cancer. *New England Journal of Medicine*, *336*(18), 1269–1275.

Toates, F. (2011). *Biological Psychology*. Harlow, Essex: Pearson Education.

Tompa, E., Trevithick, S., & McLeod, C. (2007). Systematic review of the prevention incentives of insurance and regulatory mechanisms for occupational health and safety. *Scandinavian Journal of Work, Environment & Health*, *33*(2), 85–95.

Tornstam, L. (2005). *Gerotranscendence: A Developmental Theory of Positive Aging*. New York: Springer.

Tortora, G., & Derrickson, B. (2009). *Principles of Anatomy and Physiology: Organisation, Support and Movement, and Control Systems of the Human Body* (13th edition). London: John Wiley & Sons.

Trainor, S., Delfabbro, P., Anderson, S., & Winefield, A. (2010). Leisure activities and adolescent psychological well-being. *Journal of Adolescence*, *33*(1), 173–186.

Trapnell, P. D., & Campbell, J. D. (1999). Private self-consciousness and the five-factor model of personality: Distinguishing rumination from reflection. *Journal of Personality and Social Psychology*, *76*(2), 284–304.

Tucker, P., Macdonald, I., Folkard, S., & Smith, L. (1998). The impact of early and late shift changeovers on sleep, health, and well-being in 8- and 12-hour shift systems. *Journal of Occupational Health Psychology*, *3*(3), 265–275.

Turner, B. S. (2001). Disability and the sociology of the body. In G. L. Albrecht, K. D. Seelman & M. Bury (Eds.), *Handbook of Disability Studies* (pp. 252–266). Thousand Oaks, CA: SAGE.

Ulrich, R. S., Zimring, C., Zhu, X., CuBose, J., Seo, H.-B., Choi, Y.-S., . . . Joseph, A. (2008). A review of the research literature on evidence-based healthcare design. *Health Environments Research & Design Journal*, *1*(3), 61–125.

Umberson, D., & Montez, J. K. (2010). Social relationships and health. *Journal of Health and Social Behavior*, *51*(1), 54–66.

United Nations (2013). *The Rise of the South: Human Progress in a Diverse World. Human Development Report*. New York: United Nations.

Ura, K. (2008). *Explanation of GNH Index*. Thimphu, Bhutan: The Center for Bhutan Studies.

Urry, H. L., Nitschke, J. B., Dolski, I., Jackson, D. C., Dalton, K. M., Mueller, C. J., . . . Davidson, R. J. (2004). Making a life worth living: Neural correlates of well-being. *Psychological Science*, *15*(6), 367–372.

Vaillant, G. (2004). Positive aging. In P. A. Linley & S. Joseph (Eds.), *Positive Psychology in Practice* (pp. 561–580). Hoboken, NJ: John Wiley & Sons.

Vaillant, G. (2012). *Triumphs of Experience: The Men of the Harvard Grant Study*. Cambridge, MA: Belknap Press.

van Boven, L. (2005). Experientialism, materialism, and the pursuit of happiness. *Review of General Psychology*, *9*(2), 132–142.

van den Bergh, B. R. H., Mulder, E. J. H., Mennes, M., & Glover, V. (2005). Antenatal maternal anxiety and stress and the neurobehavioural development of the fetus and child: Links and possible mechanisms: A review. *Neuroscience & Biobehavioral Reviews*, *29*(2), 237–258.

van Marrewijk, M. (2004). The social dimension of organizations: Recent experiences with Great Place to Work® assessment practices. *Journal of Business Ethics*, *55*(2), 135–146.

van Wanrooy, B., Bewley, H., Bryson, A., Forth, J., Freeth, S., Stokes, L., & Wood, S. (2013). *The 2011 Workplace Employment Relations Study: First findings*. London: Department for Business, Innovation and Skills.

Vanderslice, V. J. (1988). Separating leadership from leaders: An assessment of the effect of leader and follower roles in organizations. *Human Relations*, *41*(9), 677–696.

Varenne, J. (1977). *Yoga and the Hindu Tradition*. Chicago, IL: University of Chicago Press.

Vessantara. (2002). *Meeting the Buddhas: A Guide to Buddhas, Bohisattvas, and Tantric Deities*. Birmingham: Windhorse Publications.

Vieten, C. (2009). *Mindful Motherhood: Practical Tools for Staying Sane during Pregnancy and Your Child's First Year*. Oakland, CA: New Harbinger Publications.

Vieten, C., & Astin, J. (2008). Effects of a mindfulness-based intervention during pregnancy on prenatal stress and mood: Results of a pilot study. *Archives of Women's Mental Health*, *11*(1), 67–74.

Volckmann, R., & Maalouf, E. S. (2013). Elza S. Maalouf: Spiral dynamics and the Middle East. *Integral Leadership Review*, August–November.

Voukelatos, A., Cumming, R. G., Lord, S. R., & Rissel, C. (2007). A randomized, controlled trial of tai chi for the prevention of falls: The Central Sydney tai chi trial. *Journal of the American Geriatrics Society*, *55*(8), 1185–1191.

Vuori, I. (1998). Does physical activity enhance health? *Patient Education and Counseling*, *33*, Supplement 1, S95–S103.

Waddock, S. (2011). Finding wisdom within: The role of seeing and reflective practice in developing moral imagination, aesthetic sensibility, and systems understanding. *Journal of Business Ethics Education*, *7*, 177–196.

Wade, J., & Jones, J. (2013). *Strength-Based Clinical Supervision: A Positive Psychology Approach to Clinical Training*. New York: Springer.

Walach, H., Nord, E., Zier, C., Dietz-Waschkowski, B., Kersig, S., & Schupbach, H. (2007). Mindfulness-based stress reduction as a method for personnel development: A pilot evaluation. *International Journal of Stress Management*, *14*(2), 188–198.

Wall, M., Hayes, R., Moore, D., Petticrew, M., Clow, A., Schmidt, E., . . . Renton, A. (2009). Evaluation of community level interventions to address social and structural determinants of health: A cluster randomised controlled trial. *BMC Public Health*, *9*, 207.

Walsh, R. (2001). Positive psychology: East and West. *American Psychologist*, *56*(1), 83–84.

Walsh, R., & Shapiro, S. L. (2006). The meeting of meditative disciplines and Western psychology: A mutually enriching dialogue. *American Psychologist*, *61*(3), 227–239.

Weber, B., Jermann, F., Gex-Fabry, M., Nallet, A., Bondolfi, G., & Aubry, J.-M. (2010). Mindfulness-based cognitive therapy for bipolar disorder: A feasibility trial. *European Psychiatry*, *25*(6), 334–337.

Wedding, D., & Niemiec, R. M. (2008). *Positive Psychology at the Movies: Using Films to Build Virtues and Character Strengths*. Cambridge, MA: Hogrefe.

Weedon, C. (1997). *Feminist Practice and Poststructuralist Theory*. Oxford: Blackwell.

Weinberg, A., Cooper, C. L., & Weinberg, A. (2013). Workload, stress and family life in British Members of Parliament and the psychological impact of reforms into their working hours. In C. L. Cooper (Ed.), *From Stress to Wellbeing Volume 1: The Theory and Research on Occupational Stress and Wellbeing* (pp. 391–406). Basingstoke: Palgrave Macmillan.

Weiss, S. J., Wilson, P., & Morrison, D. (2004). Maternal tactile stimulation and the neurodevelopment of low birth weight infants. *Infancy*, *5*(1), 85–107.

Wells, J., Barlow, J., & Stewart-Brown, S. (2003). A systematic review of universal approaches to mental health promotion in schools. *Health Education*, *103*(4), 197–220.

Werner, E. E. (1992). The children of Kauai: Resiliency and recovery in adolescence and adulthood. *Journal of Adolescent Health*, *13*(4), 262–268.

Werner, E. E. (1993). Risk, resilience, and recovery: Perspectives from the Kauai Longitudinal Study. *Development and Psychopathology*, *5*, 503–515.

Werner, E. E. (1996). Vulnerable but invincible: High risk children from birth to adulthood. *European Child & Adolescent Psychiatry*, *5*, 47–51.

West, C., & Zimmerman, D. H. (1987). Doing gender. *Gender & Society*, *1*(2), 125–151.

West, M. (2000). Music therapy in antiquity. In P. Horden (Ed.), *Music as Medicine: The History of Music Therapy since Antiquity* (pp. 51–68). Aldershot, England: Ashgate.

Wheeldon, J., & Ahlberg, M. K. (2011). *Visualizing Social Science Research: Maps, Methods, & Meaning*. Thousand Oaks, CA: SAGE.

White, B. A., Horwath, C. C., & Conner, T. S. (2013). Many apples a day keep the blues away: Daily experiences of negative and positive affect and food consumption in young adults. *British Journal of Health Psychology, 18*(4), 782–798.

Whitney, D., & Cooperrider, D. L. (2000). The appreciative inquiry summit: An emerging methodology for whole system positive change. *OD Practitioner, 32*(2), 13–36.

Wilber, K. (1995). *Sex, Ecology, Spirituality: The Spirit of Evolution*. Boston, MA: Shambhala Publications.

Wilber, K. (2000). *Integral Psychology*. Boston, MA: Shambhala publications.

Wilber, K. (2001). *No Boundary: Eastern and Western Approaches to Personal Growth*. Boston, MA: Shambhala Publications.

Wilber, K. (2005). Toward a comprehensive theory of subtle energies. *Explore: The Journal of Science and Healing, 1*(4), 252–270.

Wilber, K. (2007). *Integral Spirituality: A Startling New Role for Religion in the Modern and Postmodern World*. Boston, MA: Shambhala Publications.

Wildman, F. (1988). Learning: The missing link in physical therapy. *Physical Therapy Forum, 6*, 1–3.

Williamson, D. A., Copeland, A. L., Anton, S. D., Champagne, C., Han, H., Lewis, L., . . . Ryan, D. (2007). Wise Mind Project: A school-based environmental approach for preventing weight gain in children. *Obesity, 15*(4), 906–917.

Williamson, G., & Christie, J. (2009). Aging well in the 21st century: Challenges and opportunities. In S. Lopez & C. R. Snyder (Eds.), *Handbook of Positive Psychology*. New York: Oxford University Press.

Williamson, M. (1996). *A Return to Love: Reflections on the Principles of a 'Course in Miracles'*. New York: Thorsons.

Wilson, J. Q., & Kelling, G. L. (1982). Broken windows: The police and neighborhood safety. *Atlantic Monthly, 249*(3), 29–38.

Wilson, J. R. (2000). Fundamentals of ergonomics in theory and practice. *Applied Ergonomics, 31*(6), 557–567.

Winpenny, T. R. (1999). Downsizing to corporate anorexia while dismantling the middle class: Are we in danger of recreating the 1920s? *Essays in Economic & Business History, 17*, 245–252.

Wollstonecraft, M. (1990 (1792)). *A Vindication of the Rights of Woman*. Buffalo, NY: Prometheus Books.

Wong, P. (2009). Positive existential psychology. In S. Lopez (Ed.), *Encyclopedia of Positive Psychology* (pp. 345–351). Oxford: Blackwell.

Wong, P. T. P. (2011). Positive psychology 2.0: Towards a balanced interactive model of the good life. *Canadian Psychology/Psychologie canadienne, 52*(2), 69–81.

Wood, A. M., Linley, P. A., Maltby, J., Kashdan, T. B., & Hurling, R. (2011). Using personal and psychological strengths leads to increases in well-being over time: A longitudinal study and the development of the strengths use questionnaire. *Personality and Individual Differences, 50*(1), 15–19.

Wood, A. M., & Tarrier, N. (2010). Positive Clinical Psychology: A new vision and strategy for integrated research and practice. *Clinical Psychology Review, 30*(7), 819–829.

World Health Organisation (WHO) (1948). Preamble to the Constitution of the World Health Organization as Adopted by the International Health Conference, New York, 19–22 June, 1946; Signed on 22 July 1946 by the Representatives of 61 States (Official Records of the World Health Organization, no. 2, p. 100) and Entered into Force on 7 April 1948. Geneva: World Health Organisation.

World Health Organisation (WHO) (2008). *Global Strategy on Occupational Health for All: The Way to Health at Work*. Geneva: World Health Organisation.

Wright, T. A. (2003). Positive organizational behavior: An idea whose time has truly come. *Journal of Organizational Behavior, 24*(4), 437–442.

Wrzesniewski, A. (2003). Finding positive meaning in work. In K. S. Cameron, J. E. Dutton & R. E. Quinn (Eds.), *Positive Organizational Scholarship: Foundations of a New Discipline* (pp. 296–308). San Francisco, CA: Berrett-Koehler.

Xia, J., & Grant, T. J. (2009). Dance therapy for schizophrenia. *Cochrane Database of Systematic Reviews, 1* (Art. No.: CD006868).

Yalom, I. (1980). *Existential Therapy*. New York: Basic Books.

Yang, L., Sahlqvist, S., McMinn, A., Griffin, S. J., & Ogilvie, D. (2010). Interventions to promote cycling: Systematic review. *British Medical Journal, 341*, c5293.

Yeh, G. Y., Wood, M. J., Lorell, B. H., Stevenson, L. W., Eisenberg, D. M., Wayne, P. M., . . . Russell, S. (2004). Effects of tai chi mind–body movement therapy on functional status and exercise capacity in patients with chronic heart failure: A randomized controlled trial. *The American Journal of Medicine, 117*(8), 541–548.

Yoshimoto, I. (1972). *The Method and Practice of Naikan Therapy*. Tokyo: Igaku Shoin.

Zeichner, R. L., Kibler, J. L., & Zeichner, S. B. (2013). Relationship between mindfulness-based stress reduction and immune function in cancer and HIV/AIDS. *Cancer and Clinical Oncology, 2*(1), 62–72.

Zindel, V., Segal, J., Williams, M. G., & Teasdale, J. D. (2002). *Mindfulness-Based Cognitive Therapy for Depression: A New Approach to Preventing Relapse*. New York: Guilford Press.

Zwetsloot, G., & Pot, F. (2004). The business value of health management. *Journal of Business Ethics, 55*(2), 115–124.

Zylowska, L., Ackerman, D. L., Yang, M. H., Futrell, J. L., Horton, N. L., Hale, T. S., . . . Smalley, S. L. (2008). Mindfulness meditation training in adults and adolescents with ADHD: A feasibility study. *Journal of Attention Disorders, 11*(6), 737–746.

INDEX

Lewig, K. A., & Dollard, M. F. (2003). Emotional dissonance, emotional exhaustion and job satisfaction in call centre workers. *European Journal of Work and Organizational Psychology*, *12*(4), 366–392.

Lewis, R., & Zibarras, L. (Eds.). (2013). *Work and Occupational Psychology: Integrating Theory and Practice*. London: SAGE.

Lewisohn, L. (1997). The sacred music of Islam: Samā' in the Persian Sufi tradition. *British Journal of Ethnomusicology*, *6*(1), 1–33.

Lindström, L. H., Besev, G., Gunne, L. M., & Terenius, L. (1986). CSF levels of receptor-active endorphins in schizophrenic patients: Correlations with symptomalogy and monoamine metabolites. *Psychiatry Research*, *19*(2), 93–100.

Linley, P. A., & Joseph, S. (2004). Applied positive psychology: A new perspective for professional practice. In P. A. Linley & S. Joseph (Eds.), *Positive Psychology in Practice* (pp. 3–12). Hoboken, NJ: John Wiley & Sons.

Linley, P. A., Nielsen, K. M., Gillett, R., & Biswas-Diener, R. (2010). Using signature strengths in pursuit of goals: Effects on goal progress, need satisfaction, and well-being, and implications for coaching psychologists. *International Coaching Psychology Review*, *5*(1), 6–15.

Linley, P. A., Woolston, L., & Biswas-Diener, R. (2009). Strengths coaching with leaders. *International Coaching Psychology Review*, *4*(1), 37–48.

Linton, S. J., Hellsing, A.-L., Halme, T., & Åkerstedt, K. (1994). The effects of ergonomically designed school furniture on pupils' attitudes, symptoms and behaviour. *Applied Ergonomics*, *25*(5), 299–304.

Little, B. R. (1983). Personal projects: A rationale and method for investigation. *Environment and Behavior*, *15*(3), 273–309.

Little, B. R., Leccl, L., & Watkinson, B. (1992). Personality and personal projects: Linking big five and PAC units of analysis. *Journal of Personality*, *60*(2), 501–525.

Liu, C. Y., Krishnan, A. P., Yan, L., Smith, R. X., Kilroy, E., Alger, J. R., . . . Wang, D. J. J. (2013). Complexity and synchronicity of resting state blood oxygenation level-dependent (BOLD) functional MRI in normal aging and cognitive decline. *Journal of Magnetic Resonance Imaging*, *38*(1), 36–45.

Löckenhoff, C. E., De Fruyt, F., Terracciano, A., McCrae, R. R., De Bolle, M., Costa Jr, P. T., . . . Alcalay, L. (2009). Perceptions of aging across 26 cultures and their culture-level associates. *Psychology and Aging*, *24*(4), 941–954.

Loman, S. (2005). Dance/movement therapy. In C. Malchiodi (Ed.), *Expressive Therapies* (pp. 68–89). New York: Guilford Press.

Lomas, T. (2013). Critical positive masculinity. *Masculinities and Social Change*, *2*(2), 167–193.

Lomas, T. (2014). *Masculinity, Meditation, and Mental Health*. London: Palgrave Macmillan.

Lomas, T., Cartwright, T., Edginton, T. & Ridge, D. (2013a). 'I was so done in that I just recognized it very plainly, "you need to do something"': Men's narratives of struggle, distress and turning to medication. *Health*, *17* (2), 218–236.

Lomas, T., Edginton, T., Cartwright, T., & Ridge, D. (2013b). Men developing emotional intelligence through meditation? Combining narrative, cognitive, and electroencephalography (EEG) evidence. *Psychology of Men and Masculinity*, *15* (2), 213–224.